THE INNER CONSCIOUSNESS

AND

SPONTANEOUS IMAGERY:

An Exploration of the Unconscious

DAVID W. CLINESS, Ph. D

Copyright © 2020 by David W. Cliness, Ph.D

All rights reserved. No part of this publication may be reproduced, distributed, or transmitted in any form or by any means, including photocopying, recording, or other electronic or mechanical methods, without the prior written permission of the author, except in the case of brief quotations embodied in critical reviews and certain other noncommercial uses permitted by copyright law. For permission requests, send communications to the author through his Facebook page.

ISBN: 9798613540266
Imprint: Independently published

Cover Design: Sherry Mann

ACKNOWLEDGMENTS

First, I would like to thank all of those who helped me with my research over the years. There were many who came forward to become volunteer clients. Moreover, I owe a great debt of gratitude to those whose case studies are presented in this manuscript. Their courage and determination to face their unconscious and heal their lives was an inspiration to me and from whom I learned so much. I would like to thank my family who had to endure the many hours I was away from home while conducting research. It is to them that I dedicate this book. I also need to thank my students who I loved and who informed my life during my days as a professor and Department Chair. Finally, I am indebted to the late Ross L. Mooney whose encouragement and validating support, during some of the most difficult times of my life, was immeasurable and greatly appreciated.

> Ask, and it will be given to you;
> search and you will find;
> knock and the door will be opened to you.
> Everyone who asks receives;
> everyone who searches finds;
> everyone who knocks will have the door opened.
> -Matthew 7:7-8

Table of Contents

Introduction	....	5
The Research Questions	....	6
N of 1 Research and Methodology	....	7
The Unconscious	....	8
Ego Consciousness	....	10
Personal Psyche	....	12
The Collective Consciousness	....	13
Multiple Personality Disorder	....	16
The Supra Consciousness	....	19
The Guide Phenomenon	....	22
The Healing and Growth Function of the Supra Consciousness	....	25
The Case Studies	....	26
I Sara – A Case of Schizophrenia	....	27
II Ellen – A Case of a Spirit Guide	....	53
III Theresa – A Case of the Collective Consciousness and Supra Consciousness	....	71
IV The Case of Connie	....	146
Discussion of Research Questions	....	247
Summary Statements	....	258
Notes and References	....	260
About the Author	....	266

INTRODUCTION

I began my work shortly after being employed as an Assistant Professor at Youngstown State University, in 1974. Having developed a reputation for using hypnosis, an older male student came to me and asked if I might use hypnotic regression to access his past lives. He had a belief in reincarnation and wanted to seek verification of this belief. He appeared stable and mature and seemed to be a good candidate for hypnotic regression. Hence, we proceeded on an experimental basis.

A series of hypnotic sessions were scheduled and each session was tape recorded. After several sessions, what appeared to be past life identities began to emerge. Of particular interest was one who claimed to have been a Choctaw Indian, who I asked to speak in his native language. Another past life claimed to have lived in Italy, and he was also asked to speak in his native language. For validation purposes, the Choctaw Indian language was sent to a Native American Council. Further, I knew an Italian speaking person who I had listen to the tape recording of the Italian language. A representative of the Council wrote back to say that they did not know what language was on the tape, but he was sure that it was not Choctaw Indian Language. My Italian friend did verify the Italian language.

After concluding our hypnotic regression experiment, I felt the reincarnation question was neither verified nor negated. There were several reasons for this conclusion. First, the subject of research held a belief in reincarnation and had something at stake in supporting that belief. Secondly, I believed that he felt himself part of an experiment and wanted to impress me by unconsciously presenting past life data. Third, the Native American Council did not verify the recorded Choctaw language. Fourth, we lived in an area where there was a significant population of Italian immigrants. He could have unconsciously incorporated the language from association.

While this hypnotic regression experiment did not yield significant data, it did help me formulate research questions that formed the core of future work. Further, it appeared that such questions could only be pursued in a clinical setting with individual persons.

The Research Questions:

1. What is the "Unconscious" and what is the structure of what is otherwise referred to as the unconscious?

2. What is the content of the unconscious?

3. Does the content of the unconscious affect or influence our everyday lives, such as informing our decision making and life direction?

4. Are there natural processes within the unconscious that lead to healing unresolved issues or experiences in our lives? If so, how do these healing processes function and how might we facilitate them as therapists?

5. Are there natural processes that lead to human growth and development within the unconscious?

6. How does one best work with the unconscious in order to assist in facilitating growth and healing? After all, I am by training a therapist. I was most interested in the healing and growth processes of the unconscious and how we might facilitate such processes to help the individual heal his/her life. While many have an interest in the reincarnation question, it was secondary in my research.

Ego Consciousness

The Ego system or mechanism represents one's ability to relate to the external world. Ego is very important and needs to be developed with the same degree of emphasis as any other aspect of the self. It is noted that many of the "New Age" people espouse the [idea] that one must get rid of the Ego or suppress it in order to reach higher levels of [spiri]tuality. This could not be further from the truth. In a certain sense, the stronger the Ego, [the] greater its capacity to accept the spiritual dimensions of oneself and not become [over]whelmed by one's interaction with them. The weaker the Ego the less one is in contact [with] the realities of the external world and the less likely it can express the richness and [crea]tivity of one's internal, spiritual life.

There is a difference between egotism and egoism. Egotism is a term used to [desc]ribe a self-centered person with a limited ability to see clearly the realities and [nece]ssities of both the internal and external world. It represents a weakened Ego. On the [othe]r hand, Egoism represents a person with a strong ego, one who is able to establish a [heal]thy and open relationship with one's inner and outer worlds.

The function of the Ego may look something like this. When one is hungry the Ego [searc]hes the external world for something to eat. Some people are money oriented. Hence, [the E]go looks for ways to make more money. However, if one seeks revenge or spitefulness, [the] Ego will also seek ways to fulfill these negative motivations. Whatever one wishes or [need]s, the Ego seeks to fulfill. The stronger the Ego the greater its capacity to seek and [fulfil]l the wishes and needs of the greater system. This is the role of the Ego and the nature [of it]s consciousness. The Ego, then, is in the service of the greater system and [cons]ciousness.

What creates a problem with the Ego is when one cannot decide what direction one [wishe]s to take. This can become very frustrating at the level of ego consciousness. This [frust]ration may lead it to assume direction and seek fulfillment of that direction. This is to [say,] the Ego is put in a position in which it becomes the decision maker, something it was [neve]r designed to do. Hence, we have a person who goes in one direction at one time and [then] suddenly takes off in another direction at another time. It is a rudderless ship in stormy [seas.]

In other situations, such as a dependent personality, the Ego takes on that direction. It [will] seek out relationships that support this type of personality. A dependent person who is [in pa]in may seek to decrease this pain or find some pleasure in life. Hence, one's Ego may [seek] out such fulfillment though drugs or through clinging to others who it identifies as [those] who will take care of them. Later, when the same person decides to become more [indep]endent and self-sufficient, the Ego shifts its focus and seeks out ways to fulfill this new [direc]tion.

The Ego system is in the service of the greater self. It is most content and satisfied in [fulfil]ling this role. The stronger the Ego, "egoism," the greater its capacity to fulfill this role [and t]he greater its conscious awareness regarding the direction of the greater self. The [weak]er the Ego, the inability to function in this regard. Schizophrenia is an example of when

N of 1 Research and Methodology

A major question I faced regarding the unconscious, was how does one collect data sufficient to answer such questions as listed above? The only approach that seemed to make sense to me was to utilize the Clinical setting, one person at a time. After all, most of the theories that have informed our present forms of psychotherapy, came from the clinical setting, starting with the psychoanalytic movement of Freud and Carl Jung. (1) Moreover, Freud and Jung used such techniques as hypnosis, free association, and dream analysis to access what they referred to as the unconscious. Since I was very interested in the unconscious and its healing potential, the best approach for studying it seemed to be techniques similar to what have been used for over 100 years. Hence, it seemed fitting that hypnotic techniques would be the best research tool for me to use. However, there was one problem. Most modern hypnotic therapeutic approaches, called Clinical Hypnosis, apply deep trance techniques and specific suggestions for given psychological problems. This is to say that with this approach, one is given specific instructions or suggestions. Moreover, hypnotic suggestions are often blocked from memory such that they remain as an unconscious influence upon behavior at the level of ego consciousness. The clinician is in control of the process and there is little attempt to seek or collect data that comes from the unconscious spontaneously, or of its own accord.

Over time, I developed a process by which moderate relaxation is achieved, enough to access one's inner world and to invite the unconscious to reveal itself and its processes in a spontaneous way. Further, I never block from memory anything that happens from conscious awareness, while in this state. This permits mutual discussion with the client following each session. Moreover, data were collected via tape recorded sessions. I came to call this approach, "Spontaneous Imagery Therapy," because it deals with images and experiences that spontaneously emerge during a relaxed state. While Jung did not seem to clarify his primary approach, he did refer to a therapeutic technique that he called "Active Imagination." (2) I believe there are probably significant parallels to both approaches.

I also refer to my work as N-1 research, since I deal with only one person at a time. The research design is very simple. I suggest to the subject that we are going to work with his/her unconscious for the purpose of healing his/her life and facilitate positive growth. And, during this process, I collect data on how he/she accomplishes this task, in cooperation with their inner consciousness.

Over time, one collects data from many persons such that the "One" becomes part of the "many." This is to say, one compares data from one person to another to determine what observations are consistent. Of course, there are data that are personal in nature and specific to each individual. However, there are also data that are more universal and revealing of the inner nature of all human beings. These data became of particular interest in answering the research questions that I proposed above. In order to comprehend the case studies given below, I am offering a summary of the structure of the unconscious based on the data I have collected from thousands of spontaneous imagery sessions with individual cases.

The Unconscious

The Unconscious is a common term that seems to have come out of the Freudian era. It tends to refer to that part of ourselves of which we are not conscious. It is like a vast ocean. We are only conscious of what is on the surface. Unless we put on scuba gear and dive deep into the water, we are unaware of the many forms of life that are below the surface. In fact, the ocean is teeming with life. To be sure, we are like a vast ocean teeming with life, conscious life, most of which we are unaware.

Hence, just because we are unaware of the many facets of ourselves, we should not assume that such parts of ourselves are lacking in consciousness. At times, we unknowingly communicate with our inner selves through dreams. At other times, we may have something like a lucid dream or an inner voice or thought. I am not talking about pathological experiences such as hearing voices or experiencing hallucinations, as with cases of Schizophrenia. I am talking about what many people may occasionally experience that are positive, informative and supportive of everyday life. You might be able to recall moments of intuition that help solve a problem with which you have been struggling for a long time. Moreover, when I was studying highly-creative persons they sometimes reported on hearing an inner voice, having vivid problem-solving dreams or visual experiences. Unlike pathological events, these experiences were all positive, problem solving and supportive. These are all moments of increased awareness or consciousness that transcends ego consciousness.

In order to help understand the content and processes being manifested in the Case Studies given below, I am giving an overview of the structure of what I refer to as the "inner consciousness," along with some definitive statements. Figure 1 below shows a diagram that includes the structure of the human system that has emerged in my work with 100s of research subjects over a period of 30-plus years. It is like a stump of a tree in which there is a center that is referred to as the heart wood. Extending from the heart of the tree are rings, representing each period of growth that occurs during spring and summer. By observing the rings of a tree, one can gain a good picture of the whole life of the tree. The final ring contains the bark of the tree that maintains its relationship with the world outside of itself. Hence, the heart wood represents the Supra Consciousness. The rings of the tree represent the Collective Consciousness in which individual lives are contained. Finally, the outer layer represents the present life, or personal psyche, with its own inner life and ego consciousness.

It is noted that the diagram is composed of open lines. This is to represent the human psyche as an open system in which information and communication is able to permeate throughout all parts of the system. During times of pathology, such as with the case of Sara given below, a wall or barrier is erected to block such communication. However, under normal circumstances, open communication is maintained. Further, clinical experience suggests that one function of the "Guardian Angel" is to ensure that communication between the Supra Consciousness, Collective Consciousness and Personal Psyche is maintained and in support of ego consciousness, subject to its limited awareness.

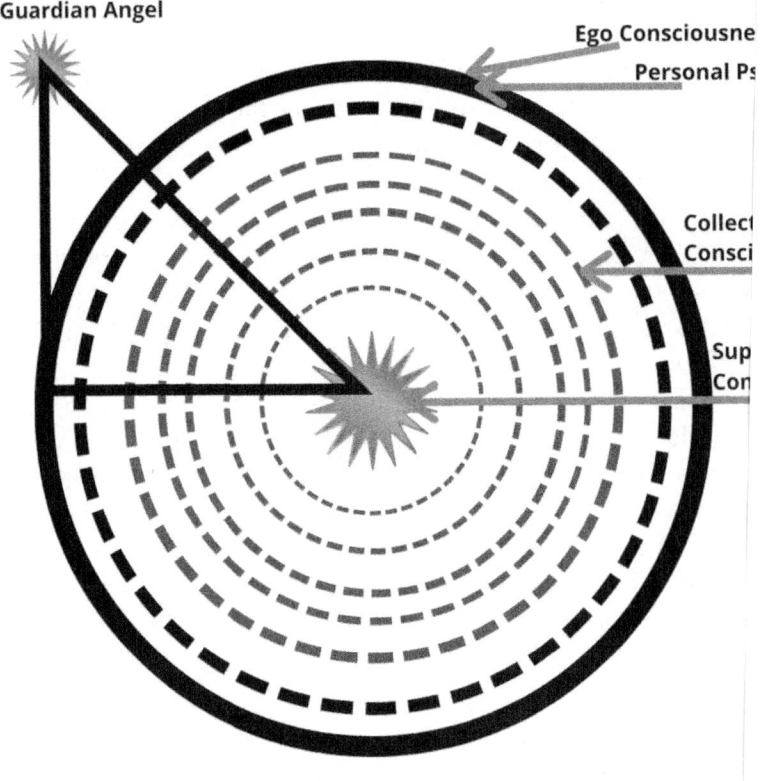

Compare with Assagioli

there is a complete break-down of the Ego system and its conscious awareness, and it is unable to discern the difference between inner and outer realities.

Finally, some people become interested in their own spiritual nature. I am not talking about seeking one's spiritual self in organized religion, which is often external to the self. Just as the Ego turns outward to seek fulfillment of physical needs and wishes, it is just as capable of turning inward to seek fulfillment of spiritual needs. However, the Ego needs to have a great deal of strength as it will be facing things that might otherwise overwhelm it, things that have been unknown to it. This may be why such spiritual desires are often delayed until later in life, when life experience has served to strengthen the Ego such that it can open to one's inner world and new experiences. A strengthened Ego is one that is more consciously aware through life experience, more open to new experience, more flexible, less judgmental and creative in its fundamental role. These are the characteristics necessary for accessing and experiencing one's own inner consciousness. In the case studies below, one may be able to observe experiences that serve to strengthen and prepare the Ego system for deeper inner work into the Collective Consciousness.

finished his hospital residency. My impression was that the client seemed to be a bit flirtatious, as well, which might cause some problems in her relationship with her fiancé. It might be noted that a common theme in such cases is that the client appears to have traits similar to those of their inner selves.

With regards to this particular inner-self, the client suddenly announced that she was going to let her take over her body, as she wanted to talk to me. Just as suddenly, I found myself talking to a young woman from Colonial times. What was interesting was that the inner-self began to speak with amazement over feeling what it was like to be back into a physical body with "so many needs." She seemed to have forgotten what it was like to be in a physical body. What she wanted to talk to me about was that she had known me during Colonial times. She said that my name was Daniel and that I was a young man who fought in the Revolutionary War. She apparently had felt some fondness toward this young man. Finally, she finished discussing her friendship with Daniel and returned to where she had come from. The client reported that she had remained fully conscious during this event and was a bit confused by the discussion. It had been one thing to interact with someone she took to be in the spirit world, someone with whom she was interacting and perhaps helping. However, this inner self suggested that she knew a part of me, and implied that Daniel was one of my past lives. This kind of thing did not fit well within her strong Catholic background. Years later, I ran across her while out shopping. She remembered the work we had shared and was quick to say that none of what she had experienced had anything to do with reincarnation.

I am mentioning this person's Catholic background because, even though what she experienced during her imagery had clear implications regarding the reincarnation question, she remained an enthusiastic participant in the work. My work with her continued for about six months to a year and she never once rejected anything she was experiencing. Hence, she represented one of many different backgrounds who accessed similar phenomena over 20 years of work. Over the course of my work with her, she accessed approximately five inner selves that helped her developed greater insight into herself and her own life. Such insight served to strengthen her ego system and eventually led to a stable sense of identity. Moreover, the work appeared to help develop greater maturity and prepare her for marriage, a career and motherhood. These two persons along with my work with many others, prompted me to consider a more appropriate descriptive statement to represent the universal presence of inner-selves. Over a period of 20 years of research, followed by work with persons I have seen on a private basis, the phenomena has remained consistent from one person to another. While the content differs from one person to another, the themes and the presence of inner selves appears universal. One thing that is consistent is that inner selves are fully conscious of who they are, their own life experiences and their relationship with the client. The only exception to this is with those who have suffered abuse or traumatic experiences as children. These persons will often access inner selves who are children, who have limited self-awareness depending on age and their own life experience. This is quite common with cases of Multiple Personality Disorder (MPD) who often have been severely abused as children. Hence, another example of the Collective Consciousness is represented by cases of MPD.

A more recent case demonstrates the relationship between the Collective Consciousness and the light (Supra Consciousness). This young man in his mid-30s, originally came to me with symptoms of anxiety, panic attacks, depression and more disturbing to him was intense anger and rage. His bouts of anger became frightening because he was very concerned about losing control and hurting someone or damaging the property of others. At times, it was all he could do to suppress his anger and keep it under control.

An examination of Jim's past revealed that he had been raised in an environment of violence, alcoholism, drug addiction and sexual abuse. His father and step father were both alcoholics, drug addicts and prone to outbursts of anger, rage and violence. To make matters worse, he had been sexually abused by several relatives. To be sure, he was experiencing post traumatic stress and what had been repressed and suppressed during his childhood, adolescence and early adulthood was beginning to surface.

I soon discovered that Jim responded well to relaxation and imagery techniques. Typically, he began to access young children within his inner world. They had absorbed the abuse of his childhood and it was recognized that he had been feeling their fear and states of panic over being subjected to violence and abuse. Other children and adolescents emerged who were full of rage and anger over the abuse that they had absorbed and experienced. Generally, the work began with younger children and progressed chronically. However, there were certain issues such as the sexual abuse that came later in the therapy and required moving back into working with children who had suffered this form of abuse. During the work, he would go through periods of flash backs that revealed the specific details of the abuse. This is quite common among such cases.

It was clear that these inner selves had been brought forward from the Collective Consciousness to help absorb the abuse in order that Jim's primary personality remain intact as he grew to adulthood. However, he would not have been diagnosed as a case of Dissociative Disorder as he did not lose ego consciousness during these emotional episodes. Rather he would most likely have been diagnosed with Post Traumatic Stress Disorder with a multitude of symptoms.

Jim was a very good candidate for Spontaneous Imagery Therapy and he began to access and process each inner self. In a certain sense, they would tell their story and then return to the light from whence they came. After working with each identity, they would be asked if there was anything left that they needed to tell or show. Then they would be asked if they wanted to "go home". Most all the children knew what "home" meant and they were eager to go to the light or back to their divine source, the Supra Consciousness, which will be described in more detail later in a following section. Some of the older adolescents or young adults were merely asked if they were ready "to go." At such time, a light would appear and they would either go to the light or was led to the light if they seemed fearful. Following the release of these inner selves, Jim's symptoms would dissipate and he would realize a period of calm and stability until the next inner self came to the surface. It is noted that this process is often repeated many times, depending on the duration and extent of past abuses, until such time that all have been processed and returned to the light. The case study of Connie will more clearly demonstrate this process and the relationship between the Collective Consciousness and the Supra Consciousness.

Multiple Personality Disorder

One of the most common forms of inner consciousness, that transcends Ego consciousness, is what I once referred to as Multiplicity, a term I adopted from Cornelia B. Wilbur, MD. (4) I used the term to explain the phenomena of inner-selves. I also intended to demonstrate that this is something that is common to everyone, with universal qualities. Since the movie, *Three Faces of Eve* and the book, *Sybil*, by Flora Rheta Schreiber, we have become aware of persons who have been described as people with Multiple Personality Disorder (MPD). While it has been considered a fairly rare disorder, I have discovered that everyone has such inner selves, of which they are totally unaware. However, they do not take over our personalities as we have observed in cases of MPD.

Dr. Cornelia Wilbur was a pioneer in the field of Multiple Personality Disorder (MPD) which is now referred to as Dissociative Identity Disorder. Her work clearly demonstrated the presence of inner selves that tend to take over the primary personality during times of extreme stress, such as with child abuse and trauma. These personalities seem to be highly specialized in their functioning, such as absorbing certain forms of abuse or taking over given behaviors that are necessary for the survival of the primary personality. Many are children who absorb abuse that would otherwise have overwhelmed the primary personality. Other, more adult personalities, may take over to achieve certain career training beyond the capacity of a troubled person. When there is sexual abuse involved, there is usually a personality who takes over during times of sexual involvement. Indeed, what occasionally drives a person to seek help is when she becomes conscious during a sexual episode, without any awareness of where she is, who the man is or how she came to be with him.

In the case of MPD, it is assumed that these inner selves were created by the primary personality and manifested as part of their own defense mechanisms. However, my work with MPDs over time suggests that this is not the case. My work with MPDs usually involved each personality, one at a time, just as I would conduct therapy with the average person coming to me for help. Hence, I would work with whomever appeared for the purpose of healing their lives as part of healing the primary personality. On many occasions there might be more than one inner self involved. However, the focus was generally on one self at a time. In the case of children, an adult or older inner self would assist in helping me work with them. What became of significant interest were discussions I had with older, inner selves regarding their own nature and the origin of their existence. In each case they reported that they had lived before and had had their own separate lives. Moreover, they had been called forward to help the present life because of their own life experiences that made them uniquely qualified to help deal with certain life situations. Further, helping the primary personality seemed to be beneficial to them in resolving issues that had been left unresolved in their own lives. There was one inner self that seemed particularly forth-coming. She was very intelligent and had been brought forward to take over and help with doing the work necessary to complete nurses' training. Interestingly, she loved classical music and reading and it was confusing when the primary personality would find recordings of classical music and books in her apartment without knowing how they got there. These were materials in which she had no interest. Also, this inner self loved entering into intellectual discussions which made it easier to gain information that other personalities might be reluctant to divulge.

It might be reiterated that each personality, especially adult personalities, expressed an awareness of who they were and that they had lived before with their own life experiences. Moreover, they had been brought forward to assist the primary personality in dealing with overwhelming abuse, addiction or difficult life experiences. Some came to bring direction and guidance. After a number of such cases it became evident that they had been brought forward by the Supra Consciousness, which I will describe more in detail below. Hence, it is the divine part of the self or the core of the self that orchestrates the direction and assistance on behalf of the primary personality, represented by the intervening personalities.

The main characteristic of a normal presentation of Multiplicity is that the adult primary personality and Ego system is fully functioning and is consciously aware of its behavior, emotions, thoughts, etc. However, one might be unaware that the painful emotions and irrational childish thoughts and responses are emanating from an inner-self or separate but related identity. Generally, one can relate such painful emotions and thoughts to a given time in his or her life when they were experiencing difficulties. Further, a given life event or decision-making experience may trigger a particular identity from the Collective Consciousness to come forward to help the primary personality to bring such life events to a positive conclusion. Such Collective identities are sometimes called "spirit guides" who help us navigate difficult circumstances in our lives.

There are other times when prominent symptoms of Multiplicity take the form of irrational obsessions, compulsions, feelings, etc., which do not seem to fit life circumstances. That is, the client recognizes that his/her behavior, feelings, and responses are irrational, immature and childish. However, he/she seems powerless to do anything about it. In some cases, a stressful event may seem to trigger such symptoms. Moreover, the symptoms appear much exaggerated compared to the event. Further, such symptoms appear completely autonomous with regard to the Conscious mind. Other forms of therapy, such as behavioristic or cognitive approaches often appear to have little impact on changing the pattern of symptoms. The problem is that an undifferentiated inner-self which represents a given response and emotional complex surfaces into consciousness with sufficient force to dominate the client's reaction. Such reactions might include anxiety, panic, phobias, anger, rage, fear of loss, feelings of paranoia, etc. Moreover, they may be inconsistent with one's personality and uncharacteristic of their normal feelings, thoughts and behavior. In one case the individual quite suddenly developed paranoid feelings that he had done something terribly wrong and the police were going to come and arrest him. After a few months of work with his Collective Consciousness, one such identity whose life had been one of criminal activity was brought forward and processed. Following this inner work his symptoms went away as suddenly as they had appeared.

As indicated above, in more extreme cases like those of MPD, the primary personality retreats presumably into an unconscious state and another personality or identity takes over. In such cases, the primary personality has periods of memory loss or "black outs" where the client is totally unaware of what happened during the takeover. One of my MPD clients expressed an experience that was disturbing to her and which caused her to feel that something was terribly wrong. One of her friends came to her and discussed an encounter with her while grocery shopping. She had no conscious awareness of the encounter and her claims of not having been grocery shopping that day was very confusing to her friend. This experience would be in contrast with that of "Multiplicity" when the client might end up in a motel room with a casual acquaintance but not without a conscious awareness of how the event occurred. The fact that the client may have felt powerless because of fear to change the course of the experience or may have felt compelled by intense sexual feelings, would not be uncommon with cases of Multiplicity. Be that as it may, the person would not have lost a sense of consciousness during the whole ordeal

My discussion on the MPD phenomenon, or more recently referred to as Dissociative Identity Disorder, was intended to serve as an introduction to the concept of "inner consciousness." Further, it is an attempt to provide insight into how our inner consciousness functions on our behalf and on behalf of the greater human system.

Hence, an inner self is an individual entity who is part of a vast collective of others. Because they are part of a collective and have their own conscious identity it seems more appropriate to refer to them as a Collective Consciousness common to each person regardless of background. To be sure, we are who we are individually while at the same time we owe a great deal of who we are to those who came before us.

The Supra Consciousness

The Supra Consciousness is at the center or nucleus of the whole human being. It might be perceived as a tremendous vastness and its entirety is incomprehensible. It is what Carl Jung referred to as the Collective Unconscious, in the sense that it is archetypal in nature and contains a vast array of archetypal patterns of life. He defines the Collective Unconscious (Supra Consciousness) as:

"The collective unconscious is a part of the psyche which can be negatively distinguished from a personal unconscious by the fact that it does not, like the latter, owe its existence to personal experience and consequently is not a personal acquisition. While the personal unconscious is made up essentially of contents which have at one time been conscious but which have disappeared from consciousness through having been forgotten or repressed, the contents of the Collective Unconscious have never been in consciousness, and therefore have never been individually acquired, but owe their existence exclusively to heredity. Whereas the personal unconscious consists for the most part of complexes, the content of the Collective Unconscious is made up essentially of archetypes." (5)

These archetypal patterns transcend both ego consciousness and our own Collective Consciousness. This is to say that its contents do not owe their existence to one's personal or transpersonal life experience. For the most part these patterns are formless and inform our lives in a natural way. However, in dreams or during the imagery process they may appear in symbolic form, such as the Jungian Wise Old Man. (6) Like the inner selves who make up our Collective Consciousness, the Supra Consciousness also contains entities who are fully conscious of who they are and their purpose regarding the whole system. These entities are divine in nature and have never been human beings, except when there is an emergence of the divine and human such as in cases like Jesus / Christ or the Buddha.

One might also refer to the Supra Consciousness as "light or fire" consciousness, because in dreams and in one's imagery it is often presented as white light or the presence of a being of light. Sometimes one will experience a fire with bluish flames. With that, it appears that there is part of ourselves that is divine in nature and which might be referred to as one's Soul. Perhaps it is that spark of light or life that is the source of our own life. It might also be the light from which each entity of the Collective Consciousness, including oneself, owes its existence.

It is also important to note that the Supra Consciousness transcends all cultural, religious, social influence, values, beliefs, and person made legal, moral and ethical standards. It is pure love, and all its actions are a manifestation of non-judgmental, unconditional love and creativity. It functions within the context of the human-based system just as a painter must paint within the limitations of the brush, paint, and canvas. Moreover, direct observations would seem rare. Rather, one more readily observes it indirectly in one's life or life direction much like the natural forces of nature. For example, the wind cannot be seen but it can be felt blowing against one's face or observed in the movement of the leaves and limbs of a tree.

The major function of the Supra Consciousness seems to be to facilitate and guide the growth, healing and creativity of each person. It appears to be cooperative in the growth of all humanity: it is growth-orientated, and is cooperative and mutually-beneficial for those around it. Further, it seems that the more highly developed the person the more growth-oriented his/her actions become on behalf of the greater humanity.

This growth function can often be seen with people who are tied together in relationships. They may be husband/wife, brother/sister, business partners, teammates or colleagues, etc. These are archetypal roles that we assume in relation to one another and often represent the many dualities in our lives. This is to say that the many roles we assume in life are often informed by given archetypal patterns that owe their existence to the Supra Consciousness. One might call them themes that permeate human life and give direction to our lives both individually and collectively.

Clinically, I have worked with many people who are in co-dependent relationships. In such cases, two people appear bound together for what seem to be negative reasons where an abusive situation may exist. In such situations it is difficult to assume mutual growth. However, when viewed in a certain way such relationships may prove to be very growth-producing. Clinically, I have found that the best way to work with persons in co-dependent abusive relationships is to support them as if they have a legitimate reason (usually unconscious) for staying in the relationship. Indeed, I have found from experience that such persons will undermine any attempt to pull them out of the relationship until they are ready to leave it. Instead, I work to discover the life issues involved in the relationship and bring those issues into conscious awareness. Most often, elements from the Collective Consciousness will emerge in images when imagery therapy is used. The person will appear unwilling to leave the relationship even in abusive situations until all of the related life issues have come to consciousness and are comprehended and resolved. At that time, energy from given archetypal patterns related to the co-dependent relationship will become withdrawn and soon there is little interest in any further involvement in the relationship. As a clinician, I have seen this process of healing and growth occur many times in the therapeutic setting.

Generally, the Supra Consciousness works in the background guiding and leading us without notice. It is important to note that freedom of choice is held sacred. Interestingly, while experiencing imagery with the Supra Consciousness when the Christ archetype is present, one often asks the question, "what do you want me to do?" The response is always, "what do you want to do" (with your life)? While freedom of choice is imperative, experiencing the consequences of our choices either positively or negatively is also exacting.

The primary intent of the Supra Consciousness is healing and growth such that each life fulfills its plan or purpose in the world of matter. We are responsible for choosing the direction of our lives and those in the divine world assist and help guide us to fulfill that direction. While it may be pleased when acknowledged or appreciated, it has no need for recognition. Its essence is unconditional love and wisdom, without judgment or condemnation. While organized religion of many faiths speak of judgment and condemnation, I have never experienced this while working with the Supra Consciousness. Moreover, I have never heard or seen any reference of hell except for that which we create for ourselves. I once asked what happens to people who lead particularly evil lives. I was told that such persons go into darkness because they are unable to face their lives. There is some reference to "life evaluation" (7) following death, and it is one's choice as to whether they are willing to go through that process. Otherwise, they will wait in darkness; I suppose in some sort of suspended state until such time when the desire to come into the light and face their lives becomes strong enough. Presumably, many lives may have passed as preparation for coming from darkness into the light of conscious awareness of one's own life.

Theresa's case study as given below is a good example of how the Supra Consciousness appears in imagery sessions. First is the appearance of the "Light" and the being of Light that is identified as the archetypal mother. (8) Next is the introduction of the "Christ Consciousness" who guides her through a series of experiences designed to help her develop a deeper sense of self and an awareness of her positive and negative traits. (One cannot change what one does not know about oneself). Finally, she is introduced to the "Father" archetype who holds her and reassures her with a sense of unconditional love. There are other archetypal images involved in Theresa's imagery such as the medieval castle, rainbow colors in the water and the ocean itself. Generally, her imagery focused on the "Light" with increasing intensity. Her case study is a very good example of how the Supra Consciousness functions within the context of one's imagery. It might be noted that combined with a sense of unconditional love is a sense of joy, and what I call divine wit.

The Guide Phenomenon

Though it may seem so, we are not thrust into the world of opposites to fend for ourselves. There is a constant and substantive theme of growth and change in relation to others in the world of matter. There has been data presented to suggest that each life is planned, (9) with a given blueprint, and with certain lessons to be learned and things to be achieved. During each life there is a need for help and guidance in achieving our particular trajectory toward given goals and the fulfillment of certain growth needs.

Clinical experience suggests that the primary guide may be referred to as the "Guardian Angel." While this is something taught within the Christian Tradition, it also seems universally true with those of other backgrounds and religious orientations. The Guardian Angel is neither male nor female and is sometimes perceived as a being of divine light. However, they can appear as male or female depending on the need of a given individual. For example, some women may feel they need a strong male or even a warrior to protect them. Others may need a feminine presence.

The Guardian Angel has never been human and while they may have some understanding of human behavior from centuries of observing it, they do not fully understand what it means to be human. I have been told that they can become totally mystified by the unpredictability of human behavior. More importantly, they know our blueprint and what we have set out to achieve during each lifetime and they are there to help us and to guide us toward fulfilling those goals. They are also there to keep us from harm or anything that might interfere with our direction in life. If a given experience, such as a tragic accident, illness, etc., is part of our plan for growth, the angel supports us and helps to guide us through that experience. Freedom of choice is held sacred, and they are not to interfere with any choice we make even if that choice might distract or undermine the original intent of our lives.

Being a creature of the divine world, the Guardian Angel loves us unconditionally and without judgment. We are the master of our own lives and what we decide with either positive or negative impact on our lives is accepted. Whichever we choose, good or evil, is accepted without intervention. This is to say that should we chose something evil, the angel will stand by until such time as we no longer want or need this in our lives. The instant we decide against something evil, the angel will intervene and rid us of this scourge on our lives. In any case, choice takes us in to an experience in which we learn many lessons leading to healing and growth. We cannot integrate what we have not experienced. It is far better to choose and act accordingly, whether positive or negative, than not to choose at all.

When needed, the Guardian Angel may go into our Collective Consciousness to retrieve a selected life that may serve to guide us through a particular experience related to something unfulfilled in its own life. In addition, a particular Collective entity may be called upon to absorb pain or certain forms of abuse that would otherwise overwhelm the present life. We have seen many forms of this kind of assistance from the Collective Unconscious.

The Guardian Angel also serves as a mediator between divine consciousness and the self. When the Ego system is too weak to allow information to filter through from the Supra

Consciousness, Collective Consciousness and even the personal psyche, the Angel provides this information in the form of thoughts and ideas. To be sure, they are beautiful creatures with tremendous divine power and energy. Connie's case study offers a good example of the Guardian Angel and how it functions on our behalf.

Another guide that we have encountered in the work is that of an entity who is not part of the self or related to the self. Such a guide was observed in Ellen's case study given below. Joseph appeared in the imagery as supportive of Julia and to help guide the process by which a tragic situation in Ellen's Collective Consciousness might be resolved. Further, there seemed to be a reciprocal involvement in which Joseph could test some of his ideas in the physical world. He appeared to be a benign character and seemed to be fairly highly developed in his presentation in the imagery. To be sure, he was helpful in the process and offered some insights into the relationship between the spiritual world and the physical world. Such guides, while occasionally appearing in the imagery with a number of persons, were generally uncommon. Perhaps they stayed in the background and their influence went unnoticed. On the other hand, we discovered that there were entities who appear as guides, but who appeared to be nothing more than those who were merely seeking attention and self-expression. While they may also appear benign, they tended to create a distraction from the growth and healing work intended in the imagery process. Once detected, they were immediately dismissed, and we would return to something more positive and productive.

We have already discussed the Collective Consciousness which comes forward at certain times when they are needed. They seem to serve several functions. One function is to absorb severe abuse or pain so that the present personality or life does not become overwhelmed with Ego destruction. The second function is clearly to serve as a guide to the present life regarding given healing and growth experiences.

Another significant form of the guide phenomenon comes directly from the Supra Consciousness and like the Guardian Angel, is divine in nature. For lack of any other description, he appears to be Christ or a being of Christ Consciousness. In almost every imagery in which He appears, He is referred to as the "Master." While his appearance is not common, it can be sensed in the background of many imagery sessions. In one dramatic case when the Master appeared, the guardian angel later stated in awe "that was the Master" suggesting that there is actually an archetypal Christ or the Son, which is symbolized in the Trinity. Otherwise, it appears that within all of us at the center of the Supra Conscious is the archetypal Christ Consciousness. He might also be referred to as the "Master Healer" because his presence always coincides with healing experiences. This is to say that He guides one through experiences whose purpose is directly related to healing, growth and creativity. In fact, it might be said that there is no healing except that it comes through divine sources that are often manifested through the "Master" or Guardian Angel. Moreover, when He appears in the imagery process the images often become more-dynamic and rich with archetypal healing symbols. Theresa's and Connie's case studies are good examples of this phenomenon.

It might be noted that most of my research subjects came from a Judeo-Christian background. Hence, the presentation of the archetypal Christ or Master would be consistent with their background. While this phenomenon is consistent among my subjects, it is likely that it would manifest in different forms with those from other cultures and religious orientations. For example, the Buddhist would probably experience the Buddha, or the Muslim might visualize the prophet Mohammed. It might also be noted that Connie, who had a background in Eastern thought and religion, experienced a Guru and other deities who served as a source of guidance and healing.

The Case Studies

There are four case studies presented below. Each person presented has their own story, with data specific to their own lives. However, there are commonalities that cut across the four persons involved. They were chosen because each one presents certain aspects or examples of the unconscious; its structure, content and processes that I have observed in many other persons with whom I have worked. For example, all four case studies include references to the Collective Consciousness. It is the most common inner content that I have encountered in hundreds of cases. It often emerges spontaneously as part of the imagery therapy process. Two of the cases spontaneously produced images consistent with the Supra Consciousness. One case demonstrated more obvious interactions with the Aura Consciousness. While not as common in my work, I am able to detect it working behind the scenes with many persons giving direction to the healing and growth process with which we are working. After all, it is the core of such processes of the unconscious.

It might be noted that the four case studies given below are women. During the first stages of my research work most of my subjects were women. Most of them had been abused as children, some sexually abused. Moreover, women tend to be more open to hypnotic techniques and, as such, become good subjects for inner work. At first, few men came my way. However, those who did were more cognitive and preferred cognitive therapy techniques. More recently, a number of younger men have come to work with me and they have become good subjects for inner work. They have come after my formal research work was terminated, as I am no longer in an academic setting.

The Healing and Growth Function of the Supra Consc

Just as the Supra Consciousness is often expressed through given Christ, Buddha, Sophia (goddess of wisdom), the Knights of the Roundta also archetypal processes that inform the different stages of human gr stages are presented as tasks to be achieved and mastered from childhood old age. These growth stages are often presented as dualities to be resol there is the initial stage of human development referred to as Trust vs. Mi is loved and supported as an infant, he/she is able to resolve this dual healthy sense of trust and mistrust. This is to say that he/she develops a when a person or situation can be trusted. On the other hand, he/she also d to know when not to trust a given person or situation. Of course, in a cer life experience one continually develops a deeper sense of trust and mistr can know when a growth duality has been resolved because one is no lon; The duality becomes one's potential for behavior and responding rather th behavior.

One of the growth dualities that are common to adulthood is duality. I have observed that many religions including Catholicism and Pr to be obsessed with this duality. It is a polarizing duality that remains unr context of such institutions. This duality is often manifested in the rigid r of the clergy who become polarized on the "good" side of the duality. observe the pedophile behavior of some Catholic priests as well as Chris are caught with prostitutes to develop insight into the polarizing effects good vs. evil archetypal duality. Others are caught in fraudulent schen money. This is to say that what one becomes obsessed with (polariz possesses them.

As indicated above, there are also healing archetypal processes tha Supra Consciousness. One process might be referred to as a process of tr; that one form of psychic material becomes transformed into another that i with the greater self. For example, there is the very common death/rebi theme in nature, where many archetypal patterns and processes are easil my clinical work I have come across many dreams and imagery that inc. death/rebirth. (10) These are common dreams and often appear in the im; might dream of dying or that someone has died. This is sometimes fright may believe that this is informing them of their own pending death. Ho dream or imagery is usually the result of something within oneself that is It may be something in the Collective Consciousness that represents a b form of psychic damage that needs to become transformed and healed. (there is often a rebirth. Sometimes this rebirth comes in the form of a bat who is whole and healthy and represents a birth of new ideas and insi serve the greater self. This process often occurs during a period of dy growth.

Case Study I
Sara
A Case of Schizophrenia

A woman (I will call her Sara) in her late 30s was referred to me by a mutual friend who described her as an example of the "Book of Job." She had faced a difficult marriage with a subsequent divorce followed by a series of mental breakdowns resulting in periodical hospitalizations, financial problems and pursuing bill collectors. She had also lost her home and clerical job because of depressed economic conditions. In addition to such stressful events in her life, she was a single parent caring for three children, one of whom suffered from a severe disability. To make matters worse she received little or no help from her former husband.

What makes this case especially interesting was an experience I had after my first phone conversation with her. She called me at home on a Friday asking for my help. This resulted in a Monday evening counseling session with her. After getting off the phone I began to feel extremely depressed. The feeling was oppressive and came over me quite suddenly without any apparent cause. I sat down on the couch in our living room and looking over to the opposite chair. I saw a vivid image of a woman sitting with her head bent over and crying. I came to the conclusion that this was an image of the woman who had just called me, and I was feeling her emotional pain. My emotional pain continued until I wrote a poem, *Be Gentle, be kind* (1), which became predictive of the journey she was going to have to make in order to heal her life. Once I completed the poem, the oppressive feelings of depression were lifted. Further, I was extremely surprised when I first met her because my vision of the woman sitting in the chair was identical to the real-life image, I saw that Monday evening.

After several counseling sessions with Sara, I became deeply impressed by the split between her conscious and unconscious systems. She had told me that she had been diagnosed with Schizophrenia. With that diagnosis, I was hesitant to work with her. After all, my work dealt with the unconscious and given a schizophrenic split, I was not sure it would be advisable. However, she told me a story of having been in and out of the hospital for the past four years and had been to numerous health care professionals with only minimal results. She declared that if things did not work out with me, it would be "the end of it." I took this to mean that she would take her own life. Indeed, if she were feeling like I had felt following our initial phone conversation I could understand why she would feel this way. She indicated that she had been told that I was conducting research, and that my work was experimental. Hence, she was volunteering to be one of my research subjects and was hopeful that I would accept her into my program.

I decided to see her for a few sessions to see if there was anything I could do to help her. I felt that hypnosis and imagery would be contraindicated, so I decided to use traditional counseling in her case. After a number of sessions, she wanted me to hypnotize her to help her stop smoking. I resisted this request telling her that I had not been successful in using hypnosis in this way, but that I might be able to refer her to others who specialize in this kind of work. Finally, she came to a session saying that she had had a dream. While she could not remember the dream she somehow knew that it was significant. This generated some interest on my part, and I decided to try to put her in a light trance and suggest that she go to the dream she had recently had and to re-experience it in its entirety. This session began a healing journey from which I learned a great deal.

Sara's divorce was of particular interest in assessing her unconscious disturbances. It seemed that she started her marriage with a given set of ideals and expectations pertaining to what a wife, homemaker, socializer, etc. was supposed to be. At the beginning of her marriage she had set out to fulfill her ideals, beliefs and values only to experience growing resentments and hostilities from her husband. The final note of unbearable rejection came when she came home one day to discover her husband with another woman. This resulted in a psychotic breakdown with a subsequent hospitalization. Her release from the hospital was promptly followed by the agony of divorce proceedings. It seemed that overnight she found herself alone, supporting three children and having to make a living with inconsistent financial support from her former husband.

The likely beginning of Sara's upheaval following the demise of her marriage seemed to find its antecedents in her childhood, most specifically in her relationship with her father. During many counseling interviews it was learned that her father, although a loving man, was unable to fully express his love for her. He appeared to be a fundamentalist Christian with a deeply-rigid, perfectionist, judgmental and self-righteous attitude. Furthermore, he seemed to have an obsession with the question of Good vs. Evil. While her father presented a rigid religious attitude, her mother seemed more passive and submissive. In fact, she rarely spoke of her mother and only once did her mother appear in her imagery work.

It seemed that Sara spent most of her childhood trying to gain her father's love, acceptance and approval. She tried to accomplish this by being a "good girl," indeed a "perfect girl," by living up to his ideals. However, she was never able to do so. Her endeavor to be a "good little girl" in her father's eyes seemed somewhat reinforced by her older sister who was the rebellious child of the family. This is to say that Sara, in contrast with her sister, was a good little girl who appeared to strive to remain so well into her adult years. As we shall see, she never seemed to develop emotionally beyond her early childhood years. Quite understandably, when she left home to enter the adult world of marriage, family and social relationships she was ill prepared to comprehend, much less integrate, the incompatible world out there; a world that served to continually confront her with the warring opposites of Good vs. Evil.

Having become so rigidly polarized by her need to win her father's love, which appeared just out of her reach, Sara never seemed to become aware of her own dark side potentialities. She became the "good girl" and evil was something that was defined as being out there rather than being something that was also within herself. Moreover, good and evil were clearly defined in terms of specific doings without reference to meaning, being, intent, etc. Since behaviors were defined for her by her father, she had little difficulty with acting out the "good" child, nor did she have any difficulty projecting evil upon the world and others in it.

with a sense of nature she might have been able to form a broader perceptual frame within which the opposites could be held as emerging from a single whole. In this way they could have been perceived as potentials for responding in appropriate ways in the world, rather than being the controlling factors of her behavior.

Secondly, Sara's religious beliefs supported and indeed may have created the good vs. evil split within her. This made it nearly impossible to examine her own dark side at conscious levels. Evil, as she viewed it, was something out there to be fought and destroyed rather than become accepted as part of one's own life struggle. In Sara's case, to examine and consciously accept her dark side, her projected shadow, might well have been to lose forever the love of her father and quite possibly her place in eternity. Hence, it must have taken extreme energy to maintain the split between herself as the "good girl" and herself as the "other woman," who she had become.

Thirdly, there was little room in Sara's thinking for creative thought which is often necessary for the resolution of opposites. For her to think in broad encompassing concepts, inclusive relationships, integrative wholes, ideas, etc., could be dangerous to her religious salvation. Rather, she must keep on the straight and narrow which was defined for her in terms of specific doings. Quite naturally, Sara was unable to maintain her restricted childhood responses when met with a much larger adult world that required making judgments beyond the capacity of her inflexible mind. Her rigid personality structures made it impossible for her to grow and change in relation to the world out there. Hence, she set about trying to force others to conform to her own ideals. The result was a divorce, alienation of friends and neighbors, and finally Ego disintegration, which occurred during her mental breakdowns.

Unfortunately, when Sara left her overprotective home and entered through marriage, she carried with her a very rigid mind-set based upon religious fundamentalist ideals. Soon she projected her unresolved relations[hip with her] father onto her husband with an unrelenting will. Her husband, who appare[ntly was no] match for her will, seemed to seize upon the natural defensive alternative of b[ecoming her] father's opposite. Hence, he appeared to violate all of her rigid beliefs and idea[s of proper] human conduct especially with regards to their marriage. His egregious violatio[n involved] his adulterous relationship with another woman.

Later on, Sara came to recognize her part in causing the divorce. Th[is helped] release her from resentment and bitterness. However, earlier her bittern[ess reached] overwhelming proportions when her former husband hastily married the "other [woman" and] seemed to enjoy contentment in his new marriage. Of course, for Sara, the "ot[her woman"] was nothing more than a "whore" who corrupted her husband and wrecked their [marriage.]

To be sure, Sara entered her marriage with some very rigid ideas of g[ood and evil] and with perfectionist notions of what constitutes a good wife, mother, husband[, etc.] When the world failed to respond in ways that reinforced her beliefs and values[, she became] intolerant, judgmental and hostile. After all, she was being the perfect wife, [mother and] homemaker. It would seem understandable that she could not comprehend the [treatment] she received at the hands of her husband and friends. As she once said to me, *I [have always] been a good girl, and I don't understand why all this is happening to me*. It a[ppeared that] she had been taught that only good comes to those who perform good deeds. [Her] confusion over this issue seemed overwhelming.

Sara's complete lack of awareness of the contradictions between her [beliefs and] behavior were amazing to observe. At times she would become the "good littl[e girl" part] of herself she often tried to display to me. However, at other times, she would s[uddenly] shift to an extremely judgmental and self-righteous person. During such times s[he expressed] her hatred, in verbally abusive ways, toward those she perceived as "bad" [or doing bad] things.

Also predictable was Sara's sexual behavior which she tried to [control,] seemingly without success. Interestingly, most of her sexual involvement incl[uded married] men. This seemed to create intense guilt and shame at both conscious and [unconscious] levels. The shadow side of her unconscious often led her into experiencing b[eing the] "other woman," whom she had previously condemned. But as we shall see, this [became part] of the basis for understanding and resolving her bitterness toward her former [husband and] his new wife. In any case, one needs to be careful regarding hatred as it often l[eads to] becoming what one hates. This is the way the unconscious engages oneself. It [is through such] ways that such issues become resolved.

At any rate, Sara seemed to be in a constant state of anger, deep depres[sion and] anxiety. Firstly, she was pulled one way and then the other by inner forces of w[hich she had] no comprehension. She was truly a victim of the warring opposites within [her. With an] extremely rigid religious background, she came ill equipped to reach resolution[. She seemed] to lack a sense of nature and the universe; a sense of something larger [than herself.] Everything seemed to revolve around herself as is often the case with childr[en.]

PART 1
The Frightening Dream - The Beginning

As I indicated above, Sara told me of a frightening dream that she had had during the previous week. Since up to this time she had been unable to remember any of her dreams, I considered the possibility of material in her unconscious trying to break through into consciousness. Either her ego consciousness was becoming strong enough to entertain a release of unconscious material or it had become sufficiently weakened and unable to block its flow. In either case, it seemed that hypnosis and imagery might be worth the risk since the Ego system and Personal Psyche would no doubt need assistance in confronting and integrating the otherwise unconscious material.

Surprisingly, Sara responded well to hypnotic/imagery induction. She was soon following a suggestion to re-experience her frightening dream from beginning to the end. During the imagery sequence she appeared frightened and distressed. In the first part of the dream everyone seemed angry although she did not know why. Her ex-husband, her father, and a friend were angry. She says, *everybody's yelling and arguing with everybody*. She also sensed that there was a wedding going on, except she could not tell who was getting married. The tension in the dream was causing a headache. I engaged some techniques to calm the tension she was feeling and to ease the pain of her headache. I also suggested that she insert me into her dream as one who would support her and help her understand what was going on. This is a technique I have often used to help with difficult imagery.

Sara begins to run away as she is frightened of all the anger in the dream. In the imagery I catch up to her and ask her to stop running and turn around and face what is there. I take her hand and suggest that she call upon her strength as we walked back to face the dream content. When she walks back she sees a courtyard and everyone is in the courtyard. It seems that there is a fight going on. She also sees an altar. It appears that the fighting is going on not among people, but among dark "terrible" creatures. It seems that these terrible creatures, demons, are fighting near a big dark hole. The demons are near the hole but they are not falling in. However, her friend Wendy is getting near the hole, and Sara is afraid that she will fall in. It is very distressing for her to watch her friend getting close to the fighting and the hole, and she does not want to watch it. Then it appears that there is something transparent like glass covering the hole keeping the demons and Wendy from falling in. During this scene her former husband is yelling and appears angry while her father is no longer angry. Rather, he seems to be frightened.

Finally, Sara wants to leave the dream and does not want to watch this ugly fighting anymore. As she leaves, she notices that her father is crying, and her friend is crying. However, her ex-husband is still angry. She says she cannot stand his anger anymore. As she leaves the imagery, she indicates that she will come back later to deal with what is there. She feels badly that her friend may fall into the hole and feels that she should try to help her. She is afraid that she will fall into the dark hole if she tries to help her. She feels ashamed that she cannot help her. Further, as she is leaving, she hears wedding music and does not understand why there is a wedding going on.

It is interesting to note that following the imagery session Sara was unable to remember even the slightest detail of the dream she experienced, despite it not being blocked from memory. In fact, I never suggest that a client will not remember even when it has been a frightening ordeal. Rather, I want to be able to go over the experience with them and try to help them gain a meaningful interpretation of what had happened to them. I believe that such insights have significant therapeutic value.

In Sara's case, the schizoid split between ego consciousness and the unconscious seemed to be well established. We would assume then that the personal psyche was the primary element of the selfinvolved in the dream and imagery. Perhaps her ego consciousness would receive the unconscious material at a later time when she has the ego strength to withstand it. At least her personal psyche appears to have become stable enough to begin searching within for possible answers. This was certainly a break with her previous attitude, which seemed to assume that her problems were centered in the world outside of herself. Having turned inward, her unconscious seems to have responded both in content and potentially with a therapeutic process.

Some key relationships in the dream and imagery session seemed to be (1) her former husband and his anger, (2) her father, who symbolically represents her religious background and related abuse, (3) her friend Wendy, who seems to be trying to help her and (4) myself, who assumed the role of standing by her and guiding her through the dream as one who is guiding her through her journey toward psychological health. It seemed interesting that presumably her unconscious used the suggested projection of myself into her dream to try and encourage her to become aware of the conflicting elements within her, while also trying to minimize her overwhelming fear.

Quite significant seems to be the anger theme that appeared to permeate Sara's dream and imagery. First, and perhaps the most important element with regards to anger was her ex-husband's hostilities, which we can assume to be directed toward her. Her father also appeared angry. However, later his anger diminished. This leads us to believe that the projection may be more related to the dream conflict rather than directed toward Sara in particular. Finally, we sense that there are many people in her imagery who are angry and as she states, *everybody's yelling and arguing with everybody*. Perhaps, without direction from Sara, her "inner collective selves" were fighting each other for control. It is of interest to note that she appeared quite surprised by the possibility that the people in her dream could be angry with her. She seemed to have no conscious awareness of the alienating aspects of her personality.

In the midst of all the inner conflict in Sara's dream imagery, she finds herself feeling alone and shut in. During the session we find her running away from the conflict rather than facing it or herself. It is suspected that running away from her problems has become one of her primary modes of dealing with life. And, secondly, she shuts herself up so that others cannot get to her with their anger and rage. These factors most likely contributed to her sense of loneliness and alienation. On the other hand, she expressed her intense dislike toward being "shut up." This leads us to believe that she is caught between the apparent safety of running away and shutting herself off, and her feelings of loneliness and imprisonment.

e point it seems as though everyone is in a small "courtyard." Finally, when ning and turns to face what is there, she finds herself in the courtyard of a ere is an altar. These imagery elements seem quite puzzling and at best we e a guess as to their meaning. However, when we combine these symbolic in the wedding that is taking place during the whole imagery episode, their ng seems more apparent. First, the courtyard likely refers to a yard where court is being held; a judgment is being rendered. Since Sara has been constantly judging others, it would seem that she would have to subject herself to the same judgments. The angry people in the courtyard could well be her accusers. This courtyard could be the place where justice is to be administered or rather where the truth of Sara's personality becomes known to her. Justice being administered could be the means by which the anger toward her could be resolved and her own anger toward others as well.

Next, she briefly mentions an altar in a church. A church and alter is the place of worship and a place where religious rituals, such as communion which is an act symbolic of union with God, takes place. This, combined with an apparent wedding taking place, may symbolize a process leading to the union of the opposites, a coming together to form a union of opposing forces of her unconscious.

Finally, we find that there are demons fighting over or near a "big hole." It is a frightening sight for Sara. We can assume that the fighting demons represent an intense inner conflict. However, they do not seem related to other elements in her imagery. Rather, they seem limited to the "hole." Hence, we further assume that the "hole" represents the opening to deeper levels of her unconscious and perhaps to her "shadow," where repressed material resides. Her friend Wendy appears to be trying to show her that there is no apparent harm involved by walking over the hole and among the demons. As we shall see later, Sara wisely knows not to venture close to the demons or the hole at this time. It appears then that the demons are there to keep her away from entering the deeper levels of her unconscious until she is strong enough and psychologically ready to experience and comprehend what is there. Sara's imagery in its entirety presents us with data that suggests a more promising outlook. Her unconscious seems to be introducing the psychological factors like pieces of a puzzle that need to be identified as part of a healing process and direction to be taken. It seems that therapeutically we need only to cooperate with Sara's unconscious processes and to encourage her to participate as fully as possible in the unfolding journey to wholeness. We will also need to help minimize the fear she is likely to experience along the way through reassurance, support, interpretation, etc. We know to be careful regarding what to present to her ego consciousness since very little unconscious material is being made available to this part of herself. We would assume that the ego system is yet too fragile and could easily be overwhelmed.

PART 2
The Red Building - The Concentration Camp and The Imprisoned Self

As Sara's unconscious unfolds, we are able to gain more insight into her condition. Another dream which she re-experienced during an imagery session was quite revealing: She finds herself alone and shut up in a red building. She wonders, *why are people never with me, David? They're either behind a wall or standing away*. She says there are no doors but windows in the building, big windows. She realizes that she could come out of the building through the windows. She does not want to come out because it is *dirty outside* and it is *very clean in there*. However, it is empty and she says, *I think I've shut myself up because I want everything nice and clean and orderly and empty. I hear an echo. I think it is a camp I built for myself; no, it's not a house. It's a concentration camp*, she says. She continues, *I built no doors. I think I built it to get away from people out there. But I left windows. That was very stupid. I left windows so I could see. If I wanted to get away, I shouldn't have built the dumb windows*. Then she realizes that maybe she needs 'a little "*dirt*" and that *maybe nobody is all clean*.

Then Sara looks out the window and sees some of the men with whom she has been involved, including her ex-husband, who are all dirty. Next, she sees me, and with laughter she comments, *I never saw you dirty before*. I am standing outside the window in the world of dirt, smiling back at her. She thinks that she does not want to be shut up anymore. *It's very clean but it's very empty*. An observation is made that perhaps the reason why people are angry with her is that she has judged them for being *dirty* and because she wants everything *so clean and right*. She says that this is what her ex-husband is saying to her. She says, *he's so full of anger. I'm frightened to go out there with those people. Maybe, I don't want them to see me with dirt*. It appears that she perceives that everyone is angry with her because she has judged them, while a part of her is just like them, "*dirty.*" *They are angry with me because they know I won't come out and show myself.* Her choice is to go where it is dirty or stay in her red house, *concentration camp*, where it is clean, with an echo from the floors. Further, it is empty and where she feels all alone without human contact or companionship.

First, Sara experiences being shut off from others. It seems that she has built walls and put distance between herself and others, which describes her schizophrenic split. Next we discover that she built a red building which she describes as a *concentration camp*. This seems significant because while she holds an image of a red building, a concentration camp is a place where political dissidents are imprisoned. Further, we find that she built the *camp* herself, and she seems to have imprisoned a part of herself in it. Since a concentration camp is a place for political dissidents, we can assume that the part of herself being imprisoned is in disharmony with the greater whole, or perhaps the governing forces of the self.

As will later become apparent, part of Sara's personality that is shut off or imprisoned is her rigid religious self. We notice that the interior of the *camp* is *nice and clean* and orderly and empty. It is a place fit only for a puritanical, self-righteous person.

toward the *other woman* upon their wives, believing that they held similar bitterness toward her. This is to say that she is now the *other woman,* the object of bitterness and condemnation. To have women present representing angry wives, despite the observation that the women were no longer angry with her, could have a negative effect on her quest for freedom.

Finally, Sara considers the possibility that things on the outside may not be as they appear: I am there in the dirt, but not dirty. Also, the dust does not seem to be harmful. Another reason for coming out into the world is the realization that it is possible for one to be a good person in a corrupt world, without having its corruption rub off. Perhaps her religious background had led her to believe otherwise.

PART 4
The Pieces Have to Set

At this stage of Sara's therapy, it was felt that it might be a good time for her to face the fighting demons and gain access to the deeper layers of her unconscious. In part, the basis for suggesting that she approach the fighting demons was that her friend Wendy could walk among them and not be harmed, nor did she fall into the hole. Of course, they are her demons and not Wendy's. Apparently, the timing was off because she continued to lack the proper Ego strength and psychic integration necessary for the task. As she said, *I am put together in pieces. I can't let them touch me until the pieces are set.* She is told, *be careful of the pieces until they are set.* As was indicated earlier, the marriage or union of the opposites had been set in motion. It would seem that the completion of this process has not been fully accomplished. Hence, the demons are very purposeful and not as Sara believes, evil; although they do represent possible destruction that could occur by accessing the deeper unconscious without the appropriate preparation.

The union of the opposites does seem to be progressing well. We can assume this because Sara's attitude toward her husband seems to be changing. She appears to feel sympathy toward him, although she believes that he wants her destroyed. It seems clear that she no longer holds him responsible for her misfortunes and even defends his bitterness toward her. She says her husband *wants me destroyed. But he doesn't know why. No, he doesn't know why. He can't know why because he is not a mean person.* Further, she is coming to realize that as she grows and changes, she will be saying good-by to her lover, Carl. She seems to sense that as she grows, she will be leaving behind a good deal of her unpleasant past.

Sara's changing attitude toward others appeared to hold firmly during the following months, even though life became more difficult for her. It seemed that she was forever moving from one crisis to another. At times I was amazed by her ability to survive the constant barrage of stress in her life. Occasionally, it appeared that she was very close to her breaking point as she often had to endure constant bouts of depression, anxiety and thoughts of suicide. It became clear that she had gained a considerable amount of psychological strength to have withstood such miserable life conditions.

PART 5
The Emergence of the Collective Consciousness

For a while, imagery sessions were suspended as Sara became mostly preoccupied with external events and progress with traditional counseling appeared to be painfully slow. Perhaps out of frustration it was finally decided to resume our imagery work, since traditional methods appeared to be of little use. At this time, I suggested that she step aside and let me speak directly to her unconscious. I sometimes do this in order to gain deeper insight into what is occurring at deeper levels of the unconscious, especially at the level of the Collective Consciousness.

Having asked Sara to step aside, we find what appears to be a separate but yet related identity emerging from within her. Its validity could not be ascertained in one session. However, for the sake of assuming therapeutic direction we treated it as such. As anticipated, it appears that this identity is a segment of her Collective Consciousness. Should this prove to be the case, its therapeutic value could be significant.

It appeared that even though Sara has shut herself off once again, the process leading toward releasing unconscious material to the Personal Psyche is progressing, albeit slowly. We could hypothesize that at some level of the Personal Psyche, the opposites are being united and the pieces are in the process of becoming *set*. That is, at some level of the psyche, the demons have been faced and access to the deeper strata of her unconscious was gained.

Of significance also is the fact that while Sara was withdrawing because of the stresses of the external world, she selected books for reading that dealt with early American history, literature, and poetry to reflect upon. Should her readings prove to be related to the emerging identity that surfaced in this imagery session, she would be progressing toward a state of preparation for establishing a cooperative relationship with her Collective Consciousness.

Noting our discussion with what appeared to be Sara's Collective Consciousness, we found that she was fighting herself. As the presumed identity of the Collective indicates, *she fights herself all the time. And when she fights, she doesn't listen to what I try to tell her. I know what she can, what she has, has to be. She's never going to be some of the things she's fighting for and she's wearing me out trying.* It seemed that this fighting is directed toward the Collective self, so as to block the flow of thoughts and feelings of the unconscious into consciousness. No doubt, Sara's resistance comes from several factors. First, the external crises of her life were constantly throwing her thought processes off balance. Secondly, her unconscious represents to her the unknown, perhaps the dark unknown, which must be dealt with cautiously. Sara's shutting off the flow of unconscious material may have been her way to establish her position so as not to risk being overwhelmed. Hence, she seems to be in the process of regulating the system's flow. In this instance, my presence may have provided the necessary security needed to open the door more fully.

During this session, we also found that Sara may have a talent for writing, which is presented as a potential life work. This identity of her Collective Consciousness asked me to *tell her, tell her she has to write*. Should this prove true it could be used as a potent therapeutic tool, a primary mode for creative expression. However, she had shown little inclination toward writing, nor does her background appear supportive of this talent. Following this session Sara was encouraged to start writing a journal to test whether she does, indeed, have writing skills and to give expression to this part of her Collective Consciousness. Subsequent sessions revealed that she was writing a journal, but she would not show me her journal until our final session.

Another source of Sara's fighting seems to be related to something idealistic that she wants to become or do. Her fighting with the Collective Consciousness may well be in defense of her idealistic aspirations. However, the necessity appeared to be to accept herself as she is, rather than what she wishes to be. This would need to be accomplished without yielding control of her life direction to the Collective Consciousness; a potentially dangerous relinquishing of responsibility.

PART 6
Resolving Conflicts of the Collective Consciousness

During this imagery session we continue our discussion, presumably with Sara's Collective Consciousness. It appears that a conflict emerges among given collective elements over the necessity for expression. At this point, these elements appeared to assume that control of her life direction rests with the Collective Consciousness. As indicated, this poses an unhealthy circumstance which can be readily eliminated if she can develop the psychological strength to order these collective elements into a whole pattern that is centered on a given life purpose. Hence, a cooperative relationship between the Ego Consciousness, Personal Psyche and Collective Consciousness might be established.

From data that surfaces in this session we are able to hypothesize that Sara is moving into a new phase of development. The good vs. evil question does not seem to be as prevalent as it was during her first phase of therapy. She no longer condemns or criticizes others during counseling sessions. This would appear especially positive because her life continued to be harsh and at times even cruel. She seemed able to accept responsibility for creating many of her own problems and refrained from blaming others for her misfortune. Moreover, realizing that she may be living her life alone in the foreseeable future, she began to take course work at the university to increase her job skills. This more realistic approach to life appeared to replace her previous hope that someone might come along and deliver her from suffering.

On the other hand, we observed that Sara appeared to be regressing to a previous state of withdrawal. At first glance, we might have concluded that this reaction was pathological and cause for alarm. After much thought, it actually appeared a healthier response to this particular phase of her development. First, she was clearly withdrawing from the external world. Her withdrawal enabled her to minimize her involvement in stressful external events so that she might have the time and energy to devote to her studies and to internal growth. Further, she all but eliminated her contact with those friends with whom she frequented bars. This served to sever unhealthy ties with those who tended to complicate her life. With the exception of Carl, for whom she had a special fondness, she seemed to turn away from all her former friendships. This paved the way for new and more enduring friendships of a healthier nature.

While concentrating on basic survival and making a more solid future for herself and her children, Sara also seemed to be shutting the door to her unconscious. This might also be perceived as unhealthy were it not for what appeared to be a conflict at deeper levels of her unconscious. Because of her vulnerable Ego and Personal Psyche, her choice to close the door when conflict emerged would, in retrospect, actually seem wise. In this way, she demonstrated to the Collective Consciousness that she is really the one in charge and when stress levels get too high she can merely shut the door. It would appear to be something akin to going on strike; by assuming control, Sara minimizes the danger of becoming absorbed by her Collective Consciousness and being controlled by it.

Having resolved the good vs. evil question to a greater extent, Sara appeared to dwell on the *life direction* question. Her answers at this time must of necessity come from the depths of her unconscious. As was observed earlier, she kept away from this realm until the pieces, presumably of her Ego system, and Personal Psyche could be set. At this time, she seemed ready to assume control over the doorway and selectively close it, sometimes by getting tension headaches. When she is ready, she can open the door for a time to see what emerges. In this imagery session a part of the Collective Consciousness steps forward at my suggestion. She refers to herself as Louise.

Louise, according to past clinical experience seems to comply with what one would expect of the Collective Consciousness. She seems open with regards to her motives. She wants Sara to write poetry, to express what she (Louise) needed to have expressed in her life. She claims to have had a life and her life represents a void, or something left incomplete in the greater system. Others seem to be present and representing other voids which seem to be creating a power struggle within the Collective, each wanting to achieve expression through Sara. On the other hand, Sara and Louise appear to have common factors in their lives such as overprotective fathers and a deep sense of distrust. It seems that her deep sense of distrust may find its primary seeds in her deeper unconscious with reinforcement from her father and his fundamentalist religious beliefs.

At any rate, we carry our assumption forward that Louise is part of Sara's Collective Consciousness. We further assume that she has a hidden talent for writing, among other talents that have not yet surfaced. Given these assumptions, it seemed that the question of Sara's life direction is gaining the greatest attention. Indeed, Sara needed to assume a primary direction in her life and take control of her life in order to stop the internal conflict, which appeared to be brewing within her Collective Consciousness.

It might be noted that at this point in therapy Sara's Personal Psyche seems to have developed the level of integration necessary to serve both as observer and participant, with the capacity to deliver appropriate unconscious material to Ego Consciousness. Louise reveals this when she claims that *I had her so close for a moment*. She later requested that I ask Sara to listen, which she presumably does as Louise continues on with our discussion.

Louise indicated that she had written poetry, *a very long time ago*. She said that *they didn't understand* her poetry then *but you would understand now. If she wrote what I wanted to write now, people would understand it. When I was writing they kept me protected. I didn't, she has so much freedom that I didn't have*. Later she said, *It was so peaceful. If you did what you were supposed to do, it was peaceful. My father was very protective, except my father didn't like for me to write and Sara's father does. Things I wrote were not acceptable then. Some of them were love poems. I wrote the way I felt and you shouldn't do that then. She could say those things now.*

While it appeared that Louise was able to express some important things about her life, there remained a force within Sara that seemed to be trying to block the process. This seemed to be creating a feeling of inner conflict for Sara and she tended to shut down when she felt tension from the conflict. Louise says, *I think there is somebody who wants her to do something else. I think it is stronger than me. It just has more energy and more strength.*

On the other hand, Sara and Louise appeared to have a few things in common such as an over-protecting father and an underlying sense of distrust. This would make for compatibility and the basis for cooperation. Moreover, what Sara did not seem to realize is that to end the inner tension, she is the one who must choose rather than wait to see which Collective element wins the battle for attention. At this point I suggest that Louise might work out some kind of agreement that would allow each one the opportunity for expression. Hence, Sara might be approached without so much conflict and tension. In this way, Sara might be able to make a choice to become more cooperative if those in the Collective Consciousness become more cooperative with each other and less combative.

PART 7
Exploring Life Alternatives

As hypothesized earlier, Sara appeared to be entering a new phase of her growth. This growth seemed centered primarily on the development of a sense of trust and personal direction in her life. During this imagery session she recalls a dream which seems to support our hypothesis. It appeared that in this dream she was presented with a number of options for her life which she might explore. Her dream is about a number of cars and it was assumed that each car, a life vessel, represents a given purpose or life direction. With the exception of one car that might have represented something external, all the drivers seemed to be unknown to her.

In any case, this dream appeared to be a breakthrough for Sara. It indicated that she, at the level of the Personal Psyche at least, has broken through into the unconscious, presumably the Collective Consciousness. The Personal Psyche, exercising its proper role and position, appeared to explore the many elements, talents, knowledge, etc. available to her as potentialities for life. It appeared that Sara was very wise not to get into any of the cars. Since it seemed that the direction of each car would have been controlled by a given element of the Collective (each car was being driven by someone else), she would have given over control of her life to something else. Hence, Sara would have been in danger of becoming absorbed by her Collective: a condition to be avoided.

Sara says, *they weren't the right cars. I think I just wanted to go, I think I just wanted to go with somebody, except none of those places they were going was right for me. It made me feel sad, but I know it wasn't right. They weren't where I have to go.* Realizing that there is a place where she has to go or something she has to do; I ask her what it might be. She indicated that, *Oh David, something I think I know, and I think I'm there and I see the girl, the little one. Remember I told you that there was a long tunnel. I don't want to wear the black anymore. I knew that if I go the right way it will be the end of that damn, I'm not, I'm not anyplace right now; I'm like in limbo.* Sara continues, *I shut those car doors. They didn't shut them. I shut them myself. They weren't going anywhere I wanted to go, so I shut them and I shut myself out.*

It appears that Sara has come to a point in her life in which she is turning away from what others want her to do, whether from inside or outside of herself. It is suggested that she listen to her own heart in deciding on what to do with her life. Then she refers to Louise's life: *Sometimes I wish I could go back in time. It was a lot safer then.* I ask her if she is referring to a time before her present life and she says, *yes, a long time ago.* To test whether I am talking to Louise or her personal psyche, I ask, "You mean before you were born?" *Yes,* she replies. I continue, "I didn't know you knew about those things." *I sure do,* she says. I suggest that, "perhaps your conscious self just isn't ready for that yet, is it?" She responds, *No, I know; I know I am going to do it. I'm gonna write. I just can't get through the burdens so the words can come out.*

Hence, it appears that I am talking to her Personal Psyche and not to Louise directly and not to her Ego Consciousness. It also seems that she knows about Louise's life and her

44

own need to write. However, she feels that her Ego Consciousness is not ready or is too weak to become involved in what is transpiring at deeper levels in her unconscious.

It seems clear that Sara's Personal Psyche is well-aware of those in her past. Be that as it may, she may not know what role they play in her present life. She is aware of her talent for writing and knows this is something that she is to express in her conscious life. At this point, I discuss with her an approach to the Collective Consciousness that may develop greater cooperation from all those who might make significant contributions to her present life. I point out that these former lives represent potentialities for action. Nonetheless, they are not there to take over Ego Consciousness and run the show. It is Sara's life now, and it is hers to do with as she wants. Therefore, it is important for her to take charge of her life and utilize all her resources in order to fulfill the life she is living right now. This is much different than her previous approach, which was to wait until someone in her Collective Consciousness wins out over the others and takes over. I suggest from my clinical experience that this is not how the system is intended to function. I have observed what happens when a given aspect of the Collective does take over. It turns out to be disastrous, and I wanted to warn her against this approach; some further healing and development needed to occur before she is ready to assume adult responsibility and take total control over her own life.

PART 8
Transformation and Future Growth

You may have noticed an apparent failure to discuss Sara's reference to the "little girl," the girl in black, the tunnel and her desire not to "wear black" anymore. As we will discover next, these references relate to an integrative process occurring within her. It seems that this process has been underway for some time, with a few occasional cues emerging into consciousness through dream material.

This imagery session occurred toward the end of our therapeutic relationship. Close attention to the content of this session reveals the ordering of the Collective Consciousness, the release of the self, the resolution of the good vs. evil opposites and a transformation of the negative elements of Sara's personality. Indeed, the data from in this imagery session seems to represent a new beginning in Sara's life. If these data are valid her present inner conflicts will be resolved, and she is released to realize her full human potential.

First, Sara finds a lot of people in her dream/imagery. She recognizes them as friends but yet she does not know who they are. It seems evident that these people are familiar to her at some deeper level, perhaps her Collective Consciousness. She says, *people, there are lots of people. I know them, I know they are friends of mine. It's the back of it.* These people who have their back turned to her are women wearing flowering dresses. The scene appears to be a path with women on one side facing away from her and on the other side are men who are facing toward the path. At the end of the line of men is Carl, the man with whom she is presently involved. She says, *Carl is there! He's bigger than everybody else. He's smiling at me, and he's reaching out. But I won't come in* (to his arms). She continues, *I think I'm supposed to be. I think it's a wedding*. She says of Carl, *he wants me to come to him but I can't. It's OK though; I'm not, I'm not unhappy because I have to go someplace else.*

A discussion commences about turning away from Carl and all those on both sides of the path. She does not know where she is to go but says, *it's peaceful. I don't know, but it's nice.* She sees a path with women on one side and men on the other. The men seem to be all the men with whom she has had affairs. Perhaps the women represent those who have been in affairs with married men or who were married to men who had extramarital affairs. It is likely that the women are part of her Collective Consciousness, and she is not ready to know who they are. They are likely those parts of herself that she had once rejected as being unacceptable to her and had been forced into the shadow side of herself. However, having become the other woman, she could no longer judge them or reject them.

The next part of the imagery is quite interesting. Sara exclaims, *I'm on the outside, David! I am outside of that stupid red house. I'm outside, and you're at the window. And, it's not me caught anymore. But, they're not mad, no one's mad. I don't understand that. I don't know who the women are though, and it's Carl. And they've all got flower dresses and hats on. That's that dumb red house. It's divided; the women are standing in front of me with their backs to me. And the men are standing, and they're facing me. You're dead center and grinning. I guess I learned why cause I'm walking away, but you are smiling.* She continues, *I wish I knew where I am going, but it's all right though. Carl doesn't understand and my dad's happy, I think. I think he is, yes, he is. It's this, hum, a lot of darkness off to the right of me. I have to go in it. It's awfully dark.*

Interestingly, Sara sees me, *you're right there. You're dead center and grinning.* While the women and men are opposite each other I am *dead center*. It might be said that I represent what Buddhists call the *middle road* (2), the transcending point of the opposites and hence, the resolution of the opposites. It might be noted that when Sara was inside the red house looking out a window, I was on the outside in the midst of all the dirt. However, the dirt did not appear to be on me. It demonstrated that one could be in the outside world, among all the dirt of humanity, without being contaminated by it. Hence, I came to represent to her the capacity to transcend the ugliness of the world. I represented a form of unconditional love to her.

Sara finally finds herself outside the *stupid red house*. Later in this session she exclaims, *that's a church David! It's a church. The red building is a church. I don't understand it but it is all right.* This is an important observation and insight even though she does not understand it. The red building represented her fundamentalist religious beliefs and values that walled her off from others who were in the outside "world of dirt." It was her own judgmental and self-righteous attitudes that walled her off and alienated her from others. While she may have felt justified in doing this, it was a puritanical lonely place, where there was nothing but echoes from one walking about; a place where there was no laughter, peace, contentment or moments of happiness.

While the women have their backs to her, they are wearing flower dresses and hats. The symbolism is unmistakably a reference to spring and a re-birth of nature, a re-birth no less in her. However, it is puzzling that the women have their backs to her while the men are facing her. That they are wearing flower dresses and hats may represent a transformation of this negative, shadow part of herself. Moreover, the men facing her may be more acceptable to her as objects of her affection. It might be noted that early in her therapy she blamed the woman with whom her husband had had an affair for the breakup of their marriage. This would have likely been consistent with her fundamentalist religious beliefs that places blame on the biblical "Eve" for the fall of "Man."

Of significance is the fact that Carl is the last man in the line of men facing her. He is also the last married man with whom she had had an affair. He opens his arms for her but she knows not to go to him. During her therapy it was determined that she actually felt a deeper love for him. It becomes clear, that she was leaving him because of her love for him. Actually, she brought their affair to an end by telling him that he needed to return to his wife and family and heal his relationship with his wife. Further, in the imagery she knows she must go through the tunnel taking her away from a world of betrayal of relationships. Clearly the tunnel represents the birth canal through which she must pass and become reborn to a new, more healthy, mature self.

At the end of the tunnel Sara sees a little girl. She says, *it's a very young, very young girl. She has blonde hair and she's very young. She's got on a black dress.* She recognizes that the little girl is her and that there are a succession of *"me's."* *It's me. It's me and I have to start over. But, this time it won't take all that time it took before.* As she enters the tunnel, a black fog closes in behind her insuring that, *I can't go back. I have to come out.* Once there, she says, *the little girl. I can almost touch her but she won't come in (*into the tunnel*). Yes, I have to finish the tunnel. And, beyond her is another one. I wonder how many me's there are? She's all black too, only she is older. I have to go into the little one in the black. That's what it is. I have to keep going into her. She's nice. She's sweet. But I can't stay there if I am going to grow. I can't stay little. I have to grow. But I have to take her with me. I have to go on to the other one and take her with me. I have to go on to the other one and take her with me, and I'll end up with all of them and I'll be me. Yes. I think me's not going to be bad. It can't be because she's so little and she's not damaged. Even the doll is not broken. She has a doll with a dress that matches and they are all OK. And she is dressed in black. She's got a* (black dress). *It's black, has a little white ruffle.*

It seems clear that Sara, by going through the symbolic birth canal will start her life again. It is assumed that the little girl represents her present level of emotional development, development that was the result of damage done by subtle abuse from a rigid fundamentalist religious environment. Hence, she will start her development anew, becoming each self from childhood, adolescence and onto adulthood. I asked her, shortly after this imagery, to look back and count the number of selves that she is to become. She counted eight selves which seems reminiscent of Erik Erikson's *Eight Ages of Man.* (3) Following this imagery, it seemed almost miraculous how her life began to change in some very positive ways. She developed deeper insights into herself and her relationships with others reached deeper levels of caring. Her feelings of alienation faded, and she seemed more connected to life and the world. These changes seemed to occur despite her challenging economic circumstances.

Summary of Additional Sessions

There were some significant moments during Sara's therapy. After about six months, she expressed some of her childhood experiences with her father. She described a disciplinary ritual her father would exercise. When she did something, he felt was wrong, which was generally behavior typical of a normal child, he would put her in a chair outside his study. Next, he would tell her that he was going to go into his study and talk to God and He would tell him what to do with her. Then he would reappear with some harsh punishment, presumably prescribed by God. This was a ritual that was repeated many times during her childhood.

First, Sara had to sit in a chair outside her father's study with mounting anxiety waiting for punishment. One can imagine the paralyzing fear that she must have felt as her father emerged from his study. Next, her concept of God became one of a punishing, Old Testament God consistent with her father's fundamentalist beliefs. It might be pointed out that if her father did believe himself in communication with God, which seems to be the case, his own personality might well have been schizoid and delusional with further damaging effects on her personality. In any case, her father relieved himself of responsibility for her harsh punishment, thus causing further confusion and ambivalence in her relationship with him. To make matters worse, much of her normal and healthy personality development was often perceived by her father as wrong and sinful. Obviously, her natural development became stunted and damaged.

Interestingly, my initial reaction to Sara's description of her father's punishing rituals in response to her childhood natural behavior was anger, even rage, as I imagined what had happened to her at the hands of a fundamentalist Christian father. To be sure, I was projecting some of my own childhood and adolescent experiences with fundamentalist Christians. Finally, I raised my fist and pounded on the table saying, 'God damn it, he had no right to do that to you!' I further explained what I felt had been done to her and that God had nothing to do with it. I continued with how such punishing behavior impacted her life in such damaging ways. She responded to my tirade with a startled look. Otherwise she gave no response. Later, as I was returning home from our session, I thought, "what did I do," fearing that I had possibly caused further damage to her fragile personality. I felt angry with myself and was determined to make amends during our next session.

During the following session, before I had a chance to apologize for my behavior, she further described her father's abusive behavior toward her. Finally, she pounded her fist on the table and said, *God damn it, he had no right to do that to me.* I was amazed as she preceded to say many of the same things I had said during the previous session. She voiced her own repressed anger and rage using the same language that I had used. Later, I realized that several things had happened. One is that my anger gave her permission to experience and express her own anger. Also, I had unwittingly validated her inner feelings. Secondly, I gave her the language with which to express her anger and rage toward her father. It is likely that her father would have considered any expression of anger or rage to be sinful and the consequences would have been severe. Hence, to survive her childhood and adolescence, she had to accept her father's abusive behavior and repress her anger and rage in response to it. This is to say that she was unable to acknowledge her anger, having repressed it, and she had never developed the means by which to express such feelings.

These two sessions turned out to be significant for Sara. Years of repressed anger and rage had been expressed and her feelings toward her father's abuse had been validated. This started the process of resolving her feelings and interestingly, she came to view her father as a victim of his own rigid fundamentalist beliefs. At the base of their relationship was a deeper sense of love and care that helped her forgive his behavior and form a closer relationship with him during her adult years.

Other significant sessions occurred close to the Christmas season. Sara came to one session very upset and angry with the woman who lived in an apartment across the hall from her. It was a time when her own judgmental and moralistic attitude came to the surface. She condemned her neighbor for engaging in prostitution, as she had observed men coming and going from her apartment at all hours of the night. To make matters worse, her neighbor had several small children who she felt were being subjected to such immoral behavior. She became obsessed with her neighbor's behavior and there seemed no way to resolve her feelings or to initiate any change in her judgmental and moralistic attitude.

Sara's ranting continued for a number of sessions, and I was at a loss to find a way to help her reach any resolution of her attitude and related obsessions. Finally, she came to a session appearing quite distressed and remorseful. She said that she felt so bad about how she responded to her neighbor's behavior. She had become humbled by the fact that she had no money and she said, *I think I am going to have to do the same thing she is doing if I am going to bring Christmas to my children.* My response was, "but you would be doing it out of love for your children." She acknowledged her own judgmental and moralistic attitude, and she could see how she had actually learned this attitude from her father. It was a humbling experience which led her to a more loving approach to her neighbor, and eventually, to her fellow renters in the apartment building.

Fortunately, an anonymous contribution made it possible for Sara to provide Christmas for her children. Moreover, she confided that she had knocked on her neighbor's door and was invited in for a cup of coffee. Her neighbor, finding a sympathetic and compassionate listener, shared that she was having to resort to prostitution in order to provide for her young children and bring Christmas to them. It was not something she had wanted to do. It was a desperate decision on her part. This was the time when the steel mills were shutting down in Youngstown and many had lost their jobs and the economy was poor. Soon Sara and her neighbor became good friends. Further, another interesting thing happened. Most of the renters in her building were single mothers who were struggling both personally and economically. She befriended many of them and soon found herself being sought for counseling and support. It was one of the most profound and sudden changes in one's personality that I have observed. On the other hand, I have witnessed a number of occasions when life experiences have had a humbling effect, sufficient to change one's attitude toward others. Such changes often happen outside of psychotherapeutic intervention, but can be validated, reinforced and supported during therapeutic sessions, helping to make the change more sustainable and lasting.

Another significant moment occurred one evening when I entered the therapy room. I often saw Sara in the evening following my workday and after classes. Apparently, I had had a particularly difficult day and it showed on my face and demeanor. She immediately responded, *Oh, David, you look terrible. You must have had a really bad day. What happened?* At first, I resisted telling her about my problems and difficulties which I often encountered in the Department Chair position. However, something internally urged me to express to her what had drained my spirit. I observed that she was listening with compassion and care, and she responded in much the same way I had responded to her during the course of our therapeutic relationship. To be sure, this was a change in roles, with which I was not entirely comfortable.

Later as I was driving home from my session with Sara, I was feeling badly over allowing a shift in roles in which she had become the therapist and I the client. On the other hand, I also had the feeling that something significant had happened. Rather than judge my behavior, I needed to examine what had really happened. There was no doubt about it, Sara was genuinely concerned about me. Her display of compassion and care was obviously sincere, and I readily verified her observation and perception that I was feeling both psychologically and mentally stressed. Then it suddenly dawned on me, she was truly demonstrating a sense of love and care for me which is not typical of someone with a diagnosis of schizophrenia. "My God." I thought, "Sara is not schizophrenic anymore." To be sure, I had developed a deep fondness for her, and I often felt compassion over her tremendous struggles. I had learned that love or an "unconditional positive regard," (4) as Carl Rogers had often said, toward a given client, often has a significant healing effect. It might be noted that Rogers had developed this kind of thinking while working with schizophrenics. In this case, it occurred to me that it is not always enough to love a client unconditionally. Rather, it is even more therapeutically significant when the client can return this unconditional kind of love in a healthy way.

It might be noted that Sara struggled to resolve her judgmental feelings toward her neighbor who had to resort to prostitution to bring Christmas to her children. Once again, she had been caught polarized in the good vs. bad duality. Finding herself humbled by her own economic troubles during the Christmas season helped her to identify with her neighbor's plight. This opened her to perceiving the situation in a much different way and she began to view her neighbor with a sense of love and care. Hence, it was this sense of love that enabled her to resolve the duality. Moreover, it was from this case that I developed the idea that the cure for schizophrenia is to learn to love others.

Unfortunately, Sara had recently lost her job as a clerk typist when the steel company she was working for shut their doors. It was the time when most all the steel mills in Youngstown were going out of business which then created an unemployment rate higher than anywhere in the US. Consequently, she was applying for any job that she could find. Since she barely made ends meet with her low paying clerk typist job, she had no financial reserves to carry her through this crisis.

Finally, Sara obtained a job interview with a steel company in North Carolina. By the time she appeared for the interview she was told, "didn't anyone tell you the job has been filled?" She told personnel at the company that she had spent her last penny getting to the interview and that she would do anything as she was desperate for a job. She was told that the only job opening was in the public relations office, and the job required writing skills. She begged to be interviewed for the job. In an effort to appease her, she was sent to the head of that department for an interview. The department head reviewed her resume and said, "what makes you think you can do this job? There is nothing in your resumé that would indicate that you have writing skills." Out of desperation, she pulled out her journal and handed it to him.

You may recall that early in our work, I encouraged Sara to write a journal. While I was aware of the fact that she was writing a journal on a regular basis, she would not share its contents with me. I felt that she was concerned about criticism. Hence, she would have had to have been in a state of desperation to share her journal, especially to a total stranger who sat in a position of authority.

Sara confided what seemed to be a miraculous story of her experience with the Public Relations department head. She indicated that he took what seemed like hours to read her journal. As he completed his review, he returned her journal with a smile and asked her, "when can you start?" Next, he began to discuss the requirements of the job and the general work of his department. Sara related to me that as she got up to leave after deciding upon a starting date he asked her, "don't you want to know what the job pays?" He told her that the job started at $16, 000, which by far exceeded her most recent salary and which was a substantial compensation for the late 1970s. Her look must have confused him because he asked, "isn't that enough?" She was beside herself with joy. It was indeed a miracle from her point of view.

Our final session came after Sara's recent return from her job interview. She told me the story of her interview experience and exclaimed, *I'm free, I'm free*. Then she placed her journal before me to read. Her journal began with descriptions of her daily activities and routine. However, as I continued to read, her writing began to become more rhythmic and then erupted into poetry and prose. To be sure, her writing was impressive, and I was sure that the public relations department head had become equally impressed. Moreover, it verified a talent for writing which had been revealed through sessions with her Collective Consciousness.

Then Sara told me of a series of dreams that she had been having. She indicated that they had been quite vivid and seemed very important. I was surprised when she started telling me of her dreams with significant details. Her dreams were extremely close to the imagery sessions that we had had. I realized that what she had experienced in her imagery sessions, dreams that she had had at an unconscious level, were now being revealed to her. She was dreaming the dreams that she had once had and which had surfaced only in her imagery. At that time her schizophrenic split and defenses were such that she had no memory of what had been experienced in imagery. This was a clear indication that her schizophrenia had become resolved and there was a free flow between her unconscious and Ego Consciousness. Hence, the feeling, *I am free*!

This final session was touching for both of us, as it was evident that I would probably not see Sara again, certainly not in a therapeutic way. Clearly, our work, which at times was painful for both of us, had come to a successful completion. It was indeed a touching moment when Sara came to me with such excitement to say, *I'm free*. She repeated this over and over again. This prompted me to write a poem as a tribute to her and our work. The last lines were, "Oh, you do not know that when you embraced me to say, 'I'm free,' what was given was in that moment returned to me. You do not know that there is something in me that loves a sprit free." (5) I never saw Sara again, although I kept up with her for a while through a mutual friend. I often think of her and find myself sharing her story with others as part of my teaching and therapeutic work. Many years later I tried to find her during the writing of her case study as I often asked clients to review their own case studies for purposes of validity. I had a friend who was a private investigator who traced her back to her home in Tennessee where her trail ran cold. Sadly, he concluded that she had died.

CASE STUDY II
Ellen
A Case of a Spirit Guide

Ellen volunteered to help in my research work. Having heard that I was conducting hypnotic/imagery studies of the unconscious, she felt that she might be a good subject because of her past meditation experience. Since she appeared to be a mature and stable person in her late 40s, I consented to work with her on an experimental basis. In fact, I felt it might be a pleasant relief to work with a more stable person and perhaps enter into a working relationship with a greater degree of mutual effort.

It was revealed that Ellen was a highly educated person and in the final stage of earning a Master's degree. She was married, although it appeared that her marriage of some duration was a source of unhappiness. Her husband was apparently suffering with chronic depression that rendered him incapacitated and dependent on her most of the time. It seems they had entered into a business together where she needed to carry most of the responsibility and burdens.

It did appear that there were several children in Ellen's life. However, there was little discussion concerning them. Apparently, they were on their own and no longer significant factors in her life and personal growth. My impression was that she appeared to be embarking upon a new life journey with a sense of commitment to fulfill some direction or purpose not yet clearly defined for her.

Ellen confided that she had spent most of her life with feelings of intense guilt, anxiety and inadequacy, along with bouts of depression. We might consider such feelings to be related to her marriage, but she claimed that they existed long before her marriage. Further, as far as she could determine, there was nothing in her childhood to explain these patterns of thoughts and emotions. It seemed that she had entered into various therapeutic relationships where nothing significant had surfaced, nor did she receive any relief from her emotional suffering. She had come to take her symptoms as a condition of life which were to be accepted rather than alleviated. At any rate, despite her marriage and chronic feelings of guilt and hopelessness, her life appeared to have been normal, and she seemed to have made significant gains in her own personal growth. As we progressed, I became impressed by the courage and strength with which she faced her daily burdens.

Ellen revealed that she was hoping I might become instrumental in helping her investigate a few of her own questions. She assumed I would be operating with a given set of hypotheses, and she hoped I might be able to help solve some of her own "mysteries of life." First, she developed a strong belief in reincarnation and wanted to understand a possible relationship between past life experiences and present life circumstances. Second, later discussions centered on the "guides" of her unconscious she had already met during previous meditation states. Third, the source of her symptoms of guilt, remorse and anxiety continued to be a question even though she had all but given up on becoming relieved of these symptoms. Since I had no difficulty taking these questions to be the primary focus of our work, we quickly proceeded to investigate her first concern.

Part 1
Julia, Joseph and the Farm

Our first investigative strategy was to apply hypnotic regression techniques to take Ellen back in time to possible "past lives." This strategy seemed to go smoothly at first. However, after a few sessions we were met with resistance. We implemented a more non-directive imagery approach which seemed the most helpful. After some more resistance, it was suggested that she might look for someone who could step forward to help us. *Oh yes, my guides can help. Julia is there and Joseph is there, too. I have known them for a while.* It seems that Julia and Joseph were previously accessed during past meditation sessions. She had developed sort of a workshop within herself where she often interacted with them, and she came to view them as her meditation "guides." They appeared to her as benign spiritual beings or entities with whom she could discuss her problems. Joseph seemed to be the older and wiser and the more intelligent of the two. Julia seemed much younger and tended to remain in the background and seemed a bit shy.

With regards to resistance to exploring Julia's life, Ellen says, *she seems to feel that I may not be ready to touch that or she might not be ready to reveal it. She really doesn't say anything. I just sense what she means.* Ellen observes that Joseph starts to talk to Julia. *He seems to want her to do it, and I have the feeling he will be there.* After some hesitation on Julia's part, it is suggested that perhaps she could take Ellen by the hand and lead her to what she might want her to see. It was also suggested that perhaps she could show her some pleasant times.

Julia takes Ellen by the hand and *it seems like we are walking through a field. It is a plowed field. It seems like spring because nothing is planted there yet. She's leading me across the field toward a barn and farmhouse. There seems to be some animals around, some horses, this kind of thing. She wants me to come inside the house. It is a big house, maybe not so old but it seems old. The house is painted a yellow-green color. It has a very high peaked roof. She is going into the house now. We are crossing a big porch. There is a double front door and half of it is open. The colors are very bright. There is a lot of color around. It must be spring because the trees outside have begun to come out in leaf. The turned earth. They must have plowed it with horses. We have gone inside but we seem to be staying in a little foyer. I ask her to show me the house. OK, we are going into the room on the left which seems to be a parlor. There is a picture in an oval frame of a man. I don't know who it is. She is not sure whether it is her father or grandfather. There is a big organ kind of thing in the corner. It appears to be walnut. It is very shiny. The organ is Victorian looking.* Julia says that the year is *1872* and the area is *Frederick County, Virginia.* Ellen says that the area *looks like that and the color of green the house is painted looks like that.*

Part 2
Julia's Resistance and Relationship to Ellen

We suspect that Julia represents a problem or void in Ellen's unconscious. We can sense the process beginning to unfold which seems dependent on Julia's capacity to face a certain experience in her life. Further, there is data that suggests the nature of her relationship with Ellen and Joseph's role in the process. This portion of the work starts with Ellen being led back to the farm.

Ellen describes Julia as being *smaller than I am, smaller boned, shorter. She has a decided widow's peak in the front of her hairline. Her hair appears to be long and when I have talked to her before, it has been hanging. But now it seems to be all done up in a knot.*

Initially, this session seems to be specifically centered on the barn. However, Julia and Ellen do not enter the barn. Perhaps the process was somewhat interrupted by my inquiry of Julia regarding her relationship with Ellen. It appears that she is relieved by the digression and seems to be momentarily lacking in courage to proceed. It is interesting that Joseph intervenes and attempts to get the process back on track. The digression had to do with Julia's relationship with Ellen, which seemed to suggest that Julia is part of Ellen's Collective Consciousness. On the other hand, Joseph appears to be one who is guiding the process and supporting Julia in doing what needs to be done. Ellen says that Julia *knows that it must be told, and she says that she'll plan how to do this*. Ellen continues, Joseph is *there as a safeguard. That is the reason he went with Julia. He seems to be fully aware of the whole situation and kind of has a hand on the rope.*

Part 3
Julia's Accident

    This imagery session with Ellen was lengthy. From the beginning we sense that there is much work to be done; a process that needed to unfold. Ellen asked Julia, *are you ready now for what you were going to do? We have to go back to the farm. We've gone up to the side of the house. There is like a driveway between the house and barn. Now we are standing on the threshold of the barn door which was where we were last week. She seems reluctant. She's climbing a ladder up to the barn floor. She says for me to come with her. Now she is climbing up another ladder; must be to the hay. She's just in the hay. The hay is loose. It is not bundled like we have now. She is kind of hiding around the hay. I can't see her all the time. I'm kind of standing at the top of the ladder watching her. I ask her if she was alone when this happened and she said 'no.' I ask her how old she was, whether she was young or older. She seems to have reverted to childhood. As I look at her she appears, ah, maybe twelve or fourteen. I seem to sense a pitchfork involved. I asked her if she was working up here or playing, and she didn't say anything. When I asked her if she was using a pitchfork, she hung her head and stared crying. It appears that there has been an accident, and she has dropped the pitchfork from the hayloft. I see why she's so upset. The pitchfork hit a man. It is the same man that was in the picture on the wall in the house. It is her father. This is why the house is so quiet. He died as a result of this, and she was held responsible as a negligent. Her own negligence caused this, and because of it she has been banished from the family.*

    At first, our impression might be that Julia's story of accidently killing her father actually represents some deep conflicts that Ellen has with her own father, conflicts that were repressed during early childhood. Perhaps there was a time when Ellen's childhood mind had fantasized about killing her father, a thought that might have been repressed but which planted a seed for a future emotional upheaval. Since the thought of killing her father could have been a horrifying experience, Ellen might have created Julia upon whom she could have projected the "thought deed." Then as Julia resolves the conflict, it also becomes resolved for Ellen.

    Another possibility which has occurred in my clinical experience is that of identifying with characters of a given drama within material that was read during childhood. In modern times, this phenomenon is much more likely to occur with television and movies which add a visual component to the experience. We may actually find in future research that this present generation of youth may experience many repressed conflicts from their deep involvement with such visual dramas. More recently, many young people spend hours playing computer games that may surface as unresolved unconscious issues in their adult lives. This could be the case with Ellen. Further, it might be assumed that she would most likely have had to contain internal conflicts in order for a given identification, such as with Julia's story, that became so deeply integrated. Hence, the framework for conflict resolution, having been fully integrated, could be used by the adult mind of the future as material for problem solving.

Symptomatically, Ellen had expressed deep feelings of guilt, inadequacy and depression. These symptoms have long been a mystery to her because her life had otherwise been relatively happy and lacking in experiences that could cause such symptoms. This would be especially true with regards to guilt. While bouts of anxiety and depression are common among middle aged persons, a sense of guilt without related life experiences or environmental conditions would seem improbable. These data then suggest repressed elements that could very easily have taken the form of Julia's story.

Given above are possible explanations of Ellen's imagery which would fit a traditional analytical point of view. However, she insisted that she had had a close, loving relationship with her parents and that she has not felt any anger or resentments toward them now or in the past. In subsequent discussions, she revealed that she considered Julia and Joseph as past life personalities and that Julia's accident may have actually happened. Clinical experience suggests that the accident had to be relived in the present in order to be resolved. Her feeling was that Julia needed her help to resolve the conflict with her (Julia's) parents. Ellen's role seemed to be typically that of intermediary, one who could look at all sides of the situation and present an objective picture to all concerned. Combined with her help, Joseph's role seemed to be that of the wise father figure. Since the accident was considered to have happened in the distant past, it appeared that its resolution needed to occur at a spiritual level. Except for her intermediary role, she could not see how Julia's accident could have affected her life or personality.

For the first time in our work with Ellen, we are able to develop an association between internal content and external symptoms. It seems interesting that it did not occur to her that the underlying dramatic portrayal of Julia's tragedy could explain her life-long bouts of guilt and depression. Rather, she felt that she was merely helping Julia resolve her conflicts with a sense of care and compassion. She had not come to sense the possibility that to help Julia was also to help herself.

Over time, Ellen's imagery work seems to have accomplished a good deal. First, the basic conflict situation and the content through which it was expressed was revealed and clarified. That is, the space within which the conflict or psychic complex could be projected and experienced as a reality was generated, quite possibly from actual memory. Second, Julia who was presumably a part of Ellen's Collective Consciousness could re-experience a tragic event in the presence of an accepting adult level of consciousness with sufficient authority to resolve the issue. Third, in subsequent sessions it was revealed that Julia's father was a harsh, cruel and an authoritarian man. His cruelty could be viewed not so much as a cause for an intentional act of life destruction, but a contributing factor for creating an intense sense of rejection from family and friends.

Part 4
Julia's Confrontation with Her Mother
and a Subsequent Journey

Further imagery continues with the same themes of the previous sessions. Ellen says, *she has taken us back to the time because he is still lying there. The time seems confused, as though we are going into this and yet it is happening. But we come in later and it is kind of a flash back. And, it was an accident but nobody thinks so. He was a very harsh man. She appears to have no brothers, so she had to do the farm work like a man would do. She was made to feel very guilty.*

The relationship between the mother and father, with subsequent consequences to Julia, becomes revealed as Ellen continues her dialogue in an imagery session. *Her mother, I sense her mother's presence. But, her mother has turned her back on her completely. I can't see her mother's face. She won't permit that. She won't allow Julia to look at her. It is as though she is turning her back on Julia. I asked her if she's treating Julia this way because she feels that Julia has done this on purpose, and she feels guilty because she wanted to do the same thing, and it's taking a lot to keep her from turning around. From her behavior it looks as though it might be. Yes, it's as though she had thought this through many times, "wouldn't it be better if?" And when it happened, the thought made her feel guilty. And if she faces Julia she has to face her own guilt. It's more a matter of how she thought this out, but it's more like she's thought this on her own and when it actually happened, she kind of feels that maybe she willed it.*

Ellen defines her role in this unfolding family tragedy. *I seem to have become involved in this as an active participant. I seem to be talking back and forth to the people in this.* Typically, in these types of situations the present life, having grown beyond a past life event, becomes the one who can intervene and bring some resolution to an otherwise impossible dilemma for those directly involved. Being on the front end of her life, Ellen can assume the authority necessary to orchestrate a process of healing.

Next in this process is to bring the father forward. Part of the problem was that, *No one would listen to her (Julia). But I called to the father, and he won't come out. He is hiding is what he is doing. I think the basic trouble is the fact that he doesn't have a son and he is bitter; bitter at Julia because she wasn't a boy. These observations are making him think about coming forth. He's beginning to see that maybe this is true. I don't see him but he is talking. He said, "but it wasn't my fault." He blames himself that he has no children, no sons. He seems to feel very keenly family pressures, and the neighborhood pressure and pressure of friends that one should have a large family and he doesn't or didn't. He seems very upset at the attitude of everyone. He feels falsely accused, falsely blamed. He is kind of like hiding around the corner of the barn talking. He really isn't that austere, vindictive man that everyone thought him to be. He has been covering that softness*

I suggest that, "perhaps what is necessary is to have them all come together." Ellen responds, *Yes, they seem to be moving in that direction. The whole scene seems to be shrinking so that they are all coming into close proximity. But nobody has moved. Mother is still standing in the kitchen, but she is not in the kitchen. It's outside where they are all together and yet she is in the kitchen. It kind of...ah...Julia seems to be in the middle, and she doesn't seem to know which way to look or which way to go. Her father has not come out yet. He is afraid of exposing his true feelings. That is the reason he won't come around the corner. I've told him that she needs his help now more than ever, and if he doesn't help her she'll perish. And, he doesn't want that to happen. He has decided to come around the corner of the barn. He is kind of caught up in the way one does things, the way one is supposed to. Men are not supposed to show emotion, or at least that is his concept of it. Mother still hasn't responded much to this. She is aware of what is going on but her back is still turned on the whole thing. It is quite a revelation. It never occurred to her that he could be covering all his feelings. He is trying to tell the mother how he feels about things. She is not truly ready to respond. She is still too caught up in herself. He has decided to let her work for a while and then he'll come back. For some reason or another he wants me to leave her now.*

Interestingly, Ellen appears able to understand each participant in the imagery drama. She is able to present the tragedy as an accident, thus relieving Julia of the responsibility for an intentional act. Ellen's intermediary role seemed necessary in order to pave the way for forgiveness from the father and mother. Also, she seems able to comprehend the father as a person who was unable to withstand the public ridicule associated with lacking the capacity to father male children. It seemed important to resolve the perception of the father as a cruel and harsh man. Rather, the father might become more deeply understood in terms of his archaic concepts of manhood and masculinity. Indeed, the father could be perceived as a product of his culture which lacked the necessary reference for transcending the social onslaughts to his weakened sense of self and manhood.

Regarding Ellen's role in this unfolding drama she says, *I seem disconnected, not involved in the whole thing and yet I was. Now, whether he was viewing me as an intermediary, a helper, I don't know.* Ellen returns to what she refers to as the workshop where she meets with Joseph, her guide. He seems pleased with the outcome of the preceding session. Further, *Julia seems much relieved. She doesn't seem to be as reticent. She seems more open now than she was before.*

After several sessions Julia's relationship with her mother emerges again. It appears that her mother is ready to face her and respond to the necessities brought about by the accident. Apparently, Julia must leave, with her mother's blessing, on a journey west to begin a new life.

In the mother we find one whose life purpose was tied to her husband; such that his loss was perhaps like losing her own life, despite at times, having wished his death. This concept of the husband-wife relationship would certainly be consistent with the historical moment being portrayed in the imagery work. Her life, although subjected to cruelty by him, was *bearable* because of her intimate knowledge of him. What seemed to be needed for resolution of the situation for her was the assurance that his death was an accident. This could pave the way to relieving the mother of her own guilt feelings over her fear that she might have *willed* it to happen through Julia. Also, Julia could be released to begin her new life given her mother's *blessing of forgiveness*.

The next segment of the imagery begins with, *I look and see the farm and the fields and the house, and the barn, just as it has been the other times that we have been there. And, she is reaching for my hand now. But she hasn't said anything. We are just going. She seems to be...ah... more than knowing whether it is time or not, she is going to see. She is kind of checking it out. We have gone around to the right side of the house. The house seems to be facing east, so we have gone around what would be the North side of the house across from the barn. We are going up the steps of the kitchen, up to the kitchen. Her mother is still there at the kitchen sink. She seems to wash an awful lot of dishes.*

Then Julia confronts her mother. *She calls to her mother, "mother, you know the whole reason. It was an accident. I would never have deliberately done anything to harm anyone. Why do you treat me so?"* Her mother responds, *Because of the loss that I have. I have no one for whom to live for now.* It appears that her mother's life was devoted to her husband despite actually hating him at times. Julia says, *Mother, don't you realize that you are free of the terrible, terrible things he would do and say.* Her mother answers, *but you only saw one side of him. There was a side that you didn't know and you didn't know why he behaved as he did. Because I knew, this life was bearable.* Ellen makes the observation, *She appears to be a very sad person.* Julia has asked her to forgive her and she says, *"Yes, my daughter, I can forgive you now because time has taken off the hurt."*

Ellen says that, *her mother seems to want her to leave. She doesn't feel that the right place for Julia is here. She seems to feel that Julia would assume guilt from the whole situation and never develop a life of her own. It isn't a question of her not loving her. It is a question of what she feels is best for Julia. Yes, but Julia doesn't understand where she is to go or what she is to do. She is asking her mother this. She is to go with relatives who apparently are moving away from the area. Her mother says it would be a better life for her. People won't know what happened and won't judge her for it. There seems to be a westward movement. I sense she is to go with a group who are heading west into a new area farther west than where they are now, into a mountainous area, but not way far west. She seems to be leaving with her mother's blessing, which was not what it was before. Things have cleared up for them.*

Ellen indicates that the mother *seems to be staying here. I don't know what the situation is going to be. She seems to have made up her mind to stay, and I sense that the farm is going to be taken care of by someone, perhaps other relatives. Yes, but I'm not sure it's all entirely family. Apparently, she may have other interests. She may marry again.*

Apparently, Ellen is confused about Julia's trip. She seems to be making preparations to go on a trip, a trip that she has already taken. But *she seems to be off making preparations for this, like she is to go right away.* Finally, her guide Joseph steps in and explains that she has been through this before. Ellen senses that, *she seems to have had lots of blockage emotionally at this point in her life. She kind of stopped emotionally when this accident happened. Now, apparently, she is going to be able to catch up with the rest of her life. I didn't know that could happen. Yes, it's going to be more of an emotional thing because she really did go but her psyche, I guess, never really went with her. She had to solve this problem and this relationship had to be straightened out before she could continue, although she really went. But it was kind of like the body went but the spirit did not. I didn't know that could happen. Yes, and she seems to be in a great rush to get herself back together again. And, she seems very happy at being able to do this. Apparently, this is the reason why she has always hung back and was so quiet and shy and unhappy looking.*

Ellen continues, *I'm not quite sure how she got with that group going west before. Joseph says that that group took her in because she had no place to go and they took her with them. The mother of course, had no words for her at all, turned her back on her completely.* It appears then, that Julia is going to re-experience this part of her life and the outcome will be much more positive, healing and growth producing. Joseph says, *she is going to be busy for a little while, but she is going to be in and out as she works things through. Then, that's going to free her to do the things she has to do spiritually. It is kind of like she has to take care of her own business and go to work to. Yes, Joseph says that I won't know anything about it unless she happens to stop by and tell me, as she has told about the incident on the farm. It is kind of like you don't understand what goes on in another person's life unless they want to open up and tell you about it.*

Part 5
Reliving Julia's Journey West
and the Process of Resolution and Healing

In the imagery given above, Julia was preparing to begin a journey westward. Having received forgiveness from both her mother and father, she is apparently free to re-experience the journey as a growth experience. It seems that she had actually taken the journey before, but she could not grow because spiritually she was consumed by an unresolved issue. This re-experiencing of the journey enabled her to achieve the growth that was otherwise lacking even though the new experience was purely at a spiritual level.

Having been released from the negative attachments with her mother and father, Julia is able to re-experience the journey as a positive growth experience. It seems that she will begin the new journey at about age fourteen and progress in age from that point. Ellen says, *she kind of stopped at this point because she couldn't get a blessing from her mother or her father. It was as if she were a spirit alone and she couldn't move on and do what she had to do without the help of those closest.* It appeared that in order to proceed in her growth everyone connected with this unresolved situation had to be released.

Ellen's imagery experience, except for the historical context, would not seem uncommon. From clinical experience as far back as Freud's work, we have learned that it is often necessary to go back in one's life and relive through dreams, hypnotic regression, or verbal expression with other unresolved life events in order to be released from them. When such experiences become repressed, it is often because one's childhood mind lacks the emotional and cognitive development to process and resolve the experiences as they happen. Moreover, clinical experience with given "past life therapies," (1) including hypnotic regression, suggest that a similar process is involved from one life to another. This is to say that some traumatic event in one life may take several additional lives to develop the growth and maturity necessary to resolve such experiences. Ellen's case would seem to be a good example of this.

In any case, Julia seems to be a fragment of the greater Self, of the Collective Consciousness, a past life rather than one having originated as part of Ellen's specific personality. Further, it is Ellen's adult development and wisdom that appears to be needed to fully understand the otherwise unconscious conflict and to serve as an intermediary among the various psychic components involved. The unconscious content of Ellen's psychic void having been brought into consciousness contains the primary elements of the conflict which makes it available for resolution. After all, one cannot resolve something that remains unconscious. While this unconscious material was held in a dark and unknown state, it could only be manifested through the emotional system as psychological symptoms without an apparent object. Perhaps one purpose of the psychological system is to respond to what filters through from the unconscious side of the personality with such symptoms as free floating anxiety, depression, guilt, feelings of inadequacy, etc., which motivate us to descend into our unconscious to discover the correlates.

It has been observed that when repressed material is released and resolved, the client begins a growth process that may proceed quite rapidly. Actually, some therapists measure their success in terms of the client's development of greater insight into their lives, along with corresponding levels of maturation, when confronted with difficult life circumstances. These observations are often noted in the face of little or no change in the person's environmental conditions. This is to say that a person's life may remain just as problematic, but he/she may develop an increasing capacity to face their problems with greater strength and creative responses. This would certainly seem to be the case with Ellen who seemed to be discovering greater meaning and a sense of renewed purpose in her life despite an unhappy marriage.

It would seem that reliving Julia's accident up to the point of departure westward was to be of direct benefit to Ellen. However, as Joseph indicated earlier, this is Julia's own experience and it will not be necessary for Ellen to know anything about her trip unless Julia decides to tell her. It appears then that once the process of resolution is underway there may be no need for the remaining details to be brought into consciousness. It seems that Julia who is presumably a fragment of Ellen's Collective Consciousness is able to grow in an autonomous way. It is assumed that what is learned and the growth that is achieved on Julia's journey will be made available as knowledge to Ellen, should the necessities of life require it. Otherwise, Ellen's growth as an individual personality would not be affected. This seems to indicate the possibility of a continuing growth and healing process throughout the whole system within the unconscious. Occasionally, such psychic material may be brought into the realm of consciousness when it is needed for conflict resolution at a level of concrete reality.

With regards to Joseph, he claims to be *simply that of a guide*. He appears to be there more out of a close relationship with Julia rather than with Ellen. Further, he states that he has somewhat of a *caseload* and there are others with whom he works such as a 10-year old boy with physical difficulties. Part of his work in this case appears to be getting him together with a particular doctor and working with both of them for mutual benefit.

Joseph seems to be philosophically oriented, and Ellen perceives him to be like a *priest, rabbi or minister*. Apparently, he is more concerned with living his religious beliefs rather than *telling what it is*. What guides his life appears to be *biblical law, Judaic Law and natural law, as well*, which he claims to be the *same thing*. While Joseph's role seems to be to bring Julia's life to resolution, with related benefits for Ellen, he does not seem to be part of Ellen's Collective Consciousness. Rather, he appears to be what he says he is-a benevolent guide in helping others heal their lives and proceed down the path of growth. As indicated, he has a *caseload* of people with whom he works. He suggests that the relationship between the physical and the spiritual worlds is very important. The physical world seems to be the *scene* of his work. He says that the *physical world is a help to me because then I can test out the things that I am working on or that I think will work*. Further, when he is in the physical world, presumably in a reincarnated state, he carries with him what he has learned in the spirit world.

Joseph seems to be a sincere expression of psychic consciousness; one who does not present himself as something of divine wisdom or righteousness. This sometimes occurs with similar but more malevolent manifestations. Rather, he appears on the surface to be trustworthy and knowledgeable within the given role that he has assumed. Unlike Julia, he does not appear to be a fragment of Ellen's Collective Consciousness. However, the fact that Joseph exists as a critical element or projection of Ellen's imagery cannot be denied. It becomes therapeutically important then to respond to him as he appears to be until such time when the projection ceases to be growth-producing. The question is whether what is occurring in the imagery process is healing and growth producing. Should this not be the case, then the imagery content needs to be dismissed.

Excerpts from the transcript with Ellen and Julia indicate the necessity for Ellen to be involved in the process of Julia's unfolding life experiences. Ellen asked Julia, *what is the purpose of my being involved in all this?* Julia responds, *Oh, I guess you don't know about that. But, you see, I was so young. They just wouldn't listen to me, and I needed someone who was enough older that they command some attention, because nobody listens to you when you are fourteen.* She continued; *I couldn't get my mother to face me. I couldn't get a blessing from her or my father. It was as if I were a spirit alone, and I couldn't move on and do what I had to do without the help of those closest to me. I had to face it and in doing so I had to make them face it.* Ellen indicated that, *it wasn't just releasing herself but it was releasing everyone connected with this tragedy.* She also suggested that *she would become released too, because her mind (Julia's), her mind could not progress, or go beyond this very far without tying together everything.* This is to say that since Julia is part of Ellen, her unresolved experiences also permeate Ellen's own personality and emotional states. Moreover, Ellen's feelings of guilt and depression would appear related to Julia's unresolved experiences and they do not seem to be manifesting from her own life experiences. Hence, when the situation becomes resolved Julia is released to continue with her life in a growth producing way, and everyone involved in this tragedy is released as well, including Ellen.

Part 6
Dialogue with Joseph
and His Role as Guide

While Julia starts on her trip west, a reliving of the trip in a much more growth-producing way, we enter into a discussion with Joseph regarding the dimensions of "reality" in which he lives and works. From my work I had developed a hypothesis that there are actually multiple dimensions of existence, and I was wondering if Joseph, from his perspective, might have some knowledge of such things. He says, *the external world and the psychic world, yes. But I don't know what those dimensions would be and perhaps again it is a matter of interpretation. Remember last, when we were talking about the circles? Well, it is kind of like this. There are dimensions of the mind. Perhaps there are people who know more than I do, but those circles keep going out and keep getting broader and broader until they grow to encompass everything. Then when you've experienced all of this, perhaps that's where the other dimensions come from. But I haven't gotten that far yet. I still have a great deal more to do.*

Joseph is next asked about his work relative to the external world and the world of the spirit, which seem to be the two dimensions in which he lives and works. He responds that, *Well, it is the scene of my work. Now my work is in the spirit world, but it must manifest through the physical world. So, if there were no physical world, I would be unable to perform or help anyone because there would be no way to manifest it. That is the importance of the physical world. Yes, now of course the physical world is help to me too, because then I can test out the things that I am working on or that I think will work. It kind of works back and forth, the two sides of the same coin. And, ah, when I am in the physical world I carry with me a lot of the things that I've learned in the spiritual world. And I can work them out, try them out myself.* It seems that Joseph represents a working relationship between the physical world where we exist and the spiritual world in which he exists. This relationship appears to depend on the interaction between the two worlds in the form of what might otherwise be referred to as the "guide phenomenon." It seems that the physical world is somewhat of a testing ground for given ideas and processes that are generated by those in the spiritual world. It might be noted that while Joseph is serving as a guide in Ellen's life, his work with her is part of his preparation for returning to the physical world during his next incarnation.

Joseph continues to refer to Julia as a fragmented part of Ellen while he is not. Presumably, there are many fragmented selves (Collective Consciousness) and occasionally there are unresolved conflicts with some of these fragments that at some time come to the surface to become resolved. In Julia's case, Ellen, the present personality and Ego consciousness was needed to help transcend the unresolved experience or memory and bring it to a positive conclusion. In this way Ellen can become relieved of her related discomfort or psychological symptoms, while Julia is released for further growth since her development appeared to have been blocked as a consequence of the accident. Hence, she continues with her life with subsequent healing and growth such that her life is brought to a successful, positive conclusion. Once this occurs, Julia, as with other soul fragments, becomes integrated within the greater system of the Soul.

According to Joseph it is quite common to have inner selves such as Julia, who are fragments of the same Soul. In addition to such fragments, it is possible to have guides who are separate identities. They apparently operate in accordance with assignments, presumably from higher sources, to help given persons through periods of difficulty and growth. It is assumed that these assignments are given with the purpose of obtaining mutual benefit for both guide and client. In Joseph's case, he was able to test some of his ideas for helping others through Julia and Ellen. At the same time, they were enjoying the benefit of a knowledgeable companion who has greater access to information needed to carry on life creatively in the physical world. Where Joseph's assignments come from is yet to be determined.

Finally, we are left with an interesting picture of the "guide phenomenon" and how it functions. Although our discussion with Joseph leaves many unanswered questions, we come away with a feeling that much has been accomplished, at least in the resolution of some psychic disturbances with regards to Ellen's life. Whether the specific data or content can be taken as valid in a literal sense will likely remain a question to many. However, in Ellen's case, it would seem that the themes running through the content are fitting.

Since it is often thought that when one dies and presumably goes into the "spirit world," they experience an increased knowledge and awareness. Joseph responds by saying that, *In other words, can you bring your awareness with you? Well, yes, to some extent. Now you remain aware of things that are necessary for you to know just as when you go into the physical world you take with you, things that are necessary to know. You are not going to be conscious of everything you did in the physical world any more than you are aware in the physical world of all you did in the spirit world.*

It appears that our spirit guides are there to help us remember what we need to know in the physical world and when we need to know it. He indicated that, *there are points at which this knowledge needs to go back and forth and this is the point where guides come in. We help you relate to things that happened in this world (spiritual world) to the things that are going on in the physical world and to integrate them as best you can with the things that are going on with you now.*

Next, I share with Joseph that Ellen's case is similar to what we have been doing with other people on an experimental basis. One of the things we would like to become better at doing is to facilitate the process more efficiently without interrupting the process. The basic process, it seems, requires that we need to go back to the unresolved memories in previous lives and bring such memories into consciousness such that they can be acted upon and, hence, resolved. Joseph responded that, *it is a question of resolving problems from a previous lifetime as Julia had to do before she could continue. Sometimes one has to do this but there are other fragments of the soul who can go on and progress without having to resolve that. But now each fragment will have to resolve it sometime or another before that particular fragment can go on.* Then we return to the subject of "spirit guides" for more clarification. Interestingly, during this discussion, Joseph confides that I have or will have 11 guides in my lifetime. I ask if these guides represent specific lives that I have had in the past such as unresolved fragments of my soul. His response clarifies the difference between guides and past life fragments. *When I was speaking of 11 guides, I meant that you would have 11 guides during this lifetime, but not necessarily reincarnated selves, no, no, not any more than Ellen is a reincarnation of me. We are two separate persons. This is a helping relationship rather than a fragmented self.*

To seek further clarification, I ask if some guides are fragmented selves or are they like him, guides who are unrelated to the given soul. In other words, are some guides fragmented selves while others are unrelated to the person involved? He indicates that, *Well, it can be either one, of course, but I don't recall being a guide to a fragment of myself. Now it occurs to me that perhaps once the soul begins fragmenting into other persons, those begin. Those develop an identity of their own and although we begin as one we are now separate just as the "God Head" began as one and decreed us and by doing so we became separate individuals and it's kind of this taking place on another scale throughout evolution. As we grow and develop and evolve and fragment, these fragments of ourselves grow and develop and become individuals in their own right.*

Next, I discuss with Joseph some of my research and how it seems to unfold of its own accord as if it were a growth process. However, it becomes difficult at times to determine whether data produced in the work is valid. It appears that all that can be done is to collect the data and compare data from one case to another to see what themes are consistent. It is like bringing all the pieces of a puzzle together to form a whole picture that has the greatest validity. He suggests that, *well when you do this all together, when you are in a position where you can sort through it, you will find that things on the left will fit with the right and things on the right will fit over to the left. You will have a lot of transposing and integrating to do. Some of what you have isn't going to prove to be valid, but it is important for the very fact that it is not valid. Some of what you need you haven't acquired yet, but that will come when it is necessary when you need it. In other words, there are a few pieces of the puzzle left to be gathered yet.*

DISCUSSION

It would seem significant that the initial encounter with Julia and Joseph included imagery of an early spring farm scene. For those who are more symbolically oriented, we can hypothesize that Ellen was being prepared for new growth much like the soil was being prepared for seeding. Quite possibly, there would be a turning over of "psychic soil" with subsequent planting of new ideas, concepts, etc., for future growth and healing. Perhaps her past was to be plowed under along with many ideas and perceptions about life that no longer hold validity in her life. Such outmoded ideas would then serve as the "groundwork" from which a more inclusive frame of reference could emerge. Whether her unconscious intended such symbolic references cannot be known. That these symbolic meanings were fitting to Ellen's work with her Collective Consciousness cannot be dismissed.

The turning over of Ellen's spiritual soil appeared to take form in Julia's story, which included a tragic accident involving the death of her father. We might hypothesize that the death of Julia's father also represented the death of a cruel and harsh father figure. He later emerged as having been a product of an inability to transcend social and cultural definitions of manhood. The result was not really a death of the father, as much as it was a re-birth of the father as a caring, loving person. Further, the guilt associated with the killing of the authoritarian father could also be resolved through verification that the death was an accident. In mythology, we often see that change comes from a tragic or unintended event that had been accidental. (2) This is to say that significant change often comes from an accidental event in which no one can be blamed, except in mythology the gods who, without human awareness, mischievously alter human events and rigid traditions.

It appears that we are dealing with a rural setting during the late 19th century with an immediate family structure of father/husband, mother/wife and child. The tragic loss of the father has also created the loss of the husband which is a different matter. Given the historical moment in rural America, a loss of a husband would create many hardships for the wife/mother. First, the mother would have to take care of the economic role of the father while raising children and assuming her traditional family role. Second, without male companionship life could yield extreme loneliness and at least a temporary loss of a sense of life purpose. With this we find Julia's mother; a person whose life purpose seemed typically tied to her relationship with her husband. Her inability to face Julia seemed due to her difficulty in facing her sense of loss and perhaps her own guilt over the possibility of having willed the death of her husband. No doubt, as presented in our story his cruelty was sufficient to create such thoughts in the mind of Julia's mother. Given the necessity of Ellen's role as intermediary, the mother was released from her feelings of guilt and probably a need to blame since the incident was clearly an accident. As would be expected, Julia's confrontation with her mother, with Ellen being the intermediary, yielded a reconciliation and her mother's blessing and forgiveness. Having obtained forgiveness from both her mother and father, she is free to start her new life journey that promised to be a more complete growth and healing experience.

A close examination of the data presented in Ellen's case study seems to suggest a few parallels between Julia's story and Ellen's life. Most importantly, there is the matter of psychological feeling states. To be sure, Julia, having been a part of a tragic accident would have had symptoms similar to those experienced by Ellen most all her life. Whether Julia's story has any literal basis in reality is a question open to debate. However, that Ellen experienced and participated in an unfolding inner drama involving the death of a cruel father cannot be denied. The experience appeared to explain in a way that fit her own system of beliefs the basis for her chronic depression, anxiety and feelings of remorse.

Moreover, being an intermediary in a reconciliation between the father and mother further reinforced Ellen's belief in reincarnation. Hence, the reconciliation among all those involved was a real experience for her and created the possibility of resolving her own chronic symptoms. Actually, within about a month of her initial imagery session with Julia, her symptoms appeared to have become significantly reduced, especially those of guilt and inadequacy.

The resolution of the tragic accident and relationships with both mother and father appeared to release Julia and Ellen for new growth experiences, as represented by Julia's journey west. It might be of interest to note that according to Joseph, Julia and Ellen would go separate ways, except for an occasional checking in on Julia's part. Further, it was suggested by Joseph that Ellen would be experiencing new insights or growth of new concepts and ideas. We would hypothesize that at some point Ellen will begin some new work in her life or perhaps start anew on some previous endeavors with a new perspective. To be sure, her marriage was one of the issues in her life that appeared of great concern, and she seemed to desire a more meaningful relationship with her husband.

During subsequent discussions Ellen began to develop further insights into her own life and with her relationship with men. While her relationship with her father seemed warm and loving, her relationship with her husband was less than satisfactory. She felt that her feelings of inadequacy and chronic depression and remorse caused her to be attracted to a man who also felt a sense of inadequacy and who manifested a chronic depressed mood. This is to say she could feel sympathy toward him and felt a desire to "take care of him." She could also see that she contributed to her husband's dependence by assuming the decision-making role and the primary economic provider. It seemed clear that her relationship with her husband was such that it tended to undermine his own sense of manhood and self-worth. Furthermore, her husband's tendency to displace responsibility needs to be considered a primary factor to which she had difficulty responding. While we might want to draw a parallel between Ellen's marriage and Julia's mother's difficult marriage, it appears that we may be dealing with a separate issue that was central to her own life. The imagery work seemed to help create an openness by which she could develop deeper insight into the everyday problems of her own life.

One question that Ellen had, was who were Julia and Joseph? Were they merely a figment of her imagination or were they actual autonomous entities of the "spiritual world." In any case, they seemed to serve as guides who supported her and helped her deal with content of her unconscious and develop deeper insight into her life. During a discussion with Joseph, he differentiated between him and Julia. He emphasized that he is a guide who is not directly related to Ellen, while Julia is a fragment of her Soul and has a direct relationship to her. The implication is that Julia is one of her past lives, part of her Collective Consciousness, who experienced a traumatic event in her life. She had been brought forward into consciousness to help heal this trauma, such that she could become released for further healing, growth and the fulfillment of her life.

Joseph indicated that we often have a number of guides, some of whom are past lives and others, like him, are guides that help bring healing and growth to the Soul and Soul fragments or past lives. The relationship between oneself and his or her guides is one of reciprocity. There is mutual benefit for all involved. Moreover, it appears that the spirit guides help us remember what we need to know in order for us to function in a growth producing way in the physical world. In this regard he says that while his work is in the spiritual world, *it must become manifest* in the physical world. Hence, the importance of the physical world is that it enables him to test ideas and possible solutions to the problems of life by helping others conduct life in the physical world. He suggests that it works both ways since he can carry with him into the physical world what he has learned by helping others while in the spiritual world.

It seems that we are fragments of God; fragmenting into other individual selves who have their own lives and identities. Such identities experience life in given cultures, and under different circumstances. This brings many different life experiences to be integrated by the soul for its own growth and increased consciousness.

Furthermore, Soul fragments, as Joseph describes them, are what I refer to as the Collective Consciousness which carries a different meaning than Carl Jung's reference to the Collective Unconscious. (3) When he uses the term Collective Unconscious he is referring to the multitude of Archetypal patterns that inform our lives.

When Ellen began a therapeutic relationship with me on a research basis, she had several questions she wanted to pursue. First, she had developed a belief in reincarnation and wanted to know if there was a relationship between past life experiences and her present life circumstances. The data produced from spontaneous imagery, imagery that was not produced by way of suggestion, tended to support her belief in reincarnation. Further, that a given past life could have a significant impact on her present life was also supported. Hence, it became clear, while reviewing the consistent themes and content of the imagery that her feelings of chronic depression, guilt, inadequacy and anxiety appeared related to a tragic and traumatic experience from a past life.

Second, Ellen wanted to know of the identities of her "guides" Julia and Joseph and their roles in her life. Were they real or merely a figment of her imagination? Data from spontaneous imagery suggested that Julia was a past life entity or what was referred to as a "fragment of her soul." On the other hand, Joseph did not appear to be a past life entity. Rather, he seemed to be a separate entity whose role was to assist Julia to resolve a traumatic event in her life while supporting and guiding Ellen in her role as intermediary in the process. Interestingly, the process was of mutual benefit for all involved. We are able to speak with a greater sense of validity in this regard, because of the consistency between Ellen's case and many other cases with which we have worked in the past. Her case is presented here as one example of the many cases with which we have experienced over a 20-year span of research.

CASE STUDY III
Theresa
A Case of the Collective Consciousness and Supra Consciousness

Theresa started working with me because of her difficulty in dealing with her husband's cancer diagnosis and probable death. Since part of my research endeavors included working with terminally ill patients and their families, she felt that I might be able to help her face the trials that lay before her.

A woman in her late twenties, Theresa was an attractive, energetic person who was devoted to her husband and his care. She had married just out of her teen years after having been overprotected, especially by her father. While her mother was a warm and affectionate person, her father was withdrawn and quiet. She later learned that he had been severely abused as a child. This seemed to have made him "pretty mean." He appeared to become especially mean during bouts of heavy drinking. On the other hand, Theresa's mother seemed to do her best to understand her children. However, she never really felt that her mother understood her, especially during her teenage years.

The most difficult problem with Theresa's father came when she began to date. He would not allow her to date until she was 16 years old and then only in group situations. She recalls that once when a boy called her, he took the phone and told the boy that if, "you call her again your ass is grass." Then he abruptly hung up the phone. Her father proved to be quite an embarrassment during her teen years with his "totally" unreasonable attitude.

It seems that Theresa's father had a good deal of difficulty confronting sexual matters. Instead of discussing such concerns with her, he tried to protect her from boys who wished to date her. She reported that he would actually become violent when boys came to see her. Apparently, he felt that each boy was a threat to his daughter's sexual well-being. Moreover, he seemed distrusting of her own capacity to deal with dating situations.

In Theresa's later years she came to feel that her father really did love her and the rest of the family. She seemed to be able to see the person beneath the meanness that he often displayed, during her childhood. However, she claims that she still must force herself to kiss him goodbye, when leaving from visits with her parents.

Other immediate family members include one sister who was two years younger than Theresa and a brother four years younger. Her relationships with her siblings appear to be normal.

A major difficulty with Theresa's family was a lack of open communication. She indicated that any problems that one had was kept inside. "All hell" seemed to break loose when one said the wrong thing. Since she was a talker she was often criticized. What input that she did receive tended to be negative. Everything was kept inward, and she said that the lack of communication remains in the present.

Theresa came from a poor background, having lived in an inner city setting in a large mid-western city. Her father was a skilled laborer with only an eighth-grade education. Her mother was a housewife with a high school education. As she explains, "there was not a lot of money around."

Despite growing up Catholic, Theresa attended public schools due to family financial problems. She was required to take Catechism classes. Religion was often a source of irritation for her. She considered it all rather "hokey" and even as a child she felt that she could see through all the "empty" rituals. The many rigid definitions of "sin" held by the Church were also difficult for her to accept.

On the other hand, Bill, Theresa's husband, seemed very religious, and she went to the Catholic Church with him after they were married. He had been an altar boy and was a strong member of the Church. Their regular attendance continued until his illness with Cancer became prohibitive. At this time, she began to become more introspective and sought out her own religious views and beliefs.

During Bill's illness they attended many different churches, wherever healing services were being offered. Theresa soon became aware of what she considers to be the "fake plastic part" of religion. She came to resent the judgmental nature of many religious people who seemed to "think of God as a person" who looks down upon the "righteous" with some sort of special favor. Rather, she appeared to believe that God is a being who dwells in each person, but who is beyond human comprehension. She perceived God as energy that is always there and which is always positive. She felt that this is a viewpoint not held by most religions, and she claims that she just has no tolerance for "self-righteous, judgmental religious people."

One problem Theresa has had in her life is jealousy. She says that she could be "possessive and obsessive" when it came to boyfriends. Her possessiveness did not include material objects. Rather, it was directed toward a boy's or man's love, affection and attention. She indicated that she always had the feeling that her boyfriends should not look at anyone else. However, after struggling many years with jealousy and possessiveness, she reports that she no longer has such feelings. This, she feels, is one of her great accomplishments in life.

Another area of difficulty was Theresa's inability to establish intimate relationships with others. She reports that she is just now beginning to develop a sense of intimacy. During her married years, intimacy was a serious problem. Presumably, this stage of growth had been strongly inhibited by her relationship with her father. Another factor was most likely the lack of communication and critical atmosphere experienced within her family. She felt that her intimacy problems have to do with a lack of self-acceptance, combined with an inability to love herself. This has been a problem that has been difficult to overcome. She indicated that her development of a sense of intimacy has been like scaling a high wall and coming down on the other side.

Maturity problems often plagued Theresa during her early adulthood. Her emotional growth appeared to have been greatly inhibited, perhaps due to her critical and overprotective father. After her marriage with Bill, she was thrust into adult situations and her immature behavior became a constant source of embarrassment. During such times she never really felt as though she were a "real grown up person."

Bill's illness and death seemed to have provided the circumstances by which Theresa had to rapidly grow toward adulthood and adult responsibilities. After such maturing experiences, she relates that she feels like a "person who belongs to the world and the

Universe," and that she can fit in anywhere. She claims to feel self-accepting, assured and mature. What bothers her now is that she does not seem to "feel a drive or passion for anything," which appeared to accompany her days of immaturity. Rather, she appears to feel more mature, adult like, settled, peaceful and loving of life.

Theresa was a good student and enjoyed school. Her grades were consistently high throughout her school career. She was also involved in a number of extracurricular activities such as the Future Teachers Association. Other interests included athletic endeavors. Her perception of herself as a student was that she was a very social person. Following high school and marriage, she completed nurses training and has since pursued a career as a hospital nurse with some private duty work on the side. Presently, she is taking additional college course work for personal development. However, she says that it is better to go to college while you are still "young and dumb" because it all seems sort of "corny." She feels that many college courses contain things that everyone should already know.

Going to nursing school also proved to be an important time of Theresa's life. It was the first time she felt as though she had accomplished something of significance. She has perceived herself as a "quitter," as she often started things but never finished them. She had made up her mind that she was going to finish nurse's training and the achievement of that goal seemed to be a milestone in her life.

Theresa's marriage has had many ups and downs. The first eight years of marriage seemed to be like a constant ride on a roller coaster. She really had not wanted to get married. She felt that she was too young having been only 19 years old. However, she was desperate to get away from her father's dominance. Once she tried to move away from home, but her parents "went totally berserk" over the attempt. Marriage appeared to be the only acceptable way out. She felt that Bill was a "dear, sweet and wonderful person" who seemed to be "just the right kind of person to have for a husband."

Her marriage soon met with problems because Theresa seemed to know nothing about intimacy, love, or personal communication. At first, she tried to settle into the routine of marriage as she felt happy to get away from home and her father's overprotectiveness. However, she soon became restless, which was somewhat sublimated in her nurse's studies. After finishing her training, she seemed to become "confused" and marital problems started to surface. This led to a separation of a couple of months. Following this period, she became pregnant with her son, Bobby, and the marriage seemed to develop more stability.

Theresa felt that her marriage problems were due to her need to be an adolescent whose development was impossible to fulfill while living at home. She appeared to want to be free to do as she wished and not to have to answer to anyone. She could not seem to realize that Bill had no intention of imposing his will upon her or threaten her sense of personal freedom. Presumably, she had projected her relationship with her father onto her otherwise gentle and loving husband. Looking back, she realized that Bill was the type of person who would not cause one to feel a lack of freedom, and that he was actually trying to help her become totally her own person.

The marriage began to mend once Theresa came to realize that Bill was not her father and was not trying to keep her tied to a "ball and chain." What seemed to make a big difference in her attitude was when she discussed her feelings with one of their close friends, a Priest. After sharing her sense of constraint with him, he pointed out that she had decided to stay with Bill even though she could have left. It was actually her choice to stay with him. It had nothing to do with anyone chaining her down or keeping her from what she wanted in her life. This seemed to be a significant concept that she had not considered. It appeared to be the basis for a totally different perception of what a sense of personal freedom really means. It seemed that once Theresa felt that she actually had a choice concerning her own life, she lost that feeling of "being locked in."

One significant event that helped Theresa to see more clearly that Bill was not her father to whom she had to answer was when she dented their car while pulling out of a car wash. Upon returning home, she became hysterical because her father would "go nuts" when she would wreck or dent the car. She said that he would go "screaming on a rampage." Bill, in contrast, was very concerned because seeing her hysterical response he thought she had been injured. He became relieved to find that she was all right.? His only response to her denting the car was, "what's the big deal?" Bill's attitude seemed to be that "everyone makes mistakes." From this experience, combined with Bill's demonstrated open and accepting attitude toward others, she began to feel the "nervousness of life" decrease significantly.

Another trait that Theresa had acquired from her family experiences was a high degree of defensiveness. Having projected her father on to Bill, it was difficult for her to understand when he tried to make a constructive criticism or suggestion. She tended to take such advice as attacks and would quickly revert to the parent/child role. In this regard she indicated that Bill seemed to have a kind of insight into her that she was not able to understand. When she responded defensively to him, he would try to sooth her by saying, "you don't have to be defensive, I am not attacking you. I am just telling you," or "I am just asking you," or perhaps, "I am just trying to help you." He seemed to understand her reactions completely and tried to help her through her defensiveness, although she had difficulty realizing it. However, this kind of response from Bill was another positive growth experience gained from her marriage.

Moreover, Bill's illness presented Theresa with what seemed to be insurmountable problems. First, her relationship with him became threatened by his incapacitation and possible death, just as their marriage was beginning to solidify. She was becoming comfortable as wife and mother. Both of them had worked hard to establish a mutual growth relationship and it did not seem fair that all might be destroyed in the near future.

As Bill's illness progressed, Theresa had to take more responsibility for making and implementing family decisions which were once his primary duty. His care alone required endless hours of coordinating private duty nurse schedules and dealing with hospital staff during his many hospitalizations. She indicated that there were times when she had to protect him from hospital personnel. It seemed that everything had to be black or white or in accordance with given rules. With Bill's deteriorating condition, the rules and procedures seldom applied. It became increasingly difficult for him to communicate, and he was unable to speak out aggressively in his own behalf. Hence, Theresa found that she had to constantly defend him and make sure he was receiving the individualized care that he needed. She reported that occasionally she had to resort to "pushing and shoving" which greatly disturbed her.

Like many terminally ill patients, as Bill's condition deteriorated, he became more dependent and childlike. It seemed that he was regressing back to childhood. Theresa's patience would become stretched to its limit by his constant demands. She found that losing her patience often became a source of personal guilt. Also, she often became deeply discouraged as the illness seemed to go on for so long without any indication of when his or her suffering might come to a merciful end. She confided that it seemed as if "it would never end." Moreover, she indicated that "he was real tough to be around." Many of her days were long and tedious. Theresa said that she sometimes felt like Bill was no longer there, although she knew that it was him on the inside. However, it was very difficult to watch the kind, gentle and insightful man who she had come to know and love during a decade of marriage fade away before her.

Theresa, having been a dependent and overprotected adolescent, now had to shoulder the total responsibility for Bill's care and all household matters. Each day was full of frustration. Nothing planned seemed to work out and instant change was the norm. She had to be nurse, caretaker, schedule coordinator, decision maker, etc., while at the same time being a mother and head of the house. Theresa indicated that for the sake of survival she learned how to delegate responsibility. She learned that the many tasks were too numerous for her to accomplish on her own. She had to trust in others to help take charge of those things beyond the scope of her time and energy.

The experience of caring for a deteriorating terminally ill loved one would seem beyond endurance for anyone. Theresa's devotion to Bill's welfare and her head of house responsibilities, given her past maturity problems, speaks well of her courage and psychological strength. Indeed, her growth and change were occurring rapidly given her life experiences during this horrible time in her life. Her feelings about her difficult experiences came through a story she told about a friend whose husband left her when she became ill with cancer. Everyone was extremely critical of the husband. However, Theresa's response was that she could "totally understand." She said that, "no one could know what it is about unless they have been there." She seemed to have no judgmental thoughts toward this man. On the other hand, it is a tribute to her own inner strength for staying with Bill during this difficult time and not running away from the responsibilities she had come to shoulder.

During the six-year period of Bill's illness, Theresa felt "like part of me was a robot, not knowing what I felt or thought." Often, she seemed to just go through the motions of the day. She indicated that it took her about two years after his death to get over these feelings. It appears as though she had endured a lengthy prison sentence. It took her some time before she could respond to the new freedom from the burdens and responsibilities that she had endured.

Although Bill's death did bring some immediate relief to Theresa, she soon had to face enormous medical bills. Their $1,000,000 dollar health insurance policy had run out with over $40,000 still owed. After a discussion with the hospital financial personnel she was able to have the rest of the bill forgiven. However, she had to become very aggressive and assertive before achieving success which created additional stress in her life.

It was during this difficult experience of Theresa's life that I began imagery work with her. Actually, I had also been asked to work with her husband. However, he did not respond as well to imagery therapy as had been hoped. He seemed to have some rigid personality structures that created resistance to descending into the depths of his unconscious. This resistance may have been related to his relative rigid religious beliefs that tended to view the unconscious as a source of evil to be avoid. Interestingly, while Bill was open and receptive to things external to himself, he found it difficult to be open to what appeared from within himself. This is not to say that he was unable to produce images, it was that his images lacked substance and a sense of growth and healing.

I do not remember what prompted my imagery work with Theresa, but she immediately began to produce rich, spontaneous images. Having discussed Bill's resistance to the imagery process, we had him listen to what we were doing from an adjacent room. While his presence in the same room became a distraction for Theresa, she actually encouraged him to listen in on our sessions. The idea was that he could monitor our sessions and determine that nothing evil was going on. It was hoped that this might help him work through some of his resistance and become more open to his own unconscious resources of growth and healing.

Part 1
A Canine Companion and Guide

Theresa's first imagery session strongly suggested that she might become a good candidate for imagery work as she was able to respond with rich and vivid spontaneous images. As we began, she found herself on a deserted beach feeling somewhat lost. Gradually her beach scene takes on more life symbols and a canine companion emerges to serve as her guide to various imagery experiences. She says, *I really love to go to the beach. I've never been to a beach like that. Yes, it's nice. I can see way out and there's nothing. All you can see is the horizon. There are no boats. I think I'll walk up the shore for a while.* Interestingly, she initially appeared surprised that she could experience such vivid images and which seemed so real to her.

Next, Theresa begins to see some *seagullsscreeching*. Further on she sees *an old tree over by the, you know, up from the shore a ways, toward the grassy area. Yes, it's just like another dead tree. There are no leaves on it or anything. Now some birds are perching on it. They are flying all over it. The bad thing is they're all sparrows, too. (Laughing) I thought they were all going to be seagulls.*

The dead tree with birds perching on it appears to be a significant symbol for Theresa. It is suspected that the tree in her imagery represents something of her life that has died, perhaps something of her youth. The death of her childhood may lead to a rebirth of a more mature adult, one who is able to accept the demanding responsibilities of taking care of her husband and assuming the primary roles of wife, mother and head of house. Further, her imagery also reveals that what has died serves in a supportive role for other forms of life, the sparrows. Possibly, these sparrows that seem a disappointment to her, represent new ideas and insights into life. What they seem to lack in size compared to seagulls is quality, perhaps growth in small increments. Moreover, they may symbolize the emergence of a more delicate and gentle side of herself; a part of her which is in contact with heaven and the nourishing sun. Hence, this aspect of her imagery seems to be a significant symbol of growth as it fits a natural theme of nature. Death becomes the process and substance by which a rebirth and new life can come into being.

In the next image, a dog of mixed heritage comes to Theresa. *There is a dog running along the beach, too. He doesn't seem like he belongs to anybody. He seems like a stray dog just running up there. I can't see what kind of dog he is. I can't recognize him as a certain breed of dog, like a Heinz 57.* This imagery appears to mark the beginning of an inner companion or perhaps a guide who is presented to her in a non-threatening way. *We are going to walk up the beach a little bit. I always like to walk up the beach. There are some people up further, sitting on the beach, too. We are walking past these people.*

With her companion Theresa seems to be prepared to walk into the world of people with whom she shares the beach. Hence, her imagery appears to be expanding with regard to forms of life and animation.

Another interesting occurrence is the brief image of a tree that has fallen into the water. *As we are walking, you know how there's a tree that goes from the land into the water?* We suspect that the fallen tree is symbolic of something in Theresa's life that has fallen, perhaps fallen into the waters of the unconscious and eternal life. Since it is a fact that her husband has contracted a "terminal illness," we are quick to assume that this tree may represent him or her relationship with him.

Next, Theresa and her companion become distracted by an old weather-beaten shack. *I see an old shack like on the beach, an old wooden shack. You know how they get weather beaten by the ocean, just an old shack. I think I'll go over and look at it. I'm looking inside. It seems all dark in there. It's real small you know, sort of like an outhouse. It is just a little old shack. I don't think the dog wants to go inside of it.*

It is not uncommon for an old dark shack to appear on the beach in one's imagery. Generally, the shack is dark because it contains repressed material that one is not ready to face. Later, when Theresa is ready, she may return to the shack and what is in the shack will become illuminated. At that time, she will be shown what is needed to be brought into consciousness. It seems significant that her companion dog does not want to go into the shack as he knows what is there and knows that she is not ready to face it. Moreover, it is possible that the weather-beaten shack with a dark interior may be symbolic of her perception of her husband's disease and potential death. That is, the shack may represent the degenerative aspect of his illness. The darkened interior may be his possible death, which she is not ready to face, at this time.

Apparently, there was a house on the beach when Theresa started her imagery. However, she did not mention this aspect of her imagery at that time. When she entered the beach, she came through a door and down some steps. Although it is not clear, we speculate that the steps to this house were the steps she used to enter the beach. It also appears that this may be the place where she first met her canine companion, a place where she first emerged into her inner world.

Theresa reports, *Suddenly, he's got a leash on him but I don't know where it came from, because he didn't have a leash before. I'm holding on to it and he's kind of running so that means I've got to run too. Yes, he is doing the leading. He's sniffing around some dead fish (laughs), on the seashore. OK, he's coming back. We're back to where we started from, but he didn't know where I started from but he just stops there. The steps are coming from a house and he wants to go in there.*

Interesting, Theresa's canine companion appears with a leash suggesting that she is going to walk him. However, it becomes clear that the leash is for her to be led by the dog which is a shift in the traditional role for dogs and humans. She is led past some dead fish to the steps of a house. Since the fish is a significant religious Christian symbol, it would suggest that many of her former religious beliefs have died and no longer inform her life, It is true that she had become disillusioned by organized religion and had developed a disdain for church dogma.

The house seems empty and deserted but otherwise well kept. She says, *we are going through this house I don't know why I came back out there because there is nothing in it. There's no furniture, yet it's in pretty good shape. There are no broken windows or anything.* She continues, *he's running through like a nut, the dog is. I think he is looking to scarf some food up. But this house is all deserted. When you go in the house, one room is like short, you know, like I expected to go in and see equal rooms on the side of this foyer. But this one room is like partial, part. I feel bored in that house, nothing doing there, so we are going to go out. I have him on a leash. I feel real cold for some reason. I'm freezing.*

Perhaps this house represents Theresa's inner-self, which she has possibly neglected most of her life having been preoccupied with external activities. Interestingly, she notices a small, partial room. Apparently, there is something of the structure that has not been completed. In any case, because of the lack of potential for substance and nurturing, it appears to lose interest for her and the dog, and he leads her outside. At this point she experiences a cold physical feeling. This experience also occurs in subsequent imagery sessions and it seems to be an expression of high anxiety. It is assumed that something about the house has created some feelings of anxiety. Perhaps the small incomplete room has triggered some memories that she has repressed. Further, it is suspected that her anxiety may also be related to sensing that she is about to go into the deeper realms of her unconscious.

The next image of apparent significance appears when Theresa's companion takes her to a hole in the sand. On the way there she sees a couple of boats on the shore. She says, *there are a couple of small boats on the shore, too. This seems like the ocean, yet it's not the ocean because, you know you don't see little boats on the shore like that. It's more like what you would see at Lake Erie or something.*

This is another common imagery with those whose primary imagery takes place on a beach. While it may seem out of place, given her experience of beaches and oceans, it is not an uncommon imagery. Often, the ocean represents God, who is like a vast body of water, whose presence is obscure on the surface but whose essence is teeming with life below the surface. The small boats tend to symbolize given aspects of God and herself being brought across the waters of the unconscious onto the shore of her conscious awareness.

With regards to the hole in the sand Theresa says, *the dog sees a hole in the sand and he's digging, sniffing in it. He's going to climb down in the hole and I'm going to climb down with him. We are going through like a tube. It is the only way I can explain it. It winds around. He's like wandering over my head coming, coming over my head, like he is climbing on the top of it and coming down. Yes, he's telling me (it's funny). Yes, he pulls me back up and out. He says, you already know. I know what? I don't know what I already know*. When asked if she has already been there, he says, *yes*, she has already been there. *I don't know that I know. (Laughs). I didn't get a chance to see anything when I got there*.

Curiously, Theresa's companion pulls her out of the cylindrical tunnel or tube that leads into the earth. Her companion pulls her out because he says she knows about what is there and she does not need to take this particular journey. While we do not understand what might have been in the tunnel, we suspect that knowledge from the depths of her unconscious is the kind of nurturing and substance that she has needed. Typically, such images tend to represent the birth canal and the potential for the creation of new life. To be sure, her journey with her husband and his illness is likely to lead to a rebirth of her personality with significant changes in the future. Further, her canine companion would seem to be a "guide dog" helping her to explore such knowledge of her unconscious and bringing it into consciousness awareness. This is a common role often assigned to animals, typically a dog, who leads one into inner experiences and subsequent growth and knowledge. They can also become reassuring companions.

Finally, this imagery session ends with Theresa's guide leading her into the ocean. *He says we should go in another direction. I'm not sure what he means. He's gotten stronger. He's pulling me harder. Now we are running in the water and the water is splashing. Now we are going a lot faster this time. He's saying, "come on." He's going out a little deeper. I'm sort of scared of deep water because I can't swim. (Laughs)* It is assumed that the "fast running" is meant to take Theresa into a situation that could otherwise be frightening to her before she has a chance to think about it. The fast running might also represent a sense of hunger or urgency in the self to find the nurturing that might be obtained from the depths of the unconscious. However, she confides that *I'm not scared for some reason.* Her guide dog seems to want to pull her into deeper water. She says, *it's over my head and he's pulling me over my head, you know. I can see fish and stuff swimming. Now he's pulling me to shallow water. I'm coming out of the water. He's a real friendly dog.*

This concluded Theresa's first imagery session. In this part of her imagery, it appears that the "guide dog" wanted her to get used to the water and its depths. Perhaps this is preparation for future journeys into the depths of her unconscious. The fact that she came through this experience with relative ease and without any apparent harm may have been a wise preparatory experience for other symbolically related adventures in subsequent imagery sessions. My clinical experience suggests that while each imagery session has certain goals to be accomplished, it also contains elements that prepares one for future sessions.

Part 2
The Old Woman

Interestingly, Theresa's first image in this session was that of a "gigantic bird flying." She describes it as *an eagle type bird with a real wide wingspan, just flying overhead, over where I'm standing*. When asked what she thinks or feels about the bird she says, *like powerful, yes, powerful*. Since the eagle is a powerful bird and is one who soars high through the heavens, we assume that it represents her own sense of personal power and ability to soar to transcendent heights, a potentiality she will need as she continues her journey into her unconscious.

Next, Theresa's canine companion joins her. She says, *I think I see him, yes, he's right beside me now. We're walking down the beach. I'm having trouble seeing things for some reason*. Soon we get the impression that something may be going awry with her imagery because of the darkness and her difficulty with visualization. She continues, *I'm just, I don't know what's wrong. I feel like it's dark. Yes, it feels dark and yet there's like a light off to the side. It's little, you know, it's not like a moon or anything. It's just lights off to the right side*. When one find's oneself in darkness during an imagery session, I usually suggest that they look for light and go toward the light. Furthermore, when one's visualization is blocked by darkness it may mean that there is something in the unconscious that feels threatened and is trying to disrupt the progress. This may actually be a good sign because distractions often emerge when one is making progress with healing and growth. I generally say that there is something in all of us that does not want to grow and change. If one presses on the distraction is usually set aside and the imagery work can continue. Such was the case with Theresa's imagery work, during her second session.

Theresa goes to the light and says, *this light is blinding me. It's like, you know when you look into the bright light of a car and you can't see. The dog is standing with me in front of the light. The light is white. We are going to walk away from the light now. The dog seems real big all of a sudden*. It is common for a guide dog to suddenly appear much bigger and formidable in imagery work. This usually means that something is trying to interrupt the work and the guide becomes more like a bodyguard or protector.

Theresa and her companion dog continue down the beach. They pass the hole that they visited in the previous session but do not stop. The dog seems to want her to follow him. *I'm just going to go with him. The waves are rolling in kind of rough. It's kind of lightened up like cloud cover but not strong. It did lighten up. I didn't realize it. He's telling me to come on. He wants to show me in this house*. Hence, Theresa comes out of the darkness, what was unconscious to her, and into the light of consciousness. *I think he had the idea to go into this house. It's got real rickety steps. We're knocking at the door. A real old lady answers the door. She tells us to come in. She says, come in and have some cookies*.

Since Theresa is led to an old beach cottage where she meets an old woman, we suspect that she has just made contact with part of her Collective Consciousness. Most likely, the experience of the eagle, going from darkness to the light, and her dog becoming bigger were all related to preparing her for entering and facing the deeper aspects of herself.

The old woman offers Theresa some cookies. This is consistent with one of the themes in her first imagery session which seemed to indicate a hunger or desire for spiritual nourishment. Therefore, we assumed that she was going to her Collective Consciousness for nourishment (knowledge) that she needs and the old woman is a source of this knowledge.

Theresa continues, *she's got a real nice table that's cherry, an old table. Cherry wood, real solid. We're sitting down at the table. She's going into the kitchen. The dog is sitting at the table like a person. She's telling me we'd better be careful* (walking on the beach). *Some of the people aren't real nice. She brings our cookies now. I don't feel hungry now. I feel nervous now. She's just too distant you know. The type of person you're not sure what to think of them.* However, as the old woman begins to talk about herself Theresa starts to feel more comfortable. *OK, she says that the house was a vacation house for her and her husband and he died. She just stayed there; sold all her stuff and is just living there. I thought she was the type who wouldn't like to tell you anything, but she's pretty open.*

Theresa is prompted to ask the old woman where she was born and where she came from. *She says she was born in Texas.* (laughs) *She says her grandchildren come up there and stay sometimes. She says let's go out back. The house looks brighter in general. She wants us to go down there. And it's right on the ocean. Right on the beach, sort of. She's got tables with big bright umbrellas on top. She's got like a real long dress on with one of those, you know, long aprons. She appears friendlier now. Her face looks real, not sullen, you know, and now it is brighter and smiling. Now she tells me that some people, some divers were diving off piers and they never came up. That's why she told me to be careful. I think she likes us visiting. She says I have a friendly face.* (laughs) *We see porpoises jumping out of the water. We are going back the other way again toward the steps where I come out to the beach*

Hence, the old woman from Texas warns Theresa of the dangers to be considered while visiting her inner world of ocean and beach. It seems that some divers were diving off of a pier and never came up. We assume from this that Theresa is being warned against blindly diving into her unconscious without proper guidance and help, as represented by her canine companion and perhaps the old woman in the future.

This imagery session seems to be an introduction to a part of Theresa's Collective Consciousness. At first, she is uncomfortable with the old woman because she seems distant and cold However, later she finds the woman to be warm and open about her personal history. As she says of her face, *now it's brighter and smiling*. This appears to help make her more comfortable with the phenomenon. Further reassurance seems to come with the image of *porpoises jumping out of the water*. It will be interesting to see how this old woman appears in subsequent sessions.

PART 3
The Old Woman takes Theresa to the Fire

In this imagery session the old woman serves as Theresa's guide, which is a typical role for the Collective Consciousness. In contrast with the previous session she steps into a *bright and sunny* day with white sand. It seems brighter than ever before suggesting a very positive and productive journey ahead. Soon her canine guide and companion joins her. *Yes, here comes the dog running over. He's ready to go right down where we were last time. Ok, we're at the house again. Now I see old stone steps up to it. I don't remember that last time. Partly cement that's broken, you know, and stones.*

It is interesting to note that instead of rickety steps to the old woman's house she experienced last time, there are *old stone steps up to it*. This seems to give the appearance of something old but solid, possibly a reference to the old but solid quality of the Collective Consciousness. Moreover, this may be interpreted to mean that she is accepting more fully her images and experiences related to the old woman.

Soon Theresa is on the old wooden porch and knocks on the door. *She's real happy to see me today. She's glad that I came back.* The old woman tells her that her name is *Sarah Donahue* and she was born in *1893*. Theresa says, *I don't know where that came from. Oh my goodness, wait. That makes her really old. Yes, but that is what she said. I'm asking all these questions. I go back to that dining room again, the same seating exactly, like I know she is standing there but there are no specific features or anything. Last time I saw her she looked different, like real old with a long nose and everything. I know she's there and she's talking to me and I can see like, her body, but I can't really see her face or head even. It's not like there isn't a head. I just can't see it.*

The inability to see the old woman's face is a typical phenomenon when encountering the Collective Consciousness. Generally, it seems to mean that one is not ready to identify this part of the self. Most likely there may be something related to this life such as suffering or guilt that might create anxiety and distort Theresa's imagery work. It is important that one remain calm such that an objective response to given images can be accomplished. In any case, since this perception is common during one's confrontation with the Collective Consciousness, we can assume that her work with the old woman may be healing and growth producing.

After Theresa asks a number of questions of the old woman, they take a walk down by the ocean. As they walk, it is noticed that the water appears to contain color, *like stripes, like a rainbow*. She says, *the most predominant color seems to be yellow. Yellow stands out for some reason. It looks like kind of like a candy strip thing, you know, where you see strips of color.* She (old woman) *says the ocean is always beautiful this time of the day. Yes, I can see yellow and blue and green and red. This lady wants to walk up the beach further, because we are standing. looking straight out at the ocean. I can see the sun shining down, all of a sudden, real clear, real bright, just a round ball, not like it normally looks.*

It is suggested that this phenomenon may be related to thoughts about God. Theresa confirms that she has been having such thoughts over the past few days. Clinical experience suggests that the rainbow is a religious symbol with each one of the colors representing archetypal patterns associated with certain qualities of God. In some Christian traditions the rainbow seems related to a reconciliation with God or a new covenant with God. The color yellow is sometimes associated with "gold, and the sun" and "it is symbolic of eternity and transfiguration." (1) The old woman says, *it's just God's beauty*.

Clinical experience suggests that this kind of phenomenon is a very positive indication of progress in imagery therapy. In a number of cases, a rainbow of colors has either preceded or follows a significant growth experience. It would seem no less the case for Theresa.

They continue their walk and Theresa says, *she wants to show me something. She is pointing out a tree and saying, "isn't it beautiful" and it's just an old, really old tree. You know how they get all crooked and stuff when they get old. I can't recognize what it is but it's, you know what kind of a tree, it's just got small green leaves on it, just an old crooked tree and the roots are sticking out of the ground. And she says, "that is God's beauty too." I'm getting overly anxious. I have to rest a second here (laughs). When I start to tense up I can't find that lady.*

It seems that the old woman wants Theresa to see "God's beauty" in the rainbow and even in an old tree. Perhaps these experiences are meant to help keep her calm and relaxed but as she senses that something significant is about to happen, she becomes anxious. Perhaps, the image of the old crooked tree is a reference to the old woman's beauty and the beauty of growing old, something that Theresa may not want to contemplate given her young age. However, these experiences of beauty may have actually intended to help keep her calm and relaxed in preparation for what is yet to come. However, sensing that something significant is about to happen she becomes anxious.

Next, they come to an opening in the ground. Theresa says, yes, *she is definitely showing me, like this area into the sand that goes down. I don't know how to describe it. It's a hole but it's like a scooped-out hole. She says, "let's go down there." So that's where we are going to go. It's a tunnel. We are bending our heads because it's so low. She's telling me, "come on and don't be afraid." She says, "feel how warm it is," which it is warm. You expect it to be cool because you are going underground. This seems weird but there's fire shooting out from inside of there, yet it's not burning. She is holding my hand taking me down there. The fire is like orange and red and it has blue spots in it. I ask her what it is and she said, "you'll see." She says, "it's warm and beautiful and loving." We are going deeper into this fire. The fire is coming up and we are walking into it. And I see us getting little, it's getting bigger. It fills up the whole area that I can see. She told me to take my shoes off and sit down a while. There's like benches on the sides of the cave and we are still in the fire. I asked the old woman when she first discovered the fire. She says, "it's been many years ago." She says, "I only show it to people who I think can appreciate it and accept it." Yes, this fire isn't hot. She says, we'll rest a little bit and then we'll walk around. She keeps patting me on the back and saying, don't be scared. (laughs) I'm not really scared, I just don't know what to think, in a way.*

This appears to be a very significant imagery experience for Theresa. While it is like nothing she has ever seen, she seems to accept the fire and its "loving" warmth. It is assumed that the fire represents the essence of her life, the fire of her own Soul, the Supra Consciousness. Like the yellow of the rainbow it is symbolic of the sun and light, which is at the center of everyone's life. In Eastern traditions it is considered "sacred, purifying and renewing." In Christian traditions, God is sometimes represented by fire. Hence, we conclude that Theresa has been led to the fire, the spiritual source of her own life because of her openness and ability to accept it as part of her own, otherwise, unconscious life. (2)

After resting for a while, the old woman leads Theresa further into the tunnel where there are torches on the wall. *There are torches on the wall where we are. Now the fire, we're not in the fire anymore. It's higher than us, up further in the cave and we're like underneath it and there are torches on the wall and we are sitting on that bench looking at these torches. She says, "That's the beginning, these torches." Now, she says, "Come on we're going to go deeper." It's like a cave but it is a tunnel. It's hard to explain.*

As they proceed deeper into the tunnel, Theresa sees people. She says, *I see figures of people. I can't see their faces but I know they are people and they are big people. She says, "they are nobody to be afraid of," because I'm getting uncomfortable, you know. She acts like she knows these people. I ask her and she says, "Yes." She says to just keep coming on. They sort of back off. She says, "they won't hurt you."*

It seems that having come out of the fire the torches serve to light the way and provide warmth for the rest of their journey. Interestingly, Theresa is told that the torches are *the beginning*. Perhaps the torches are meant to represent individual lights that have come from the larger fire experienced earlier in the tunnel. This is to say, each individual life may be a small flame from a larger, greater source.

Soon Theresa sees *figures of people*. She is told by the old woman that they are *nobody to be afraid of*. Once again, similar to her experience with the old woman she is unable to see their faces, suggesting that she has come across additional parts of herself, her own Collective Consciousness. A further verification of this hypothesis is in how the old woman refers to them as, *this is your family,* while walking through the tunnel. Next, they enter a maze where they seem to be walking back and forth. It is strongly suspected that Theresa has been taken into a Labyrinth which tends to represent human life with all of its trials and detours. The center of the labyrinth might be taken to be symbolic of the spiritual center of the self. Her center as represented by the warm, all-consuming, but non-burning fire which also represents something very *loving*. The old woman says, *its warm and beautiful and loving.* Finally, Theresa says, *now we pass right alongside of the fire, and we're coming out and it's bright daylight again*, as this session comes to an end.

PART 4
Theresa is Taken to Meet Her Mother

Theresa returns with her canine companion to the Old Woman's house. It seems that she is going to spend more time with the woman from Texas. She says, *OK we are at the house again. She's opening the door and she tells us to come right in. Her hair is different today. She's got braids on. But it is like I am looking at her but I can't see her face.* I suggest that she ask the Old Woman why she cannot see her face. Theresa says, *This is ridiculous. It sounds like there are all kinds of answers coming like nothing. She's saying, "you don't know why?" She says specifically, "you are not ready to."* This is a very common reason given for not being able to see faces. In any case, it is common when one is dealing with the Collective Consciousness. The old woman says, *"come on and quit asking so many questions."*

At the beginning of the session, I had asked Theresa if she might be able to see a castle on her beach. She indicates that she does see what looks like a castle. My suggestion actually came from an imagery session with another person. (The significance of the castle will surface in subsequent sessions). However, the old woman also sees the castle and says, *I know you are interested in that castle.* Theresa asked if *we could go in there today but she said, "not today, I'll take you somewhere else. Come on honey, you don't have to be scared." I'm not scared. She says, "let's go to your mother."*

They start walking on the beach. Theresa says, *she wants to go back down that same hole we were in. She wants to go a little bit further than last time, as far as you can this time. The old woman says, "Now, don't be afraid. Just take things as they come. There is nothing there to be afraid of anyway." We are going down in. We have to stoop to go down. There are lights on the side. There is an old chair sitting on the side against the wall in the tunnel. It's old wood. She says, "see this, this was your mothers."*

The old woman's announcement of going to her mother, appears as an interesting surprise to Theresa. She says, *my mother is still living by the way. But, this lady talks like it's somebody who is not living. But she keeps referring to my mother.* Hence, it seems that this mother is not her living mother. Perhaps, the old woman is referring to the "Earth Mother," or the "Archetypal Mother."

Theresa continues down into the tunnel. She says, *we are going deeper and deeper past the areas that we were in before. It looks darker. I feel like I can see her more than I can see myself, you know what I mean? I mean I know that it's me but I can't see me.* At this point, it appears that as she goes deeper into the tunnel, she has left her body image behind and is experiencing herself as pure spiritual consciousness.

They pass by people playing cards or a game of chance, which may be symbolic of life being such a game. However, the Lady says, *you don't need to bother with them just keep going.* A more important image appears to be a dish, which is described as her dish. The dish is described as having four sections to it. The old woman says, *"This is your dish."* Theresa expressed that *the dish, it's hard to explain. It's a dish like in four parts. It's got lines down and across. It's got four parts to it.* Theresa asked the lady, *is this my life? She says, "Yes." One part of the four is like it's almost like the plate has lids in four sections and one part is partially open. She says, "Do you want to see what's there?" I think I do. (Laughs) I'm going to climb inside this dish. There's like nothing though. It's like I'm surrounded by black, like darkness, you know. I'm getting back out. She says to me that I don't have to worry about these things.*

It is suggested that the dish represents Theresa's life. It is assumed that the four parts to the dish represent four parts of her life. The first part with the lid partially open may suggest that the first part of her life has not been completed and is only partially open. When she goes into this part she is surrounded by darkness. It is likely that this indicates that she is not ready to become conscious of what is there. Moreover, it may also represent the dark period of her life in which she is having to deal with the difficulties of her husband's life-threatening illness and the responsibilities which she is having to assume as mother, wife and care taker running a household and managing finances matters. Such responsibilities have been visited upon her quite suddenly. Further, having been over protected as a child and teenager, she had little life experience to prepare her for assuming these responsibilities. To be sure, this partition of the dish represents this part of her life in which she finds nothing but darkness and loneliness.

The next part of Theresa's imagery seems to be much brighter and she is told that it is going to be a part of her, a nurturing part, the mother, presumably the "Archetypal Earth Mother." She says, *it brightened up in that area. Like the part we're in got real bright. She says to me, "So do you want to know or don't you?" (Laughs) I tell her I do and she's telling me to have faith in her. She says, "Have faith in me." I said, OK, where are we going to go. She says, "we are going to part of you."* At this point Theresa loses her concentration and becomes anxious and unable to relax. Interestingly, during times when she is told that she is going to see a part of herself she tends to become anxious. Perhaps her anxiousness is related to self-esteem problems and a religious background that tends to degrade one's own sense of self. On the other hand, there seems to be something within ourselves that does not want us to know who and what we are, since to know is to assume responsibility for who one is.

The old woman tells Theresa to "*go in there." We are going to a door that's in the tunnel and it's a door that's got a rounded top. It's not like a regular door. I don't know where you would see those kinds of doors and it's got one of those brass knockers on it. I can't see exactly in the door. I can see through the crack where the hinges are. I see, bright, bright light. We are standing in front of this bright light. It's like a flame, but it's not.*

What Theresa describes is an ancient door that one might find in a castle or underground passage. She refers to a brass knocker which is reminiscent of what Jesus said to his followers, "Knock and it shall be opened, seek and you will find." She is certainly seeking, and it appears that she may find what she is seeking within her own inner consciousness.

As Theresa stands before the light, she realizes that she seems real little next to this light. *In fact, I look like a little tiny girl and this lady still looks like an adult. I don't feel warmed by this light. I just see it. The old woman says, "this light is you and you are it."* Theresa asked the light what it is and the light responds, *I am the One*. Then she asked, *Do you want to help me? And the light says, "I do." I ask the light; will you help me find where I am and who I am? The light says, "I will." In a way this light seems three dimensional and in another way it is flat. Part of it is flat, and it' turned for me to walk by it.*

It is interesting that Theresa becomes like a little girl in the presence of the light, while the old woman remains an adult. Perhaps this is symbolic of her level of spiritual development, while the old woman, with much more life experience and wisdom, is expressed spiritually as an adult. It is important to note that the light is actually Theresa, a part of her, and is the "One" at the same time. What she may be experiencing in this imagery sequence is the archetypal mother within herself, a part of herself not yet realized and what she is to become. To be sure, this is a time in her life when she needs the capacity to love and nurture herself and others, especially her husband and young son. Indeed, the archetypal patterns that are within all of us, and which Carl Jung referred to as the "Collective Unconscious," (3) but which I refer to as the Supra Consciousness, inform our lives and represent our capacity to act and respond to given situations that we may encounter in our lives.

It is interesting that Theresa asked the light, *will you help me find where I am and who I am.* This is a fundamental existential question regarding the meaning and purpose of our existence. One would think that she would have asked questions more directly related to her present life circumstances, including caring for her terminally ill husband and having to assume the responsibilities of being head of the house and being a mother to her young son. The light says to her, *"come on Theresa, I love you. Let's find out who you are,"* Theresa says, *I seem like a little tiny person, partly like a child, but I'm really not a child. I said to the light, "are you my mother?" The light says, "yes I am." It doesn't make sense to me but I am getting hyper again.*

As noted earlier when Theresa seems to sense that something is about to surface from her unconscious that may result in a change in her life, she becomes anxious. Change and growth often takes us into the unknown which results in a change in consciousness and with such changes comes responsibility.

The light says to Theresa, *"Let's go up these stairs." You see, we are underground in this tunnel, but now we are going up through an old wooden trap door, up and out. The light says, "this is the other side." Now we are on real green grass and the sun is shining real bright, and I see little children playing all over. Swings, and I feel like I'm sort of lost. Yes, it's like they don't even see me. It seems that way.*

Theresa seems to be confused by what she sees: little children at play. Apparently, she is being shown what her life has been, like a child at play when everything appears perfect, *real green grass and sun is shining real bright*. The life as a child is one which is carefree without adult responsibilities. The light says to her, *"it is you."*

After the light shows Theresa the children at play, she says, *"you will not grow here. Come here, and I'll show you how to grow." Oh, I'm starting to get cold*. Once again when growth and change is suggested, she becomes anxious. It is obvious that she is being shown that her life has been like a child at play without responsibilities or the kind of difficult life experiences that lead to growth and change. She says, *the light's calling me in a different direction, saying, "here you are again." I can't see* (anything). She continues, *the light is saying, "your mother is here." I don't get that mother thing. Ok, I can see half of a house like looking at the side of a house, but I can only see half of it. The light said, "that's all you need to see."* Theresa says, *you know it's there but it's like when someone takes a picture and you only get half of it in the film, but you know the whole thing is there. (I don't know why I start to shiver and stuff). The light told me, "Come on now you can go back." I would stay and see more but the light says, "No, you've had enough for one day." Alright, the light is sending me out. OK, I'm going to come up those steps.*

In this imagery segment Theresa is shown a house, but she can only see half of the house. The implication is that the house is her, or the structure of her life. She knows there is a whole house. However, it is like a picture in which only part of the house is caught on film. Further, she becomes anxious while being shown the house. Presumably, the half of the house that she is able to see is that part which represents her life as a child and young adult. The rest of the house, of which she has no conscious awareness, is made up of her life experiences yet to come. The part that she cannot see may reveal her future as a responsible adult when her life will become more fully realized through difficult life circumstances and experiences. It is likely that at an unconscious level she knows what the rest of the house looks like. However, she must experience it to become fully conscious of it.

Of great significance, is the emergent presence of the, "Archetypal Mother," (4) who is a differentiated part of Theresa, but who is also herself. She is loved unconditionally by this mother, who is leading her into growth and change. Given her background, it is not likely that she was loved unconditionally as a child. Hence, in her imagery experience she is able to experience a mother's unconditional loving presence. Moreover, she is introduced to the archetypal mother within herself that may inform her life during a time of difficult life circumstances. It is what she will need to respond to what she will be facing in the future. Presumably, we will be observing changes in her personality that will reflect a more loving and nurturing mother and person.

PART 5
Theresa goes to the Castle

Theresa returns to the old woman with her canine companion and they visit the castle on the beach for the first time. When she opens the door to her imagery *it is brilliantly bright out today. The ocean waves are rolling in, sort of foamy. I see the castle down there today, too. It looks the same except that there are more little buildings on it.* She says of the old woman, *I can see her face a little bit, sort of but not really.* She says, "*Let's go out in the sunshine."*

It might be noted that with each imagery session Theresa's beach appears to become progressively brighter. In this session the sun seems to be all-consuming. Since the sun is sometimes associated with the Christ Archetype, (5) it is assumed that she is coming closer to an experience with this phenomenon. Interestingly, she is told by the old woman, "*you will know the sun."* This response seemed to be related to my suggestion that the sun may get even brighter as she approaches the castle. It seems that the castle has a particular association with the sun. In some cases, the castle represents the place where one's wishes become fulfilled, a place where one becomes nurtured as the sun nurtures all life. (6) She said, *today you can go up to the castle if you want to. So, we're going to. This one tower that sits on the side of the castle that I can see real good, I have this thing that I want to go in there. OK there is a wooden door right on that tower, round at the top with a big brass round knob on it to open it with. So, we'll go in.*

Theresa and the "Lady" as she calls the "old woman" enter through the door to a dark space. The Lady says, "*don't be scared of the dark, come on."* They proceed through square doorways and archways as they go deeper into the castle. Finally, they come to a room with a round table. Theresa says, *it looks like a game table of some sort because it has round cups all around the edge of it, like cups that something goes into.* The Lady says, "*see this table, this is you."* Theresa indicates that *the area where those cups are is almost like a border, and it drops below that middle circle. You know, the round table is almost separate from the place where the cup area is and it looks green in the middle.* It is suggested that every place there is a cup there is a place for a person. She concurs, *that's what it looks like exactly, and there are a lot. That is why I couldn't tell you what kind of game table it was because it looks like 18 or more people could sit there, 20 or so. I don't know exactly.*

It is implied that Theresa is becoming involved in the exploration of different aspects of herself. It is assumed that the large round table where about 18 to 20 people sit represents the wholeness of the system around which given elements of the Collective Consciousness sit and take council. Each place is represented by a cup. It is interesting to note that later on in the imagery session it is revealed that there is a place for the Old woman who appears to be her designated guide.

They move on to another room where Theresa finds plants and flowers. The Lady tells her that the flowers are not important and directs her to a mirror. *There is a mirror like a full-length mirror. She wants me to look in the mirror. Oh, I look ugly in the mirror. It doesn't even look like me or a person at all. This is freaking me out. I don't like that.* The

Lady says, *"that is what you were."* Since the image seems to represent what Theresa was it is suggested that she be shown who she is now. She says, *before you said that Dave, she is saying, "this is what you are." This is crazy Dave (laughs). It looks like a fairy god mother, like in Cinderella. It's in that mirror now with a magical wand in her hand.* The Lady says, *you'll make things happen.* It appears that Theresa is being shown two images of herself, one which is like *a monster type thing* and the other is *very beautiful, with the capacity to make things happen.* When asked if she could imagine herself as a beautiful person with the capacity to be and act in creative ways, she says, *I think so. You know, I never really have, but I think I have the potential of being that way.* She continues, *I have trouble with that sometimes, from looking back, you know, reminding myself of bad things. I really have to work on that. There are things that I don't like or things I didn't like before about myself that I have to try to put out of my mind.*

Further, it might be noted that while the important thing was for Theresa to realize who she is and what she can become, reference is made to the plants and flowers that seemed to be prominent in the room with the mirrors. The Lady tells her that *"yes, that's what those plants represent, growth."* Theresa's ongoing growth. She says, *"now you can start moving right along."* *She wants to go into another room. Each room seems to be something different. This room looks like a planetarium with a ceiling with stars in it. Is that the right word, "planetarium?"* It seems that this room represents the natural order of the universe and the natural arrangements of life. Theresa continues, *the word nature and natural keeps popping up.* The Lady says, *"you will be able to use nature's best."* It is concluded that this room represents a kind of natural wisdom which she contains and will be able to utilize as she grows toward responsible adulthood.

The Lady asked Theresa if she is *happy with her life* and she says that *I am.* Then the Lady says, *"well then, let's go on."* While it seems to Theresa that the old woman is referring to her external life it appears that she is actually making reference to aspects of her life being represented by the tunnel experiences and the rooms of the castle and tower.

Soon another room emerges, and it seems that they are making a circle. This would be consistent with the structure of the tower first observed at the beginning of the imagery session. Theresa says, *now these rooms we went into Dave, sort of, I just realized have circled around. And this room enters a little different than the other ones. And it's green inside. I can see that, it's like green on the floor, and the lady says, this is the beauty of love. There's green grass and the sun shines right into this room. It's like, what it is is all windows and you can see everything outside. Yes, there's all kind of little windows and you can see the whole beach area and the sun shining in. The sky is real pretty.* The Lady says, *"you are loved," how did she say that? "And you do love."* As the scene unfolds, it seems that there is an attempt to represent the relationship between the sun nurturing the green grass of the room and love. This is to say that the sun nurturing the green grass is an expression of love, the unconditional love of the natural world. This theme continues in the image through the windows of the sun shining on the beach and the ocean along with the blue sky. Such images are apparently being used to demonstrate and define love as that which nurtures life. Since it seems clear that this room is meant to be viewed as another aspect of Theresa's life, it is assumed that she is being shown her own inner capacity to love and nurture others.

Next, Theresa and the Old woman go down some steps. She says, *we are going down steps, stairs. They're so steep that it's like it's not even an angle, it's straight down, and you know what would be a cellar way. It looks like a tunnel with stairs going straight down it.* Soon they find a number of transparent people who seem to be those who sit around the round table. The Lady says, *"see all the people here?" There are all kinds of people, but they look sort of transparent and they don't take on any shape of a person I would know. They are sitting in chairs*. The old woman confirms that these are the people who sit where the cups are at the table. She is also asked if she has a place at the table and she responds with a *definite yes*.

Then Theresa sees strips of colors. *I see like, I want to say a flag, but it's not really a flag and it has colors across it hanging above a doorway area. I think we'll go in there. There are people in there, too, and they are saying, "Hi Theresa," like they know me, but I don't know them. There is a man who is saying that. He looks like a middle-aged man and it makes me sort of uncomfortable. I don't like men that age (Laughs)*. She is greeted by the people as if they know her, but she has no memory of having known them. This would suggest that she is dealing with her own Collective Consciousness.

One in particular, a middle-aged man, approaches her and makes her feel uncomfortable. It is likely that middle-aged men remind her of her strained relationship with her father. However, he says, *"I'm no one to be afraid of,"* He just told me I'm paranoid *(laughs). OK, he says he's my friend. He says, I come from your subconscious mind. Now the Lady is telling me that he is my friend*. Suddenly, the middle-aged man becomes younger and tells her that they are *"going to put things together for her."* Theresa continues, *the thing about him is he keeps looking older, then gets younger. (laughs) He's got gray hair and yet he has brown hair. I can't see the purpose of all in this. He's telling me not to be so anxious. I do feel over-anxious, too. Yes, the guy looks totally different now. He looks young with blond hair. He says, "I am different people, but you know me as one."*

It appears that this man is projecting himself as being at different stages of human development such as an old man, a middle-aged man, and then as a young blond-haired man. Presumably, this man along with the other transparent people seem to represent her Collective Consciousness who are going to become active forces on behalf of her own growth. However, this particular "middle-aged man," given his description in her imagery seems to be a blend of many people. He may be more of an archetypal image rather than a specific aspect of her Collective Consciousness. Supporting this hypothesis is the indication that he is the creator of the castle or the one who is behind given conditions for Theresa's growth.

Finally, Theresa says that the man wants to go back out. *You see we are sort of down under right now, and we are all going to go back out, himself, the Lady and me. Now we are out at the beach and the sun is shining bright on the beach. He's saying, "this is where your love is."* When asked who made the castle, the man tells her, *he did and he said, "you are supposed to come down here." He told me, "you and your lady friend can go back now and we'll talk another day." It's like he just had that short little bit, a bit part.*

PART 6
Theresa meets a "Christ Like" Man

This session appears to represent a change toward greater light and in the guide function as compared to previous sessions. First, she finds herself alone on the bright sunny beach with pure white sand not knowing for sure where to go. It seems that she has been left to make her own decisions as there was no one to meet her when she stepped out on her beach. And she feels so *tiny. I sure look tiny like a little ant. I sort of don't know where to go. I'm just standing there.* It is suggested that she go toward the castle and she responds by saying, *Ok, I feel like I look like a little girl. I am even skipping.* It appears that she is a little girl in the midst of the infinite. Moreover, from this session on it seems that her guide becomes a higher level being, in the form of a "Christ like figure." She later refers to him as "Jesus."

Theresa continues down the beach toward the castle as a little girl acting like a carefree child skipping along. It is suggested that perhaps she may actually be a child in terms of certain aspects of her maturity and growth. We shall see later that this is a source of embarrassment for her as this is how she presently perceives herself, as an immature child.

Then Theresa comes upon a big tunnel. *I'm going to go into it. It's round, the opening is round, totally completely round. I'm going down. Its winds. It looks like there is green moss growing inside on the walls. I keep seeing a lot of green stuff. I don't know why. But I am not seeing anybody. I don't know why, but I see myself ironing some clothes right in the tunnel. Yes, on a little ironing board. I stop right there to iron it. I hate to iron clothes (laughs). I don't know why I am doing that. Someone seems to be coming up now from the other direction of the tunnel. It's the man with the blond hair. He says, "come with me," and we have left there. He's real nice. He's got his arm around me and we're walking down there. I feel this love, it's love, when I am with him here. Yes, it's a back and forth love. But I feel that I'm receiving more love.*

Theresa and the man continue through the tunnel. They walk around a U-shaped part of the tunnel and down some stairs. He says to her, *"come on and see where you began."* She appears to be going down into a basement where there are a lot of people sitting around. She says, *they are sort of invisible. I don't want to say invisible, transparent. They seem to be holding candles.* It is suggested that perhaps each one of them is a little bit of the greater light. She responds, *Yes, and he tells me, "these are my friends."*

Next, Theresa is standing with the blond man as she sees a beam of light coming through a window. They are standing in the beam of light. She confides that *this man seems like Jesus to me, because he's warm and loving.* They proceed into another room which has walls that seem like dirt. The man says, *"this is you"* and he is going to turn on a movie projector. She starts to laugh, *here's me jumping around skipping like a little girl, (Laughs), skipping in a circle making faces in the movie, (laughs). This is too much.* He says, *"here you are growing"* and it's me, a picture of me real big, but l look like a child which I could very well know what that could mean. And he says, *"this is you now,"* It's completely an adult person.

It appears that Theresa is being shown that at one time she was a child and acted like a carefree child, skipping and jumping around. She has grown from a carefree child to an adult person. However, in many ways she is still a child. She is embarrassed by her childlike behavior of the past and also feels embarrassed over what she feels as childish behavior during her adult years. The blond man seems to want her to realize that there is nothing to be embarrassed about, as it is all about growth. He appears to imply that one cannot hold oneself accountable for what one lacks in maturity at any given time. In a certain sense, those life experiences that are otherwise embarrassing to her are actually growth experiences through which she can acquire maturity and wisdom. She says, *he tells me there's nothing to be ashamed of. "We all have to grow," he says. I do feel embarrassed about that, about being immature and stuff like that*. It is suggested that he is showing her that part of herself that she is ashamed of and embarrassed by. Further, it should be noted that often parents shame their children for their childlike behavior making them feel self-conscious and embarrassed by their natural behavior. Under such conditions children often become shy and stifle their behavior. They mature more slowly because they learn to avoid natural childlike behavior to keep from being criticized and shamed. Theresa seems to have had this kind of experience in her childhood, when she was expected to act like a mature adult while being a child, thus delaying her natural growth toward adulthood. This is to say that having been unable to explore the natural growth experiences of childhood, the immature child would often surface after becoming an adult.

Theresa notes that the blond man is wearing a white gown with a red tie. She asked him about the red tie on his gown and he said that *"it's love."* He says, *"come on now we are going somewhere else."* He says, *"that is the simplified portion."* Next, they emerge from the tunnel. She comments that the tunnel was really long going down, but that they have come out of the tunnel *real fast*. Laughing, she says, *nothing is impossible here*. This is an observation often made by those who enter into the imagery process. The blond man says, *"you will love this,"* and he gives the impression that he loves to show her things about herself as they proceed further down the beach to the castle. He says, *"we are going to go there."* The door to the castle is already open. They enter into a grassy area inside the castle. He tells her, *"come on Theresa and quit worrying about what everybody thinks."* She responds that *that's true (laughing)*. She continues, *we are standing by a window with a lot of little panes in it. Some of the panes are colored and there are plants on the windowsill.* He is asked if the colors represent her and he responds, *"definitely yes."* She says, *it's real pretty in here because it's got real old big bricks in it. I love old stuff, you know, the bricks are real old.* It is suggested that she is the light coming through the windows with colors such that she is being grown by the light, yet she is also the light that which is causing the growth.

They then proceed into a room that is round. The walls are round and the whole room is round. Further, *the ceiling is a dome, again like that planetarium, remember*. She says that *he pushes a button and the walls start going around*. He says, *"you are round." I hope not (laughing)*, she responds. She continues, *it's so definite. The floor stays still and these walls go around and now the room looks sort of pink. He says, "you are pink" and there is like lace in it. I can't explain it. I guess it's like girly stuff, and the room went like heart-shaped. He says, "you are heart-shaped." He keeps pushing this button and different things keep happening, color changes and shape changes.* It is implied that these are all things about herself, that when she looks at all these various images, she is looking at herself, presumably, the qualities that she possesses.

Theresa indicates that, *I'm sort of bewildered here. He is really enthused. He says, "you just aren't getting the drift are you"* (laughs). *Next, she says, there is a definite sky light here. Now, I see. The sun is shining through the ceiling. I love skylights, too. He says, "come my little ray of sunshine." This guy is loaded with energy and enthusiasm, I'll tell you. Now, I'm in another room and it sits up from the other. It sits up high and it's real small and it's got a round floor. But it's like windows all around it, like little panes of windows. There is a sun, bright as can be, shining in one spot real bright right on me. And a voice comes from that light that says, "come up with me,' and it's hugging me real tight. It makes me want to cry (begins to cry), it's so goofy. He says, "don't worry about Dave, he doesn't care." The light says, "you are so afraid, and you have nothing to be afraid of."* Then the light puts her back on the floor.

This session ended with a touching, emotional experience for Theresa: being hugged by a being of bright light. The theme seemed constant throughout, which was to help her explore and become aware of different aspects of herself. One primary theme is that she is a feminine person who is capable of growth and creating the conditions for growth in others. She is also "round" a symbol of wholeness. All these things appear to "bewilder" her as she seems to have difficulty attending to the symbolism within the context of what appears to be concrete images. Moreover, she seems to have a guide, who she refers to as Jesus, a "Christlike" figure who appears to love her unconditionally. He also seems to demonstrate a good deal of energy and enthusiasm in helping her learn things about herself. Finally, we are introduced to a "being of light" that appears to be a higher quality of being who embraces her with deep love and a reassurance that she has nothing to be afraid of.

PART 7
A Light Consciousness

In the previous imagery session Theresa interacts with a bright sun or light. This session seems to be a continuation of this phenomenon, as the light seems to show her more of what she is and contains.

As Theresa opens the door to her imagery, she is met with a burst of light. She says, *there is a light shining around the door again. When I open it, it is like a burst of white light. This sounds crazy Dave, but when I stepped out into that light a voice said, "hi kid" (laughs). This can't be. The light is like stretching out and telling me to go down the beach. I feel real warm. That's a switch too. You know what the light told me? (Laughing) "You're doing too much talking and not enough working." (Laughing)*

This "white" light seems to be a being of consciousness who appears to be the same source or perhaps the same light that Theresa experienced at the end of her last imagery session. Hence, we see a continuation of the phenomenon previously presented serving as a guidance function in subsequent sessions. The theme of exploring aspects of herself and developing a sense of self-realization remains the major emphasis of her imagery.

Next, Theresa is described as "something green," which is suggested as being associated with growth and healing. She indicates, *I see grassy green, a large grassy area and this light says, "this is you." He keeps saying over and over, "something green, this is you." The light says that it is both healing and growth. Then the green area takes on the shape of a hand. The light says that this is me. It seems like there are little children on the fingertips of this hand shape, that's like green or it is green. And this light tells me to sit in the middle so that's what I'll do, of the hand. And he says, "these children are all yours, did you know that?" There is one on each finger so there are five, but I can't specifically see them. I just know they are there.* Presumably, this image illustrates her capacity to offer growth and healing to her own child traits or aspects of herself.

Then the light tells Theresa to *"come on somewhere else."* He says, *"I want you to see everything, but I don't know where to start you." I feel like I am walking back to where I started again. There seems like there is something stretched out over the water now. Maybe it is a bridge.* She begins to walk over a brown colored bridge. She notices that the bridge has high cobble stone sides. Also, it appears that she has become a little baby who is just starting to walk. She says, *you know what? This light like thing says, "come on, come on." I feel like I'm a new baby starting to walk. He's trying to edge me on, and I'm walking like a little baby.* It is suggested that she is just starting the process of her own growth and healing which is like being a little baby just learning how to walk.

Moreover, the presentation of a bridge out over the water presumably extending from the land of consciousness, of which she is familiar, over the water of her unconscious that contains that which she does not know about herself. Further, a bridge typically crosses from one shore to another such that both shores become accessible. For Theresa, it appears that the bridge is expanding, perhaps toward another place of new and more highly developed awareness, consciousness. She says, *the light keeps talking to me, Dave, saying things like, "this is all yours, everything is yours, just appreciate it and love it."* It is suggested that all that she is experiencing; the beach, the bridge leading out over the ocean, the sky, etc., is all hers to enjoy and appreciate. While it is for her, and it is hers, she does not own it. This is to say that it is not hers to possess and is there for everyone. Theresa continues, *this bridge, as I keep walking keeps extending out further and further and he keeps prompting me further, like, yes this bridge is going over the ocean across the water. He's holding me like a baby. I'm going to fly through the sky with him. Yes, this is like a fairy tale because he sprinkles out like stars and he keeps saying, "these are all yours, all these things of nature." Now he's taking on more of the form of a person with his arms outstretched like around the world. He's saying, "it's all yours and you need nothing." There's that excitement feeling again. He's says, "come on, come on, come on in." We're back on the ground again and now he's like the form of Jesus, the man I saw before.*

    The message seems to be that Theresa has everything she needs and that all she needs is within herself. Further, all that she is experiencing in her imagery is herself. Soon, they are back on the ground and the light seems to take on the form of the historical Jesus. This would appear to suggest a relationship between the light and the archetypal Christ in the form of Jesus. As they proceed to enter another tunnel which becomes a maze, she sees brilliant colors and a rainbow. Everything is very bright with animated colors. He says, *"just keep coming down. Don't say you don't know who I am because you do." Everything is so bright. It's like, ah, certain bright animated colors. OK, he says, "this is God, your God."* For a brief time she becomes distracted by images of puppet like animals. *He says, I'm not getting the message about it. "Let's see," he says I have to calm down or he can't show me these things. I know that is true. Now we are sitting on a park bench looking out. Now it's like we are floating in the air. We are and we are looking down on the Universe. We see clouds. Something looks black underneath, it sort of gives me a yucky feeling. I ask him what the black is. He says, "it's all the fears and doubts that you keep putting in your mind." He says, "just ask them to go away." He says, "you need to be over here," and he turned that whole bench around another way so I don't see that. He has like the power to turn it without doing anything. I feel like we are near the Master. I feel really warm, and I feel the light on us, a great white light, and we are both there inside the light. We are both there, yet it's just me. You know, he says, "you are not ready to learn today." (Laughs) Oh boy! That comes across loud and clear.*

PART 8
Theresa's Negative Concept of Men

The light on Theresa's beach appears to have progressively increased from one imagery session to another. She says, *there is light shining around the door again, real white.* She opens the door and says, *this light tells me (laughing). I can't tell you, (laughs). OK, I'm flying through the air all by myself. The light is there but I mean, I'm flying.* When asked if the light told her to fly, she said, *no, he says, "it's OK, you can love Dave, he is a nice guy."* This implies that she has developed feelings of love toward me. However, she is unable to express them. This is an important moment during the imagery session given its theme. There is no indication that her feelings are romantic. Rather, it was just a feeling of warmth and love toward a man. Given her attitude toward men it may have been somewhat confusing to her; to love a man while not being sexually involved with him. Moreover, her flying on her own at the beginning of this session is assumed to be a new feeling of personal freedom within the context of her inner self and perhaps her increased capacity to love.

Soon Theresa is walking with "Jesus." They go to the castle to review her concept of men, which she admits to being unhealthy. She indicates that, *there is the same door that's always been there with the arch top. When we go in there are ripples of water, and we are walking on top of it, the water. (laughs) He walks ahead of me and tells me to come to him. I get the feeling he's going to tell me about men. (laughs) I did get the feeling for some reason like I don't have a real healthy view of men. You know, I get that idea. I could never figure them out.*

Next, they walk down a narrow walkway to a room that has fruit hanging from the ceiling, like bunches of grapes. Theresa's says, *Ok, now we are in the room that has, it's like fruit hanging from the ceiling like bunches of grapes. It's got big wood beams. It's old like a, I don't know, maybe like a wine cellar, yes. And the saying is coming to me, "fruit of the vine and works of human hands," as clear as can be.*

It would seem that one of Theresa's concepts of men may be reflected in the narrow passageway. This could indicate a possible difficulty in relating to men because of a feeling that they are narrow minded. Moreover the "fruit of the vine" may refer to the male role of going out to work and receiving the fruit of his labors.

A second concept of men appears to build upon the previous one. Theresa sees a square door in the upper half of the wall. Jesus says, *"that door up there is very important."* Theresa says, *it's like, a door that doesn't go to the floor. It goes halfway up the wall. You know, the door is complete but it's like a square door in the upper half of the wall and it's wooden.* She asked Jesus if it has something to do with men and *"he says it does."* He says, *we're going to go in there. I wasn't going to but he told me (laughs). Ok, when we get in there it's like a tunnel, but it's square in shape, a square like shape and the walls are made of medal and they are hot. On one side, there is a burning light, bright, and we have to crawl through it because it's so small. I don't know what this has to do with men (laughs). OK, we get to an area where we can stand up, but it's still a square room, square tunnel.*

The theme of this portion of Theresa's imagery is that everything is square and narrow with hot metal walls. Further, the tunnel is so narrow that they have to crawl through it. This would suggest that she views men as square, rigid, conventional and narrow minded. The square door that is presented as being halfway up the wall may indicate that she feels that men are square and not down to earth or aloof and not readily accessible since one must climb up to reach them. Also, the burning light and hot metal walls presumably represent her concept of male intelligence and analytical thinking as being critical and "burning," especially during disagreements with men. It is likely that this may have been consistent with her experience with her father as a child growing up.

The next image Theresa experiences is that of a wall with five vertical narrow wooden beams. At the top of these beams is a shelf with three little birds. She says, *He's pointing out one wall in this area. It's dark and it has, they look like narrow wooden beams going down the wall. There are five of them and they are going up vertically, but they don't look like anything I know of. He particularly points those out but doesn't say anything about it. Oh, at the top of those strips, there's like a shelf and there are three little birds on it, ceramic looking birds and the birds are different sizes.* It would appear that this imagery suggests a rather narrow male role of father, one of supporting the children of the family. It is interesting that a mother bird is not included in the image. Perhaps this indicates that Theresa does not perceive herself as a mother receiving the same kind of support from the father or husband. Moreover, it appears that she perceives the role of the father as one which is primarily that of support and not one which includes closeness, intimacy and loving care.

As Theresa and Jesus continue down the next hallway, she finds the walls covered with brown animal fur. She declares that, *these images are real clear today too.* This indicates that she is relaxed and well-focused during this imagery session. She continues, *now as we are walking down this hallway tunnel, it looks like fur on the walls, like animal fur. And it's brown, right.* It is assumed that this part of her concept of men is that they have a primitive, animal nature which she may perceive as being related to their sexuality. My experience with dream interpretation suggests that young girls who are entering puberty sometimes have dreams of a brown bear that is chasing them. I have theorized that such images come from deep within the Collective Consciousness. During the days of the cave dwellers men often wore bear skins. Hence, young women were often pursued by men dressed in bear skins seeking sexual contact. It would stand to reason that such dreams are informing young girls of the onset of puberty and the development of their sexuality.

In this regard, I recall a mother telling me of a dream that her ten-year old daughter had. The girl was running down a path with a brown bear chasing her. Her parents were standing by the path looking at her as she approached them. She stopped and told her parents to watch out because a brown bear was chasing her. Interestingly, she did not seem fearful of the bear. Rather she seemed concerned for her parents. Of course, my interpretation was the bear chasing her represented her approach to puberty and potential for sexual activity. She was warning her parents of the problems this may cause them in raising her.

Next, Theresa's imagery reveals a light shining through the roof which appears to be a grass roof. *Now we go into an area where the light is shining through on the roof. It's more like it's a grass roof. I can see the sun shining on it and it's real bright and lively. And he points to this round table. The light is coming from both sides of this roof and is crisscrossing on the table. The table, it has a checker's game, but it's got black and white checks, for sure it does. Now the table looks square instead of round. It changed shape and it has grooves around the edge of it like if you were playing a game, it would look like you would put chips in it. And hanging on the opposite wall is a square blanket.* Oh, he says, *"put two and two together." And what did he say? Wait, he keeps saying, "men are people, too."*

This imagery seems to reveal Theresa's perception of men as playing games, such as checkers and poker. One can draw a parallel with a poker table in which several overhead lights are shining down with concentrated light focused on the table. The table is first revealed as round, a typical shape for a poker table. However, it changes to a square table with black and white squares which resembles a table used for playing checkers. Again, we find the theme describing her perception of men as being square with rigid black and white thinking playing at games of chance with other men. This is to say that checkers and poker is considered a "man's game" reflecting their nature of collecting together to play card games. One is reminded of the "man's night out" with his buddies in a dark smoke-filled room playing games of chance. To reinforce the square image is a tapestry or square blanket on the opposite wall.

To be sure men, especially by way of tradition, do gather together to play such games. It is often perceived as something that masculine men do. Hence, Theresa's perception of men has some basis in reality and perhaps her husband having been an athletic, masculine man participated in such activities with other men on a regular basis. However, it is her critical and judgmental attitude that she projects upon men that distorts her perception of them as people and fellow human beings. This seems to be the point that is being made during this imagery sequence.

Jesus says to Theresa that, *"they don't need you to cater to them." I don't think I do that*. It is pointed out that her husband has often accused her of mothering him. She says, *Yes, that's true. He's putting his hands on my shoulders and is talking to me like a child. You know how you kneel down and talk to a child. I do look like a child.* He says, *"I don't want to scare you but you see them all wrong." Yes, in my image I look like I'm getting ready to cry.* He says, *"don't feel bad about it."* This imagery sequence suggests that her perception of men is related to immaturity, being like a child. Indeed, at an emotional and developmental level, she remains a child, having been overprotected by a rigidly strict father. Perhaps the grass roof of the tunnel represents new growth that is occurring as a result of her imagery experiences.

Then Jesus says, *"OK, this part you are not going to like."* Theresa indicates that, *we go into a room that's round, and it's dark like, black, you know dark. Now the floor starts spinning around and there's a light. There is like a round hole in the roof and the light is shining through that and shining on me.* He's says, *"you need to be turned all the way around."* It is suggested that perhaps her thinking and attitude needs to be turned around. *But it's me spinning around in here, my whole body. You know, he's right, I don't like to spin around. He knows what I don't like. It looked like nails were coming out of those walls.* And he says, *"don't be scared because it can't hurt you." And then they retreat. I feel like I am in a James Bond movie or something (laughs). He says, "that is the way you perceive me and it is wrong."* Apparently, Theresa's perception of Jesus as represented by nails coming out of the walls is also wrong. Presumably, her religious background has caused her to believe that Jesus has a piercing, judgmental side to him, a side that can hurt her, which he tells her is wrong.

They proceed down some steep stairs toward what seems to be the same place where she previously saw the transparent people. Theresa says, *there are people down there again. It's like a scene I've seen before. People are clapping, but they are translucent and there are a real lot of them. It seems like they are saying, "you've made the grade." And we went back into the room where I first saw him. Remember when he looked different, then he changed, the same exact room. Yes! And he's saying something about that now. He said, "you saw me differently than I was." His whole physical features changed. We are hugging each other here, that's what's taking so long. He's telling me, "people are people." In other words, no matter what sex they are. I think we are done now.*

This session obviously dealt with Theresa's negative view of men and of Jesus as well. Her perceptions of men have come from her limited experience with men having been overprotected by her father. The problem is generalizing her past experiences with men to the greater population of men. To be sure, some men are rigid and narrow minded as would be true of some women. The primary theme of this imagery session was to examine her limited perception of men and to recognize that men and women are just people with individual characteristics that specify differences among people. Theresa's concept of Jesus most likely came from her religious background and reinforced by adults during her childhood. Her view of Jesus seemed to be two- sided. One was of Jesus as a loving caring deity, while the second view was of a judgmental, critical deity. The theme regarding Jesus was that he is indeed a loving, caring, healing archetypal presence whose character is totally non-judgmental.

One may question the need for Theresa to be led through many symbolic journeys in order for her to examine her perceptions of the world and others. Why not just tell her about these things. After a great deal of clinical experience, I have concluded that such symbolic journeys are necessary. They are something to be directly experienced by the client. One cannot integrate something except that it be experienced. Experience is what created her negative concepts of the world and others. Hence, experience is needed to change those concepts and replace them with more healthy perceptions.

PART 9
The Father

Theresa responds to the bright light as the *Father* when she opens the door. She says, *this time there seems to be a bigger crack at the top of the door because I can see more brightness at the top than around it. When I open the door it's real bright, white. I find myself saying, "hello Father," to the light. The light seems like now that it encompasses more than it ever did before. It seems to extend itself further and further out. Yes, I feel real little compared with this light. The light tells me to go back to the castle and that's where I'm going. I'm walking down. I seem to see flowers along the way, different colors, mostly red, which I never saw before. A deep red, they seem to be tulips for some reason.* It is assumed that tulips represent spring a time of rebirth and new growth. As was suggested in previous sessions, red represents love. Moreover, the white light appears to be increasing in its brightness, from one session to another as *it encompasses more than it ever did before.* Also, of particular interest, is that she addresses the light as *Father*.

The light tells Theresa to go to the castle. She enters the castle, *when I go, the door this time is a regular castle door that falls down with chains on it. It wasn't like that before.* When she enters the castle, she perceives brown to be the dominant color in contrast with the grassy green color of prior sessions. The brown being an earth color may be related to the Collective Consciousness which has been encountered in her imagery in the earth, e.g., in tunnels. This hypothesis finds additional support as the imagery session progresses.

It is suggested that Theresa start moving toward the upper level of the castle. She says, *it is a lot brighter up here. The sun is shining down through the windows. It is different* (than before). *It's almost as if this level isn't even connected with this castle,* as it is very high. She continues, *I think I hear the Father's voice talking to me, saying, "I am your Father and you love me and I love you." It is more distinct than it's ever been, as far as words go. I say to him, what is going to happen to Bill and he says, "he will be all right." I ask him, what shall we do? He says, "follow your own instincts." He tells me, "you are not to worry about Bill right now."* It seems clear that her own growth is of greatest concern in her imagery work. It is suggested that perhaps she can best help her husband, if her own life has been healed and she becomes more highly developed. She humorously verifies this assumption, *he says, follow David and listen to him he knows what he is talking about. (Laughs) He told me to go back down to the castle.*

Theresa proceeds to the lower levels of the castle and comes to a room where there is a brown area in the middle of the room. She says, *this room, I came into in the castle has a green outer rim and it seems like, oh, the inner part of this room has brown in the middle of it. I don't know how to explain it, it sinks down to a point like in the middle of it almost like those games where you spin little balls, just like that.* (Like a roulette wheel). Further, there is a person sitting *real high*, with whom she appears to be passing a big ball. Then the floor seems to sink and the ball goes down with it. She follows the ball to an open round porch area. She says, *this is open. It is definitely like a veranda like thing. I can only see a part of it. I know it is a circle but I'm only seeing one quarter of it and the rest is dark. The light only shines in on one side. I hear that the darkest part is what I do not know. I flashed a light on this and there was a lot of people standing, sort of those translucent looking people. He says, "they are people to come. They are the future."* It is suggested that she may be of help to these *translucent* people who are part of her future.

Quite possibly Theresa is gaining some insight into the process of life as represented by a give and take type of ball game with the one on high. Moreover, the chance aspects of life may be symbolized by the roulette wheel which interestingly leads to her collective selves. The circle aspect of her imagery would suggest the infinite and wholeness of life and even the cyclic nature of life.

Next, Theresa is standing in the part of the veranda that is lit while the translucent people are standing in the dark part. She says, *these people I see, I can never see specific faces. I just know they are there. And it's never one sex or the other. I mean it's just a mixture of people.* Clinical experience indicates that this is the most common description given for the Collective Consciousness. While they can be seen, their faces are vague and not definitive. This generally means that one is not ready to know who they are. Their identities will become known as she works with them for the benefit of mutual growth. She asked how she can help them and she is told, *"you can help them to know life."* Then she asked, *"what kind of help do they need."* She is told, *"they need help to lessen their fears." Oh, is that me because I am fearful of the future. I know that. I get the feeling that those people are me for some reason.* It is suggested that by dealing with her fears, she will be able to help *those people* in dealing with their fears. She continues, *I get the word from the people that says, take one step at a time. They sort of lighten the area around them and there's more of them now.* This is a consistent theme when working with the Collective Consciousness. The one whose life is in the present engages in experiences that not only helps them resolve their own fears, but also helps to resolve the fears of those from the past. Further, those of the past are brought forward to assist or perhaps guide the one in the present through given life experiences that help to resolve similar fears of the past.

Then Theresa says, *it seems like they are saying, "come and we will have a party." I seem to be going with them and they seem to be walking downstairs. They seem real big, and I seem real little. The stairway seems so narrow we can hardly fit. When we get to the bottom there is a flower garden.* It is suggested that this is her flower garden. She continues, *the flowers all seem white instead of different colors. All the people are walking through the garden but I seem to back off. I'm hesitant. I don't know. I don't feel scared. They encourage me to go with them. As I go I feel I'm flying over top. Seems that some of these flowers have turned into somebody's mouth and they are opening up and down like talking real fast. It's real silly. I can't understand it.* It is suggested that the flowers are trying to express something and they are trying to get it out as fast as they can. She responds by asking the flowers, *are you trying to tell me something? They say, "yes, but you are not listening." I get the feeling that they mean the whole message.* Accordingly, she is asked to try to put herself in a mental state of openness, such that she is willing to hear the message from the flowers. After a few moments she says, *I can see myself in a white robe, very angelic looking, and words are coming, "life is beautiful. Life is nothing to fear and life is forever."*

It appears that Theresa tends to focus on the finiteness of life. This seems to be creating a good deal of her fears. Rather her imagery seems to be trying to lead her into a more inclusive perspective of life, the infinite forever aspects of life itself. Further, we are given the impression that she tends to struggle with life rather than cooperating with it. It is suggested that in the garden you have pure life trying to express itself and trying to tell her of itself, of herself. Given her continuing struggles, she says, *the words are coming, "you are such a tired child and you bring it on yourself."* Yes, seems like the word is coming, *"you need to see the blue light."*

Presumably, the blue light is meant to bring her a sense of peace and calmness. She continues, *I see a square tunnel type of thing, but it's not really. It is more like a square room and it seems like the Father is sending a ray of blue light through it. I seem to want to go stand in it. It seems like there are white birds (doves) on either side of this cubicle, while I am in it and they are shining light in it too, but there is more white. I'm floating in the sky. I look like a holy type person as I fly in this cubicle, and the doves are pulling it up in the air. Now, I feel like I'm getting close to the Father. I feel like he's holding me again, the light. He seems to feel sorry for me. (Crying) I don't know but he treats me like a baby. He says, "you do have a lot of burdens right now." And he says, "they will all be lifted." But he doesn't tell me when. (Laughs) He always holds me like a baby.* It is suggested that one often seeks the Father when one's burdens become heavy. To be sure, her burdens of responsibility and that of caring for a terminally ill husband and a young son are great. Finally, she says, *I feel like he's giving me energy. I sure need it. (Laughs) He always draws tears from my eyes for some reason. (Crying) I never feel like I want to get down but he always makes me. (Laughs).*

This imagery session seems to be full of rich images of growth, wholeness, and calming peace. It offers a lot of hope for Theresa's future. Apparently, she has come to realize that the Collective Consciousness is also part of her and that she will have much work to do with them in the future. Fear of life appears to be one of the major collective themes, which may be manifested in her own fear of the future.

PART 10
Theresa's Growth and Healing Blocked by Fear and Negativity

The light has become so intense that it is now penetrating through the door. Theresa says, *I can see the rays, the actual rays shooting down on everything making it sparkle. I keep getting the words, "let's take a walk down Primrose Lane." (Laughs) I keep trying not to hear that. (Laughs) Off to the right, as I walk down the beach area, I see vaguely, real ugly black trees. But it doesn't scare me at all and it's so vague. It's sitting way back almost as if it would like to scare me, but it can't. It's so far removed from me, the ugliness of it. It's hard to explain. Like I know it's there, but it doesn't matter. I feel very joyful walking down the beach area, just in a very happy, good mood and feeling all the goodness that nature has. I ask if I shall go to the castle and the answer is, "if you want to, that's fine." I don't really know where else to go. He says, "go with the castle today." (Laughs)* When asked who is talking, *All he says is, "I am you and you are me." That's all he says, "I'm nameless."*

Theresa's interaction with the light, which calls itself "*Nameless,*" seems to create a mood of joy and goodness and an appreciation of all that *nature has*. It might be interesting to note that there seems to be a shift in her concept of the "Light." Her initial imagery first presented the Light as the "Mother," followed by the form of "Jesus" or "Christ." Later, she began to view the light as the "Father" and now the term "Nameless" is applied. Perhaps what is being displayed over a number of imagery sessions is the archetypal forms that the "One" light may take at any given time. It appears significant that the Light suggests that "I am you and you are me." By this we assume that the Light is implying that it is a divine part of herself, the Supra Consciousness. Moreover, Theresa seems to associate the light with Jesus or Christ. Her imagery over the past few sessions would tend to reinforce the development of this perception

A very consistent theme in Theresa's imagery is the increase in the intensity of light that she experiences at the beginning and throughout her imagery sessions. On this occasion, the light or sun is so strong that it penetrates the door. It appears that she is becoming more comfortable and trusting of the being of light, and her interactions with it carry a higher degree of clarity and emotion.

Also, of interest is that Theresa encounters something negative in her imagery in the form of *ugly black trees* in the distance. However, the positive effects of the sun/light appear to outweigh any fear that she might have had regarding this phenomenon. She continues, *he's anxious to get me in that Castle today. I feel like I'm being pushed down these stairs. (Laughs) This time as I enter the castle, I am definitely going down large stone steps and going downstairs. Normally, I didn't go down to enter. There are very wide steps. There appears at the bottom to be real murky water. I find myself running back up the stairs. I hear a voice saying, ugliness and dirt. But it's not scary. I mean I'm not really scared, but I don't want to. It just totally repels me. He says, you need to come to the higher levels. I see a winding staircase to the upper level on the outside of the castle.* She is asked if she has been thinking about the ugly things of life and if she tends to dwell on the ugly things of life. She responds, *I do, I think. I haven't thought about it but I do. Yes, I don't like to do that either because it doesn't help anything or do any good. I get into those ruts, I guess. I find that I'm getting more control over getting over it though than before.*

Theresa goes to the Castle and down some stone steps where she finds murky water at the bottom. This appears to be an additional form of ugliness, symbolic of the ugliness and dirt that repels her. However, this time she is not frightened only repelled by it. This would suggest that she has become more comfortable with her inner world and its related journeys. It is recalled that she seemed easily frightened during the initial stages of her imagery work. This may also suggest that she has developed a greater sense of trust and faith in the guides of her inner world, especially in the "being of light" that has recently emerged. It seems that she needs to rise above her thoughts of fear and ugliness. Hence, she is encouraged to go to the top of the Castle where she can be with the light and where she can rise above her fears and the ugliness of life.

Suddenly, it appears that Theresa is on top of the Castle. She says, *I feel I'm on top of the Castle. The voice is saying, "you are here with me now." I feel like I see a red and white flag blowing on the top shaped in a triangle.* She feels that the flag has a significant meaning such that the color white may suggest purity and perfection while red may be symbolic of life, love and warmth. Of course, the triangle would suggest a triad with symbolic religious meaning such as the Christian God in "three persons." It might be noted that the encounter with the light that called itself the *Nameless* one, might be a reference to the Holy Spirit, a third aspect of the Trinity.

Next, Theresa expresses her concerns regarding her husband's illness and of times when she falls into a state of negativity. She asks of the Light; *I ask him why I get in the bad states of mind or into ruts. He says, you are not fully grown. I asked him why Bill is sick. He says, it's a learning lesson.* It is suggested that it is a learning experience for both of them. *He says, "It sure is." (Laughs) He says, "You love and need love." I don't know why he said that.* It is further suggested that they both have lessons to learn through their relationship. *Yes, He says he's trying to teach me patience. (Laughs) That's a toughie. He did say, "Do you have any more questions?" (Laughs) He never said that before. I feel like he doesn't want to hear about my questions. He says, "Let's go downstairs and see why you are becoming fearful." At times, I guess I do. The steps I'm coming down are rod iron like with open spaces between them. I don't like those kind.*

Theresa comes to a brown room. She says, *the first room I come into is brown again. I've had other brown rooms. And the ceiling is so low that I have to crouch way down to walk in it.* It is suggested that she may be afraid of life circumstances pressing down on her, compressing her. She responds, *maybe, and he says, "You can go on the other side," and when I do it's wide open and there are no ceilings and walls or anything and the sun is shining real bright.* Further, it is suggested that the room is the way that she perceives the world, but the wide-open space is how it actually is. She confirms this assumption, *right, it was made to appear like a room but it really wasn't because there was nothing closing in at all.* Hence, it was something that she had created to express her feelings that her life circumstances were pressing down on her. *He says, "Theresa I love you, stop fearing." Well, it is hard not to fear when things around you appear the way they appear.*

This part of Theresa's imagery seems to be helping her face some of her fears. First, as she descends to the lower part of the Castle, she finds wrought iron steps with open spaces. This seems to represent her fear of falling, perhaps falling psychologically and spiritually. Next, she comes to a brown room, the color of the earth. The ceilings are so low that she must crouch to walk. It is assumed that this is symbolic of being oppressed by earthly matters. As she comes to the other side of the room, she discovers wide open spaces where there is plenty of room and bright sunlight, representing her ability to transcend her fears. To be sure, her imagery represents her difficult experience with her husband's illness. In any case, these fears and feelings of oppression seem to be of her own creation. On the other hand, her experience, rather than her response to it is very real in terms of her earthly circumstances.

Moreover, the Light seems to be trying to comfort Theresa in the midst of her fears. It is suggested that she try to project more into the future rather than become so absorbed in the immediate situation. She says, *he's holding me real close again (starts to cry). He keeps telling me that I look at the immediate rather than the future. I look at what is immediate. I never like to look at the future. My fear is in the future (laughs).* It is suggested that she is afraid of the future and that she has been that way her whole life. She confirms this, *yes, that's exactly right. Now could be bad and the future could be good.* To be sure she tends to project into the future based on the ugly stuff that she sees now. To her the unknown future will likely become even worse, given her present circumstances. Hence, we have another example of her fear and negative thoughts with which one would have to be sympathetic given her present life situation.

Theresa continues, *that's right and it's back to dwelling on that ugly stuff. I feel like I have to really sift through that. I feel like he has hands, and he's putting me down into the castle like I was up there with him, and his hands are reaching me down, and I feel real tiny and he's gigantic. This room has carpeting of all different stripes of colors, green and pink and yellow and it's hard to make out all the colors. I just know that they are there.* As indicated above, this part of her imagery reminds us of the colors of the rainbow, a religious symbol related to Christ and a reconciliation between God and humanity. (7) Presumably, this room is meant to indicate that she has the love and support of the divine side of herself throughout her time of struggle.

Next, Theresa experiences an interesting image of a gigantic drinking fountain from which it appears that she is to drink. *Now I feel like I'm standing by this gigantic drinking fountain, and I'm standing at the bottom and I can't reach it.* It is suggested that the drinking fountain must be for her and that she might need to become as big as the fountain in order to drink from it. This is to imply that she is much bigger than she seems to feel that she is. Then she says, *OK, now I'm real big. (Laughs) The water seems to be wine, back to the winery. (Laughs)* It seems clear that the fountain represents a source of nurturing and sustenance for her. However, she needs to change her perception of the child self perhaps to a more worthy adult person. When she does drink from the fountain the water appears to be wine, which could possibly refer to the biblical story of Christ transforming water into wine. Further, wine is sometimes associated with the blood of Christ. (8) These symbolic representations seem to be very deep and positive religious symbols for her given her Catholic background.

Theresa is then reminded of an earlier imagery session when she was given a magic wand for making things happen. It seems to be symbolic of some of her hidden abilities that are not yet available to her without future growth. Presently, it appears that her fears are causing her to fall short psychologically. She continues, *he's saying, "wave your magic wand and make it happen." Remember that time I saw myself with the wand? I feel that it is there now, too. Well I want to see Bill well. OK, I see Bill well and he's saying, "I told you I'd be well." How does he say that? "I told you, you didn't have to worry." (laughs) That's what he said. Wait, let's see, He (Light) says, "the ability is there. That's all I want you to know." He tells me, "you're falling here and falling there. I keep having to pick you up." (laughs) That's true. He has to really hit you with the truth doesn't he. (laughs) More like between the eyes if you ask me.*

Finally, Theresa is taken into a pure white room. *He tells me to come here into a room that's all white. It looks like it's snow on the walls, just sparkling white. It looks like a fairyland room because it just doesn't look real. It's all white and fluffy looking, the walls and floor. It doesn't seem right. He keeps saying, "these are all things you fear." I don't know. It's like a room of beauty, really beautiful and the message comes across, "those things you fear are actually beautiful."* The message seems to be that much of what she fears, if viewed more in terms of what they actually are, would appear beautiful.

Theresa continues, *I told him I love to grow. He says, "I know that but you keep letting things stop you." He says, "I know you love to grow but you are the very person who stops it." I feel like he is in that room because it is so white*. This would suggest that she is fearful of purity, perhaps because it makes her feel by way of comparison, that she does not measure up or is not worthy. She asked him how she stops her own growth and he refers to her fear. She says, *I get the feeling that that is exactly what he's talking about, too. I keep doubting and questioning*. It is suggested that she wants her future to unfold for her before she goes into it. *Right! She says, is that so hard. (laughs) I can't believe it. He says, "no one knows their future, absolutely no one." He says, "don't worry, I'm God, follow me." Oh, I said, "where are we going?" He said, "we are going to the other side of you, to the other side of the Castle," which he says is the other side of me. He takes on a form. I mean I can't see a face or anything, but he takes my hand and he's pulling me. We are flying. A white robed person. What I see I don't like. (laughs) I see like a wall and its got like all these prickly things sticking out that makes it look like they are like hard core shaped things. He says, "you appear." I ask him what it means. He says, "you are too sharp." Oh boy! I know that! That came through loud and clear, the tongue. I hope Bill doesn't hear that. (laughs) He'll be confirming it. Now he goes to another section. These aren't rooms, they are hollowed-out sections. This one is totally smooth.* It is suggested that she fluctuates going from smooth to sharp. She is told that both traits can be equally deadly. It is assumed that she is being shown some negative traits, which she may need to work toward accepting and changing; her sharp cutting side along with what might be taken to be a sort of soft, permissive nature.

PART 11
Confronting a Duality

Part 11 is a short imagery session which seems to deal with Theresa's ability to differentiate between the Light and its opposite. As consistent with previous sessions the intensity of the light increases, such that it permeates the door. She says, *the bright white light just disintegrates the door at the bottom of the stairs. He's telling me not to be frightened. The ocean is exceptionally blue and it has white sparkles in it. He keeps encouraging me to swim in the ocean, but I can't swim. I feel like I am swimming, jumping in and out like a dolphin. He says, "I want you to freshen up. You haven't been here for a while." (laughs) He told me to get out and dry off and go to the castle. So that is what I am going to do. The castle seems to have a red line around the doors that it never had before. I'm going up the stairs on the outside of the castle to the top. It sort of winds around.*

It is assumed that this aspect of Theresa's imagery is meant to demonstrate that she is able to do something that in the past she was unable to do. She swims in the waters of the unconscious and it seems with a high degree of skill. Further, it may serve to demonstrate that many things can be done in the world of imagery that may not be possible in the world of matter and duality. In any case, this segment seems to serve to calm her and wash away all the clutter and stress of her daily routine. It would seem important to note that she accomplished these tasks on her own, with some encouragement.

Theresa ascends to the top of the castle. When she arrives on the roof, it seems cloudy and she appears to be confused by two voices calling her in separate directions. She says, *I don't know. I feel like there are two voices. One says, "I'm over here and the other one is saying over here." I'm looking back and forth.* It is suggested that she go toward the voice that comes from the light. She continues, *I know, that's the one I want to go to. The other one scares me. He says, "Don't be scared of him, he's just a jerk. Don't even think about him, think about me."* Hence, she makes a conscious choice to go toward the light. When she goes toward the light the clouds appear to go away. Moreover, her brief experience on the roof seems to be a kind of test to determine whether she can differentiate between the "Light" and whatever the opposing voice represented. We are reminded of the Good vs. Evil duality.

Next, Theresa says, *I feel like he's taking me by the hand, and he's putting me on his back. And, now it looks like the back of Jesus. But it looks like him in his state, when he was carrying the cross. I don't know the word, sort of emaciated looking and yet he's putting me on his back like a child. You know how they like to be carried on your back. And he says, "I'm not hurt anymore," like for me not to worry about it because it sort of makes me uncomfortable. He hugs me and holds me and tells me, "we are lovers," he says, "you and I and the world," he says. Now we are flying through the air. I'm on his back. He is telling me, "we are all one, the sun, and the sky and you and me."*

This imagery of being carried on the back of Jesus appears to be significant regarding Theresa's perception of him. The interesting feature of this perception is that it is of Jesus as the suffering Jesus. Further, it appears that she views herself as if the cross (child of humanity) being carried on his back. Apparently, this viewpoint represents one of her concepts of Jesus, which seems to be one that needs to be altered in favor of a Jesus who is strong and healthy, one who is able to carry her when needed. Moreover, he tells her that the two of them, along with the world, are lovers. From this, we create the idea of a triad in which there is the divine (Jesus), Theresa as humanity and the Earth as the ground on which this human/divine duality is being expressed. Next, as they fly through the air, Jesus further presents another triad, but in the sense that all is ONE. This triad contains the Sun (Divine), sky (heavens) and Theresa (humanity).

Theresa then sees *a pinpoint of light that's shooting warm beams of light. It almost resembles those lights from airplanes because it's moving around like that too, up and down. It sort of looks like it has a laser eye on it. Oh, he tells me it is not a good light. This doesn't make a lot of sense but he says, "It is a foolish light."* Hence, it is implied that some lights are not necessarily good. This we take to be an extension of the previous good vs. bad duality.

Finally, Theresa says, *now we're back on the ground because we've been up in the air all this time. I have a hard time coming to the ground. He's got to pull me down.* She is asked if she likes to fly. She responds, *I must, contrary to belief. I see an old man walking by with a real long beard, like to his knees and he takes real short steps. He walks with a cane. He reminds me of an oriental person. He keeps telling me that I can come out now.*

The image of the old man appears to be a passing image and might have no significance. However, it might be assumed that the old man may represent wisdom or the ability to make judgments concerning right and wrong or good vs. evil. It might be imagined that this session was actually about the development of such wisdom.

PART 12
Developing Faith and Trust

For the first time we find that the door that separates Theresa's outer and inner worlds seems to be gone. Now there appears to be a bright opening. *It is just wide open.* This may suggest that there has developed a new openness and freer flow between her conscious and unconscious systems. Presumably a much healthier relationship between these two aspects of herself has been established. Also there seems to have been a gradual attempt to help her develop a deeper trust and faith in the transcendent elements of her unconscious, as represented by the light and the form of Jesus. Moreover, earlier in the first few sessions there seemed to be an endeavor to assist her in understanding and accepting the collective components of her unconscious. Theresa sees two people playing on the beach, playing ball. She says, *the light is shining on them.* She continues, *they are real friendly to me. They are throwing the ball to me. For some reason the ball is going in a triangle shape, going to three people. It stands out very much that the lines of the ball are shaped like a triangle, the direction that the ball is going. And it keeps getting bigger and bigger. And he tells me I need to remember that, the triangle. He said, "the father, the son and the holy spirit." He says, "you will not forget this for eternity."* Hence, the emphasis once again is on a triangle or triad relationships, which is presented as a ball being passed to each person or point of the triangle. Its expansion may illustrate a quality of becoming more expansive, inclusive and transcendent. It appears that the triangle is related to the biblical father, son and holy spirit. The passing of the ball may also indicate that energy or light is continually flowing from the various points of the triangle.

Theresa is taken to the castle and finds that the outside of the castle is gold. It is suggested that gold is precious and beautiful and that the castle is her, symbolic of her own beauty and worth. *The Light tells me that's true and that precious and beautiful is me. I hate taking all those compliments. (laughs) I told the light that I want to be with Jesus. He said, "you are always with Jesus. He will never leave you." That's what he said.*

Theresa seems to have trouble getting the door to the castle open. When she enters the castle, she sees an angel. She says, *that's the first time I've ever seen an angel with big white wings and blond hair, kneeling. And the angel is telling me, "don't ever be afraid. We are here to protect you." It's a glowing white robe. The angel says, "I'll walk with you." Now when I am walking, I feel like, I feel like someone is looking down on me from like a balcony that's way above me. I see myself walking with the angel and I feel like it's me looking at me.* Hence, in this imagery segment she is both participant and observer suggesting that something significant is about to happen. With regard to being a participant/observer the angel says, *"it will make it easier for you to understand."* Soon they come to some dark rooms. She says, *the rooms are so, they just seem dark to me or something. There is like a void. I can't get anything. The angel is taking on some ugly form for some reason*

It is suggested that Theresa face whatever is there and to have faith that she will not be harmed. However, she begins to falter as the angel takes on an ugly form. She says, *I don't know. It's just jumbled up. I can't understand it. I feel like the light is failing me out there. Now he grabbed me up with him. You know what he's telling me? I don't need to go in there. He says, I just need to stay by him and I don't need to go in there. He said, "I went through enough times."*

It appears that Theresa was being taken to face something dark within herself. It is the first time that she has encountered an angel, which suggests that this part of the divine world is being introduced to her, as one who is there to protect her and that she does not need to feel afraid. However, it seems that when confronted with the dark rooms, which generally means she is to face what is contained in the rooms, she falters. The darkness suggests that it is something that is unconscious to her, but which needs to be faced and brought into consciousness. It is likely that the rooms contain what she has repressed from the past and which is otherwise unacceptable to her. Further, it is probable that her fear was projected onto the angel which is typical in such situations. Unfortunately, it was not those benevolent forces who abandoned her, rather her fear caused her to abandon them. This also suggests that she was not quite ready to face such dark elements of herself, and she becomes withdrawn from the situation.

Theresa says that when, *He puts me on the ground, He takes on the look of a king. He has a crown on his head. He held me like a baby and then put me on the ground.* He tells her, *"You and Bill will work this all out and he said, Bill needs your love and understanding."* He said, *"I know you get impatient but you have to work on that."* And he said he understands that. He said, *"You are a very good person in spite of those qualities that you don't like about yourself. He says, "They aren't bad things they are just things." He's saying remember, I love you."*

PART 13
Theresa's Potential for Reflecting the Light
and the Beauty of Love, Friendship, Relationship and Purity

The theme in this imagery session is that Theresa seems to be reflecting the Light that she has been experiencing in previous sessions. The idea is to reflect the Light to others through positive traits. Also there is the concept that some of the most valued things of the world are the most plain and simple. She describes her experience as she opens the door. *Today, when I open it up, it's like a blast of white light. I feel like the white light is beaming off me. It's going out all over me. It's not just one light like a beacon. It is just reflecting all around me, like a halo type look.* It is suggested that when people enter into a relationship with the Light, they reflect it to others. She is told, *"You are a child of the universe. You can bring that to others."*

Theresa reports, *we are going down to the castle today. The outside of the castle looks real dark today, with real little tiny windows in it which I never saw before. The door of the castle is beaming with light too, and its real white.* She is reminded that the castle represents her and is a reflection of herself. She acknowledges this and continues, *somehow when I walk in this castle I feel like a big ugly monster, sort of like a Frankenstein thing. I don't know why that is, but it's not scary. It's sort of clumsy looking.* It is suggested that sometimes things that look good are not always good and things that look bad are really good. Then she says, *I think I will turn normal again. OK, we got into the foyer and it's barren looking. There are hardwood floors in it, but there is nothing on the walls. It's just very barren, very empty. I say a foyer. It's the first room you enter but it looks like a room. I'm bringing a beam of light in there with me. The light is behind me.*

Theresa finds that she is able to illuminate the dark and barren foyer of the castle with her own light. Whereas in the past, the way had been illuminated for her. Now she seems to be the source of the light. This seems to be significant because during the last two imagery sessions she has been given the task of doing things on her own, without help from others. First was swimming in the ocean, and now she is becoming a source of illumination in her own castle. The next few images seem to represent her capacity for actualizing given aspects of the inner light within the world and with others.

The next room I go into, there is a man sitting on a throne. He's dressed like a king. He has a scepter in his hand and the room is very ornate. This guy definitely looks like a king. He is asked if he were the king of the castle. *He says, he's the king of power. "The power to heal,"* he says. Theresa asked about healing Bill and he says, *"Within Jesus Christ we can do all things."* He says, *"Bill can heal himself. He has to work a little harder." I said, how can I help Bill? He says, "You can help Bill by learning how he feels and understanding how he feels and just by understanding him." He says, "we have to continue our faith," and he says, "Don't let what seems to be get in the way." I assume, when he looks worse or bad.* It is suggested that healing can take place in an instant. *Yes, he's saying what you are saying. Yes that's true. He says, "Believe in Jesus Christ. He can do all things." He said, "I am his messenger."*

With regard to the king, Theresa reports, *I really don't see a face on him. I just see the king and he's sitting there on the throne. I feel that there is a lot of gold in the room*. It is suggested that gold is symbolic of something precious and of great value. She responds, *OK, then I think that room is of great value, too. You know what he said? "Gems of this life are not in this form," meaning the gold and there are jewels, too. Now I am seeing symbols of people. Like just in front of my eyes, between the king and I. I see symbols of people and it's like Mary and Joseph and the donkey and they look real plain, very plain and humble. It seems like there is a message here. There is such a contrast between the gold and everything and the plainness of this vision.*

One aspect of the power to heal appears related to knowing what is of true value in life. The room containing the king seems to be full of gold, which earlier represented Theresa's own beauty and self-worth. Further, it appears that real beauty may actually be in what is plain and humble. An image of Mary and Joseph seems to have been shown to illustrate how much impact something that is plain and humble can actually have on the world. It is suggested that what she is seeing is something of real beauty, very precious. Further, what doesn't seem to be of very high value, really is. She says, *yes, really. That's exactly right because they look, in the vision, they are made to look exceptionally plain, and their heads are bowed down, very serious nature, the picture. And he says, "This small family changed the world," that's what the king said.*

Theresa continues, *He tells me to go into another room. That's what I'll do. I'm getting a lot of this ornate vs. plain, because that first room was real plain, too. It just stood out as being empty, plain. The next room doesn't come into focus for some reason. The next room is something plainer. It is definitely plainer, and there is a man standing there with a long beard. He says he is a wise man. Incidentally, the floor is green in this room or carpet like. The walls look pink for some reason. He's telling me that I have wisdom but I don't use it. (laughs) He says, "Wisdom comes with years." He says, "if you ignore it (the wisdom within), you never gain it." He told me to go to the next room.*

In keeping with this theme, the next room that Theresa visits is much less ornate than the previous one. In this room is a man with a long beard who seems to be a wise man. The floor is green and the walls are pink. The man tells her that she also has wisdom which he apparently represents. Presumably wisdom is needed to reside over the use of power, as symbolized by the king. Wisdom comes with years of experience which quite possibly is accessible to her through the Collective Consciousness, if she does not ignore it.

Moving to the next room Theresa says, *This room has a very wide door. In fact, it's not even a door. There is no door. It's just wide, you just walk right into it. It's just wide open and it seems like it's white, and the curtains are white. It seems like there is an angel sitting there, white too, with wings.* She asked what the angel represents. *He says, "the beauty that you don't even know about." He says, "the beauty of this world." He says, "the beauty of love and friendship." I know about that though. He says, "you think you do." (laughs) He says, "you don't know the beauty of letting someone know you, really know you and accepting you for the whole person that you are." Which I do only let people get so far. I let them get so close and then I don't tell them everything. He says, "if they don't respect you for who you are then so what?" "God loves you," he says. He says, "God loves you no matter what you do or say." He said, "He may get upset with you but he always loves you.* It is suggested that sometimes you can get angry with the one you love, but it won't damage the relationship. She says, *he sort of implies that those things are purity. Love of friendship is beautiful, too. He is saying to me, "Why don't you see your Father today. He is in the next room." And there is light coming out of that room. I just felt pulled toward him and he's hugging me.*

In the following room Theresa visits with an angel who seems to represent the beauty of the world, the beauty of unconditional love, friendship, relationship and purity. She is encouraged to let others know her, such that she learns the beauty of letting someone know her and accept her as a whole person. Further, ultimate love is being loved by God. This is to say that she can let others know who she really is since it does not matter if they are unable to respect and accept her, as she will always have God's love.

Theresa is hugged by the Father in the next room. He says to her, *"not to fear anything." He said, "I sent Jesus Christ to protect you from all that is evil." He knows why he's saying that, and I know why he's saying that. (laughs) He says, "focus on us and you can't waiver. We are Love." He says, "It seems hard to understand but it is not really." He says, "I am the master of this universe and every universe to come. I was, I am, and I will always be." That's what he said.*

In this imagery session, Theresa appears to have been introduced to a number of things that are assumed to be related to her own human potential. First is the capacity to be a healing influence in the lives of others through understanding and feeling. This seems to be related to seeing worth and value in the plain and humble things of life. Next is the attainment of wisdom, which may be related to the unlimited experience of the Collective Consciousness. Wisdom may be needed as a necessary quality in the application of one's own human potential. Perhaps related to wisdom is the beauty of love and human relationships, love being a fundamental aspect to transcendent functioning.

The idea of unconditional "Love" appears to lead Theresa to a concept of the Trinity. This may be a product of her Christian background but it nevertheless has significance for many different cultures and religions. The Trinity or Triad is sometimes considered to be a basic building block of the Universe. Given the two previous imagery sessions, she has become concerned about matters of good vs. evil. The Trinity as pure love appears to have surfaced here as the fundamental element that transcends the good vs. evil duality. That is to say by establishing a relationship with the Trinity, which is consistent with her personal belief system, she is able to transcend duality.

PART 14
Theresa's Black and White view of the World

This imagery session appears to continue with demonstrating Theresa's human potentials. Moreover, she is confronted with her narrow viewpoint based on Christian beliefs. Such black and white perceptions seem to be one reason why she is unable to realize her mental abilities. She appears to be preoccupied with growing old and wishful thinking rather than devoting herself to more intellectual endeavors.

First, Theresa finds the outside of the castle to be black. She seems bothered by this because she tends to associate black *with something not good*. She continues, *I have a hesitancy about the color black. I know I don't like dark. I don't like night. I have a thing about that*. It is assumed that her religious background suggests that black or darkness is associated with something evil. *He says, "black is a beautiful color, also. If it bothers you we'll change it."*

Theresa goes into the castle and finds a white room. She says, *the first room is white that I come into, and it looks like it's almost white fur on the walls. It's just a brilliant white almost like what white carpeting would be over the whole room, walls and all around. There seems like there is a white kitten in it, real white and fluffy. It seems like there was some reason that the black exterior made a contrast with the interior. There was some sort of message there.*

It appears evident that Theresa is being presented with a contrast between white and black, a duality that she seems to associate with good vs. evil. It may be significant that the color black is associated with the external presentation of the castle, while the inside is experienced as white. This is to say that the outside may appear black or evil while the inside is actually white and pure. In any case she seems to be presented with a form of rigidity in viewing certain aspects of the world based on religious beliefs. This would also cause her to view the world in terms of "either-or." Hence, she would be unable to view the world as it really is, rather than what she believes it to be based on a rigid, narrow point of view.

To accent this way of thinking Theresa is presented with an image of those from a different culture. *It seems like there are two oriental people sitting there with their legs crossed. You know how they do that when they meditate? It looks like there are two of them sitting there. But I don't know why or anything. He says, "they are wisdom in a different sense than you know." He says, "their knowledge is different, but not wrong from yours." I think the oriental philosophy is what is being referred to. Their belief system is all different.* She continues, *that's something else I always think about and question, it's comparison with Christianity. He says, "they are loving. That is what's most important." And he also told me, I don't have to fear those philosophies. I don't have to have anything to do with them, just not concern myself with it. It is nothing right or wrong.*

Apparently, Theresa has harbored some fears regarding Eastern Philosophy. Indeed, Christian Churches often refer to Eastern thought and Philosophy as something evil and to be avoided. The idea of reincarnation, central to Eastern thought, seems to be considered contradictory to Christianity. Moreover, to believe in such things may put one's salvation into question. Her imagery suggests that she has nothing to fear and that her black/white point of view has no basis in reality. It was also suggested that there is much that she could learn from such philosophies. She indicates, *yes, He says, you can learn a lot from everyone, something from everyone. What he tells me is that most Christians don't understand that philosophy. They think they have to make a choice and that isn't true.* It was further suggested that Jesus himself had studied those philosophies. *He said, "yes, he did." He said, "they were integrated within his philosophy and his teaching."* It was also suggested that Jesus knew of the Muslim religion. *He says, "he loves them all."* The message seems to be that one can learn from everyone if there is an openness to ideas and beliefs that differ from one's own. The idea that Jesus integrated many different religious orientations and philosophies within his teachings may not have occurred to her. The Christian Bible may only hint at this. However, the Gnostic Gospels, which represent a split in early church doctrine would tend to strongly support this idea. (9)

Theresa goes into another room. She says, *the next room appears to be canary yellow. The yellow stands out for some reason.* It is suggested that yellow is associated with intelligence. She indicates that, *He says, "it refers to my intelligence," which I have a lot of but you wouldn't know it sometimes. (laughs) I know that it true. He says denseness and intelligence are two different things. Oh boy! He just told me I'm lazy intellectually. (laughs) I know that. The room is just blank, because I'm looking like wall to wall. It is very long and rectangular.* It appears that the room represents her intelligence which she does not use as much as she should. The fact that the room is empty would suggest that she has not used her intelligence. It may be implied that using her intelligence would be to learn more about differing philosophies and religious beliefs and the wisdom of others. This may also be one of her abilities that she has not cultivated and developed.

Then, Theresa goes into a room full of antiques. He says, *"come on into this room. You are going to like this one." It's got all kinds of antiques in it, no wonder. Wooden floors, real wide planks, sort of ornate, not really over done though. It gives more like a darker effect, you know, because of the old furniture. The word stands out for some reason. Old things too, yes. Old things hanging from the ceiling everywhere. Oh, it has to do with an obsession with getting old. He says, "how can you like antiques and think that getting old is ugly?" It's not an obsession but it does bug me though lately for some reason. It never did before, but I'm seeing lines and symptoms of age that I don't like. Bill just gave me a reprimand on that yesterday. He told me to take the beauty of every facet of your life and enjoy it. It is short enough. He says, I have to liven up a little bit. (laughs) He's got me in my best mood for some reason. There is an old staircase there that he told me I could go up. So that's what I'll do.*

It is implied that one of Theresa's preoccupations seems to be with growing older. It appears that she equates growing older with growing ugly. The comparison of her love for things that are old, such as antiques, with her view of growing older is interesting to note. At times she seems to be wishing that she were different or that she could have something that she does not have. Her husband who is ill with cancer tells her that she is too wishful. It is suggested that she needs to be more accepting of who she is and what she has in her life right now.

Theresa continues to go up the stairs but says, *there is actually no upstairs. There is just open light. The light is shining real bright. He says, "it's you and me again, kid." (laughs) I said, when is Bill going to get better? He says, "Bill is better." He says, "when are you going to realize it?" He told me that "when you ask me a favor, I do it. Now I am going to ask you a favor." He said, "I want you to live your life filled with love." He said, "love everyone. You are still too picky and choosy about that." He told me, "love is my middle name." (laughs) He just told me, "Bill will see wellness again." He's holding me now. It's like, he seems like he is a person. It seems like there is a divine halo of white all the way around him and he seems real big. He's saying to me, "we are the Universe." He says, "don't forget Jesus. He made you who you are. You are all of mankind." He says, "you can go out now, but don't forget me."*

It is noted that a constant theme in Theresa's imagery is the transcendent experience with the light, which usually occurs toward the end of each session. It is generally a touching experience of being loved, feeling secure and encouraged. Sometimes there is some last-minute advice given. In this case, she is asked to "love everyone" and not to be too picky and choosy about it. As we come to review some of Theresa's human potentials, it seems that there is an encouragement being offered to begin to actualize such abilities. Perhaps acting on her inner abilities is what her husband needs in facing his own ordeal, along with facing the prospects of her own future.

Further, there is a theme of unity that seems to permeate Theresa's experience with the transcendent light toward the end of her sessions. She is continually told that "we are the Universe" and "all of mankind." That we are all love and that He is "love." She is encouraged to view all of life with love and that to be open to life and Him. It might be noted that what is being described in this session, to love unconditionally, is highly characteristic of the Supra Consciousness.

PART 15
Growth and the Trinity

This imagery session begins with the door appearing transparent because the Light is shining so bright. The Light tells Theresa to walk on the beach. *The Light is telling me, "I know you like the beach so let's go down it." And I do. I can hear the waves coming in. That's why I am being so quiet here. He told me to enjoy the water because this is part of his life, He said, or not his life but his world. That's what he said, "this is part of my world." I think meaning natural things.* It is suggested that the ocean is symbolic of God. Theresa responds, *so he could mean that, yes.* Hence, it seems that there is an attempt to equate things of the natural world as metaphors for God. This would especially appear to be true of water because it is lacking in form but yet is full of life and a potential for life. It is also considered symbolic of "the primal origin of all being." In some traditions water is considered to be the "spirit of God." (10) Interestingly, it is suggested that the experiences with the metaphors of life in this world may be preparation for functioning in the next, presumably life after death. *He says, "are you getting your head straight about the way things go, or are you still worrying about every little thing?" (laughs)* Meaning, the answer to what's going on in this world is in preparation for or understanding the next. That is what he is referring to. *He's hugging me, and I told him I love him. He told me he loves me too. (laughing) He says, "go in the castle with me today. But if I go, we go from the top," He says. (laughing) He lifted me right to the top.*

After going to the top of the castle she is shown a small garden. She says, *on the top of the castle he pointed out a small garden of vegetables and he said, "See how they grow from small to big. And that's how we grow. We grow from small to big but being small doesn't make things wrong. It is the fact that you grow. That is important."*

It is assumed from this exchange that Theresa has some resistance to growth, as defined by starting from small to something large. We know from previous discussions that she feels embarrassed by her lack of maturity and childishness. Perhaps her resistance has to do with the idea of taking on the position of being a small shoot of life, rather than assuming full adult growth as she is an adult physically.

It is suggested that Theresa has grown out of the soil, just as the vegetables grow out of the ground. Presumably this is a reference to the ground or field of the unconscious, more specifically the human part of the self, the Collective Consciousness. The reader may recall when she was being introduced to the Collective Consciousness she went into the earth through a tunnel. There were also colors of brown and green associated with such earth images to symbolically tie the earth and growth (green grass), together. This theme appears to be woven into this imagery session as described below.

Theresa continues, *He said, "you grew out of the soil just like the vegetables but that's the part that you don't know about, and that is the part that Bill doesn't know about." I ask what he means. He says, "learn to know the earth. The answers are there." He says, "He shines down on the vegetables and makes them grow just like us."* It is suggested that our roots go into the ground, as well. *Yes*, she says, *we need both, the earth and him.* (The Sun, the "Light"}

Next, Theresa sees an image of Jesus knocking on a door, presumably to suggest the biblical reference to "knock and it shall be opened." In this case it appears that Jesus is knocking on her door, but she does not open it. Apparently, she is not opening herself to the inner, spiritual help that she needs for her growth.

Theresa says, *all of a sudden, I see a vision of Jesus. You know the one of the painting where you see him knocking on the door. It just came right out. I seem to get the thought that I'm just not opening the door, in reference to help, as far as getting upset with the situation. He said, "you are not allowing the spiritual help that you need. You keep closing the door on it. It's like he's saying, you keep expecting things of this world to help and they can't. Jesus picks me up and holds me here like a father picks up a child and bounces them, like throws them in the air, very lovingly. He told me I let silly doubts come over me, but it isn't wrong, it's just things that I have to work out. He says, "do you see how we are all one?" I really don't. He's giving me the impression of feeling that God the Father is in the Supernatural state that we will never understand and that Jesus is him in a state that we can understand. He seems to be surrounding Jesus and me, the light is.* It is suggested that we perceive the light of the Father through Jesus. She says, *yes, and, Jesus is like living in him, this light. And he holds me there, too. It makes it a little clearer.* It is suggested that Jesus is one with the light yet he's separate and an autonomous being. Theresa responds, *not only that, yes, to give man the understanding because he said it is way beyond our understanding. And I'm sure it is. Anyone who is always and always will be is pretty tough to understand. But we think of things as beginnings and ends, ourselves, rather, in a way, because we only know this earth part of us. The Holy Spirit keeps, I feel that's what it is, the white bird over Jesus' head, and it seems to want to land on his head. It's very white, whiter than any white I've seen. He belongs in there, that's for sure. And, I feel I belong with them, but in a very different way.*

Interestingly, we find that the image of the Trinity or Triad becomes reinforced and further discussed in this imagery session. It is suggested that the Father is beyond human understanding. The second element of the Trinity, Jesus or the Christ, seems to be a manifestation of the Light in the World. He is presented in a way that might be comprehended by humanity. The third element, a white bird over Jesus' head, presumably represents the Holy Spirit.

The reader is reminded that a concept of the Trinity has been emerging in the past few imagery sessions. This session seems to contain another attempt to incorporate it within Theresa's thinking, as an image of transcendence. It was also suggested that her husband needs to integrate the trinity, as well.

Theresa continues, *it's a real good feeling to be there. I said, does Bill belong here too? He says, "of course he does but he has to learn that yet." And he said, "Bill belongs here too. We are all one." He says, "that is why man does not have to fear separation from his loved ones, because we all are one." I said, can Bill get better? He definitely says, "yes. But he has to do it himself." He says, "I'll help him." He says, "the earth is the earth. It is separate but it also belongs to me. We are all one in that we have life." He says, "Bill has to wake up." That's what he said. "Wake up," meaning to become aware of something or something like that. "You all come from me."*

PART 16
Theresa takes Communion

Theresa enters her imagery with the usual intense light which seems to increase in its intensity from one session to another. At times this light is so intense that it causes her eyes to burn. After a while her eyes seem to become acclimated and her *eyes are not burning as much now but they are burning a little bit*. Then Theresa says, *I feel myself looking real little and like a tiny figurine and the beams of light are all around me. For some reason the light seems to be coming from an eye, you know.*

The eye is not an unusual symbol that sometimes emerges in the imagery process. Some clients merge with the eye in order to see the world from a different, more transcendent perspective. We are also reminded of the eye of the Pyramid. In Christian Art an eye that is surrounded by the rays of the Sun is symbolic of God. (11)

Theresa continues, *He said, "you don't need to see the eye. This is the eye that watches you always." He says, "the eye of the world." Oh boy! He says, "it is the eye that can burn as well as do good." Maybe that is why my eyes are burning. (laughing) I don't know. He told me that he's going to let up on me a little bit. (laughs) I hope so, please! He told me I don't learn lessons very easily.*

Next Theresa sees an image *like an angelic being in a white robe. She asked, are you Jesus? He said, "I am the Christ, Jesus lives within me." When he refers to himself, it is I and we at the same time.* It is implied that Jesus is part of the Christ Archetype and that presumably there may be other parts of Christ. Perhaps the Christ Archetype has a collective makeup that includes all of humanity. To be sure we tend to think of some highly developed human beings as Christlike people. It is suggested that a distinction is being made between Jesus and himself, yet the two are the same. Theresa says, *right. He says, "you can call it whatever you want but we are the same thing." (laughs).*

Theresa indicates that *I keep floating but I'm not comfortable floating. I feel like I want to get on the ground. He told me I'm not very adventurous. (laughs) I know that. I am a conservative. I see a stripe of rainbow coming. I can see. It comes right off the side of the light. I shouldn't say stripe but a strip with colors and clouds. I'm feeling a lot of weird physical symptoms today. He's telling me to quit worrying about things and trust in him, which he has told me a million times. "Your humanness is limited," he said, "I am not."*

As indicated above, the rainbow is a significant symbol in a number of religious traditions. In Christianity it has a number of meanings. The rainbow has emerged in imagery with a number of people and tends to represent Christ's relationship with them as a binding covenant. Moreover, it appears that the colors of the rainbow represent the archetypal patterns of God.

In keeping with the theme of the rainbow, Theresa feels that she is at an alter upon which sits a chalice. She says, *I get the feeling that I am at an alter that opened up real wide like an alter to a church in front of him. In fact, that's just what it is. And the Light, it looks just like this chalice that the priest takes note of. I think it is called a tabernacle, in the church. It looks just like that. It looks sort of like the sun shining you know, but it is brighter, and I get the feeling that that was a message in some way.* She continues, *The Host, the unleavened bread that they use in communion sets in the middle, and that's what's in the middle and all the beams of light are coming off the side of it. That represents the body of Jesus Christ in the Church and a brilliance surrounds it. He said, "it represents the same thing in every Church." (laughs) "You are talking too spiritual," that's what he tells me. (Laughs) I can't even have a fleeting thought, can I? (laughs)*

Theresa asked if she is going to take communion. *He said, "every time you ask for me, every time you look for me, we are having communion whenever you are seeking me." "Yes," he said, "it is our interaction." I get the feeling that that Host also represents him. You see, in the Church, that represents the body of Christ, and I get a real loving feeling from that. "Yes," he says, "you are receiving love, Jesus' love." And now I see a beam of light shooting from him through the Host and then into me. We're all one and the beam comes at a downward slant. And now I'm kneeling at that alter and that light is coming down on me and a real spiritual, like a strong, I can't even explain it. It's just a very strong spiritual feeling of goodness and love, and pureness and all those good things. (laughing) I feel like it's coming all around me, making like, ah, like an aura around me, you know, almost the way you know, how you watch those movies, like outer space movies when it disintegrates. This shiny stuff comes and surrounds their body. It is a holiness is what it is in a word. Now there is like a white veil over my head, but it's very plain, and this good feeling. My eyes are starting to burn again. He told me that, "you are my child and I'm always close and that's all you need to know. And that's all."* To be sure, her experience regarding communion a feeling of communion with the Christ or the Light was very moving to her. It was obvious that it had a significant impact on her.

Next, Theresa asked about her husband, Bill. *He said, "Bill has to come to him, himself." He said, "He's part way there." He said, "Bill has to seek him only and keep his mind open. He can't let religion blind him." He says he doesn't knock religion though. He said that "it's good and it's a good guide. Just don't let it get to the point that it blinds you from closeness with me." He said, "don't let anything get in the way of closeness with him." He said, "that goes for parties, too." (Laughs) He said, "in fact, I'd rather you be blinded by religion, if you are going to be blinded."*

It appears that Theresa's husband may be having a difficult time keeping his mind open because of his religious beliefs. There seems to be a warning that religion, presumably organized religion, can cause one to become blinded to a close relationship with God.

PART 17
Love Each Other

Part 17 represents the final imagery session with Theresa. The Trinity and Light theme continue with a final suggestion to love, to love each other. It appears that Jesus comes up the stairway to meet her. Perhaps this represents a willingness of the unconscious to meet her halfway. At any rate the Trinity theme continues with this session. It seems important for her to note that the Light can be transformed into any of the three archetypal patterns: the Father, Son and Holy Spirit. It is in this way that they are all one.

Theresa begins the session by starting down the stairs and says, *I feel like Jesus came part way up the steps to meet me. He's explaining to me about the Trinity again, and he said that he can transform into any one of the three, but they are all one, the Father, Son and Holy Spirit. I see them like, as three with their backs to each other and then sort of forming into one light beam, and he says," I am the way, the sooner you know that the better off you will be." (laughing) I feel a smiling person. I feel a smiling being. He told me that I need to lighten up a little. (laughing) I'm too serious. He told me that what I want to know is far beyond my comprehension. All I need to know is like, what I'm seeking or what I'm after, and to just live for that and everything will work out. I guess I just want to know more about the Father, Son and Holy Spirit, the relationship. I can accept what he says.*

It is suggested that Theresa is being given an image of the Father, Son and Holy Spirit in response to what she desires to know. She continues, *yes, the beam was like in the shape of a monument, sort of like a pyramid at the top. Oh yes, I just realized that.* It appears that she is making reference to the Egyptian pyramids or perhaps the Washington Monument, that may be symbolic of the archetypal triad. Perhaps the Hebrew Essenes and Egyptians shared this commonality within the context of their own religious traditions. Theresa said, *He says, "yes." But he said, "they were still somewhat off. They didn't have the completeness." He said, "the greater understanding came after Jesus walked the earth."* It was suggested that Jesus may have represented the next step in the evolution of humanity. Theresa continues, *yes, but it goes deeper than that. He said that, ah, the funny part is that I had a lot of questions about the far Eastern religions before and now he is answering some of them. He said that they sort of got stunted in their growth because they didn't look beyond this point. I think he means after Jesus walked the earth. They stayed where they were.* It appears that each religion had a concept of the light but did not identify it with humanity. This is to say that they may not have realized that each human being contains an aspect of divine light.

Right, Theresa said, *he says, "yes." He said, "Do not allow growth to stop." He says, "grow up and gain a strong foothold." He said, "Do not waiver from the truth. Stick by what you believe and understand." He told me that I listen to too many people. He is saying to me," you know what is right and just allow that to penetrate you."* It appears that it is being suggested that one's truth comes from the inside. *Yes, he told me in a certain kind of concept, the understanding is inborn in you. It's there. Just allow it to surface.*

It was suggested that Theresa may need to evaluate what she reads according to how fitting it is with what she feels from within herself. She says, *yes, there were times when I read the Bible before, there was fury and wrath in it and it would scare me. He says, now I know what the words will mean. They will have deeper meaning, more than most people understand. I need a base to go by. He says, I'm too conservative to just, I don't know what he means. To be open to just ideas. I need a base to give myself.* Theresa may be referring to needing something concrete to hold onto. However, the world of ideas and concepts is not a concrete world.

Next, Theresa continues her dialogue with Jesus. *He said, "You are my flower." And he is showing me a picture of all the different kinds of flowers and one is just as pretty as the other, but they are all different, a whole field of flowers but all different kinds. He said he likes flowers. (laughs) Me too. I said that when I see a field of flowers it reminds me of heaven and he said, "heaven is much more beautiful than a field of flowers. It is all beyond what you understand." He told me the thing I like most, as far as beauty and nature, is just a pinpoint of the beauty of the next world and of heaven. His sun light is shining on one particular white flower and it makes it glisten like artificial almost. It glows. Yes, he told me that flower standing, I'm still seeing the whole field of flowers, is how I am to him and that each person is like that to him, special.*

Theresa asked about her husband. She says, *He wrote in big letters in front of me, all capitals, he wrote, "FAITH. Keep it and don't lose it," he says. He says, "I don't mean small amounts either." (laughs) He says, "Bill has better faith than you," and I know that Dave. (laughs) He says we underestimate him. (laughs) I don't think we do that. He says, "when Bill comes through this, the whole world will rejoice." I don't know about the whole world. I got the notion that he loves all people no matter who they are. That was really loud and clear, too. He said they are all important to him, but something else too, <u>they are all needed</u>, I think. He said, "Mankind is beyond mankind's comprehension. Why don't they just leave it to me?" And he says, "love each other, period." That is not an easy thing to do, always. He says, "yes it is. You haven't tried hard enough." (laughs) I know, oh boy. He said, "you better work on patience Theresa, I'm warning you (laughs) Work on patience, having patience."* At various times I have been working on that.

SUMMARY AND DISCUSSION

Theresa proved to be a very good candidate for imagery work because of her ability to experience vivid images with color and with a sense of sound and smell. Initially, she approached her unconscious with apprehension and distrust, probably because of her rigid religious background that seemed to view the unconscious as something dark and sinister. However, with her deeper sense of openness combined with the painful experience of her husband's illness, she seemed to respond to the imagery process very well. It is assumed that having already resolved many of her childhood and adolescent problems during the first eight years of marriage, she did not encounter such painful and intense images of childhood trauma, common in more pathological cases. While she did deal with issues such as her perceptions regarding men and lack of maturity, her imagery work appeared to focus more on developing a sense of personal growth, strength, spirituality, faith and trust in the wisdom of her own inner resources. This was combined with a process of change with regards to her religious beliefs, leading toward establishing a greater acceptance of and faith in Divine Love.

The Guide Phenomenon - Theresa's Canine Companion

As we have seen, the guide phenomenon is quite common in Imagery Therapy. It takes on many forms such as animals or everyday appearing persons. Moreover, each guide is generally specific in its function and purpose. They seem to carry one through given phases of the imagery process with given content and experiences. The most enduring guides appear to be those parts of the self from the Collective Consciousness. Some appear as animals and there is the "Guardian Angel Phenomenon." Also is the "Wise Man Phenomenon" or "Christ Like Figure," that seems to be part of one's Supra Consciousness.

Theresa's first inner guide came in the form of a "canine companion," apparently of common ancestry. This companion, in her first imagery session, appeared after a short time of getting acclimated to her inner surroundings. The dog, a non-threatening animal, seems to be the perfect projection in the face of her fears related to the unconscious. At first he serves as a benign companion as she further explores her inner world. Then he gradually begins to take on a guidance function. The most significant example of this was when he appeared with a leash. It became apparent that she is being led by him rather than the other way around. Interestingly, he is also able to talk which is quite common in such situations. They go into a hole in the ground and then he pulls her out into the ocean. She feels a little frightened because she does not know how to swim. However, everything happens so rapidly and she is led to shallow water before her fear can take over. As we observed, the ocean plays an important part in her imagery

It appears that one purpose of the dog was to help Theresa deal with her initial fears of the unconscious as represented by the ocean. A second function or major purpose, appears to be that of leading her into her Collective Consciousness in the form of the Old Woman from Texas. Another aspect of the dog as demonstrated when he became "real big" was that of protector. This is also a common function in the imagery process. This helps reduce fear and anxiety during uncertain situations.

Once Theresa begins to develop a comfortable connection or relationship with the grandmotherly woman, we see that the dog begins to fade into the background. Actually, it is not clear when the dog ceased to appear since she becomes absorbed in the images presented by the "Old Woman."

The Collective Consciousness and Supra Consciousness

The transition from the dog to the Old Woman as guide seemed to be well orchestrated. There was the initial period of getting to know her and becoming comfortable with her. One role that the Old Woman first assumes is that of a nurturing grandmother to which Theresa responds positively. Just as the dog appeared non-threatening the Old Woman seemed to represent a similar benign, trustworthy person.

Another major role that the Old Woman appears to assume is to introduce Theresa to her own Divine Self (Supra Consciousness) represented by the fire in the tunnel. Further, it seems clear that she is being led to her own sense of humanity which is represented by her Collective Consciousness or as she is told, her "family." To accomplish this task Theresa is led into the earth, the ground of her own being and humanness. Further, it is assumed that within the earth is the source of spiritual nurturing that she needs.

One significant event is when the Old Woman leads Theresa back into the earth to meet her "mother." Presumably, this is the archetypal earth mother who gave birth to her spiritual self rather than her physical self. Finally, the Old Woman takes Theresa to the Castle which seems to be a reflection of herself and her many personal traits. It is also where she meets a "middle-aged man" who appears to be an archetypal figure. He appears to be a blend of a number of men. Hence, it seems clear that the guidance function of the Old Woman gives way to a Christlike figure.

During the next phase of the imagery work Theresa begins to experience a "Christlike" man with an increased level of sun light. This is a common phenomenon which coincides with such archetypal projections. This person appears to her with blond hair and a white robe, most likely a male image that suggests goodness and purity fitting to her religious background. The primary function of this guide seems to be to help her discover and experience the many facets of herself, as represented by the different rooms of the castle.

The next projection of the "Christlike" man takes on the form of the historical Jesus which is Theresa's primary image of "Christ" or God. This image seems more closely associated with the sun, the "Light," which becomes a more prominent occurrence as her imagery work progresses. It is noted that there is no real distinguishing difference being made in her imagery between the middle-aged man, the man with blond hair and Jesus, and the Light. This is because they all seem to be different projections of the same phenomenon progressing from a more human appearance, including the Christian image of Jesus, toward a more abstract image of a divine presence, Christ or the Light. There seems to be an intent on the part of her unconscious to represent these various images as being interrelated. It might also be noted that such images seem to fit with the Jungian description, at least in function, of the archetypal "wise man." (12) The primary role of this guide is to bring one's unconscious aspects of the self into conscious awareness, including one's own "divine" nature.

Another important function of the "Christlike" guide is that of bringing the individual to such knowledge as would be needed for healing oneself. This generally is presented as distorted beliefs, ideas, or perceptions of life which do not fit the realities of one's life and life circumstances and which cause tension and disharmony in oneself and others.

Finally, and perhaps most significant, is in facing and dealing with one's own religious beliefs and relationship with God. The "Christlike" image often becomes instrumental in the development of one's relationship with God and with one's own divine self. It would seem clear that Theresa's "Christ" guide served well in this capacity.

The initial session seems to present images that appear to describe some of the life issues facing Theresa. It is noted that she is casually led by each symbolic image as if on an exploratory walk. It is assumed that the dead tree represents that part of Theresa's life which has died or needs to die, especially her overprotected childhood and adolescence when she developed a distorted view of men and the need to remain a child. We find that the dead tree has become a nesting and perching place for tiny birds, sparrows. Such birds might be symbolic of the new thoughts, ideas, concepts and beliefs that may emerge from the inner process of death and dying. Since sparrows are creatures of flight, we assume that the emergent values and beliefs will be of a higher nature and will be simple and plain in their appearance.

A second tree that had fallen into the water appears in Theresa's imagery. It is believed that it may represent her husband's potential death. The tree has fallen into the ocean, the waters of God, from whence his life had originally come. Moreover, she sees dead fish lying on the beach. Fish are creatures of the water and may be related to the spiritual nature of the unconscious. It is well known that a fish is symbolic of Christ and Christians. (13) Those who have been baptized sometimes view themselves as being transformed into fish, presumably swimming in the spiritual waters of Christ. In Theresa's case the fish are presented as dead. It is felt that the dead fish represent the death of her own misconceptions and distorted religious beliefs, especially about Christ and Christianity. Such childhood beliefs need to die and give way to a more open and inclusive view of Christianity and spirituality.

Next, Theresa and her companion find what appears to be a deserted house which they start to explore. There is no furniture and it seems desolate and cold such that she begins to feel "real cold." We assume that this house may represent feelings of emptiness and boredom regarding her role of housewife, mother and caretaker. Her feelings of being cold may be a symptom of anxiety associated with the house, but we have no indication of the source.

A gigantic eagle appears at the very beginning of Theresa's second imagery session. This image seems to be archetypal in nature and may carry more of a universal meaning, especially since it appears in a spontaneous manner without any apparent relationship to any other part of the imagery session. Her feelings of great power associated with this bird are also common and further support our archetypal assumption. This would be symbolic of the power that she possesses, but of which she is unaware.

As indicated, the eagle is also a mythological creature and is often associated with the sun, a consistent theme in Theresa's imagery. In Christianity during the middle ages, the eagle was symbolic of rebirth, Christ and his ascension. Moreover, Jungian Psychology regards the eagle as a father figure. (14)

My clinical impression is that when the eagle is presented, as it was in Theresa's imagery, it marks the beginning of a journey into the unconscious. Joseph Campbell refers to this as the Hero's journey. (15) The eagle is a symbol of the ever-watchful divine power that has the keenest of sight and is capable of striking its prey (evil) in an instant. Perhaps like the watchful father, it observes its child during its exploration and discovery of the world and allows it to experience failing and suffering. However, it is keenly vigilant of circumstances that might be overwhelming or truly threatening. Knowing that the father is there observing may be the significant factor that gives the child the faith and confidence necessary to boldly explore the unknown, so vitally important for his/her own growth. It is suspected that this is also the case with Theresa, since she was often presented as a little child at play, a child of consciousness and spirituality, being thrust into the unknown world of the unconscious and adult responsibility under the watchful eye of the Christ and the divine Father.

At one point in Theresa's imagery everything turns dark, except that there is "light off to the right." Her canine companion joins her and they walk toward the light. The light, white light becomes bright and blinding and the dog becomes *real big all of a sudden*. White light often represents the purity of divine consciousness. It also appears to be a stormy day which tends to be symbolic of the turmoil in one's life or in one's own unconscious. In Theresa's case it may be symbolic of internal conflict developing over her entry into the unconscious. As one begins the journey toward wholeness, when one's unconscious ideas, beliefs and experiences, etc., are subjected to a process of transformation, (death and rebirth) inner conflict often surfaces. There seems to be something in all of us (human weakness as represented by the dark side of the self), that does not want us to grow and change and which must be confronted at different stages along the way. This may account for the presence of the Giant Eagle just prior to one's entrance into the unconscious.

Toward the end of one imagery session, Theresa is led down to the ocean where she sees porpoises jumping in and out of the water. This seems to be a fitting completion to an imagery session since porpoises are generally perceived as a positive symbol. Their presence seems to indicate that all is well and safe. They are often considered helpful to humanity and one need not fear sharks or primitive creatures of the unconscious when they are swimming close by.

It is noted that when Theresa encounters those of her Collective Consciousness, she is unable to see their faces. This first occurred when she met the "old woman." This observation is noted because it is one of the most consistent experiences in the clinical setting, from one person to another. It appears that one experiences the Collective in this way, because he or she is not ready to recognize them. In time, facial features may become clear and identifiable.

Once while walking near the ocean, Theresa sees bands of color in the water like a rainbow. Yellow appears to stand out. The rainbow is always a positive symbol and according to Christian tradition, from which she has come, it represents a reconciliation with

God such as the rainbow that appeared at the end of the Great Flood. Yellow is associated with the "Light" and symbolic of eternity and transfiguration. (16) Also, the sun suddenly becomes *"real clear, real bright just a round ball, not like it normally looks*. Perhaps the sun represents the light of Christ, the Son, which nourishes life. (17) The old woman refers to it as God's beauty, just like everything in nature. In a certain sense Theresa seems to be shown the essence of her relationship with God, the God of beauty, reconciliation, growth and nourishment.

The old woman points out a "really old tree" that is crooked with roots sticking out of the ground and she says that this is "God's beauty too." To her, all things in nature have beauty, even things that are old at the end of life having grown through life experiences with increased wisdom and awareness. As they walk further down the beach, they find a hole in the ground that opens to a tunnel. Tunnels often represent an opening to the ground of one's own being, the ground representing the earth which contains the nurturing substance of one's life. In nature, the earth is composed of the many generations of life having died and returned to the ground of its origin. So it is the ground of the human psyche that contains many generations of human life, having died and returned to the ground of its own being, to become the source of nourishment for future generations of human life.

Within the tunnel is a fire that is orange, red with blue spots in it. The fire is perceived as warm, beautiful and loving. It is believed to be representative of the source of one's life, the divine fire of human life, the archetypal earth mother who gives birth to human life. The torches in the tunnel appear to represent each individual life, having been created from the greater fire, the Light or Earth Mother of the human Soul. It is noted that as Theresa preceded through the tunnel, she perceives forms of people who were described as parts of her, or aspects of her Collective Consciousness. Theresa is introduced to her own divine light and her Collective Consciousness

The divine light seems to be related to what Theresa is told to be "your mother." Soon it becomes clear that the mother being referred to has nothing to do with her biological mother who is still living. As she continues further into the tunnel, which is a theme during the first phases of her imagery she comes to a plate that has four sections to it. The plate appears to represents four parts to her life. Occasionally in imagery work, one's life is represented by a circle or sometimes a wheel with four parts. It is assumed that those partitions are symbolic of the four seasons of one's life: childhood, adolescence, adulthood, and old age - or the period of generativity and wisdom. Theresa perceives the first part of the dish as being dark where she feels alone. Presumably, this represents the first stage of her life when she was in a very oppressive situation. The experience of the area becoming bright most likely represents the resolution of this part of her life through her relationship with her husband and other life experiences outside of her childhood home.

Next, Theresa finds herself standing before a bright light, like a flame. She is told that this "*light is you and you are it*." Further, the light says, "*I am the ONE.*" The light tells her that it loves her and that it will help her find who she is. The light tells her that it is her mother. Perhaps this light represents the essence of her own life, what gave birth to her spiritual self. Perhaps she is one of the torches, a spark of light or fire from the greater fire, one's spiritual, archetypal Mother.

Then the Light leads Theresa out of the tunnel to where there is green grass and the sun shining. Apparently, this is the world of matter where lots of little children are playing. This suggests that the world in which she lives, is like little children at play. It should be noted that this has been a theme in the imagery of others, indicating that we live in a world whose development tends to be that of children at play. However, Theresa is told that she will not grow there, suggesting that she must leave her childhood behind in order to grow. Moreover, we form the impression that she is being booted from the nest, the secure playground of the child where she is taken care of without responsibilities.

Finally, Theresa is shown a house but she can only see half of it. She is told that that is all she needs to see for now. It is implied that this is her house that is only half developed. Hence, she will be working on developing the rest of the house throughout the remainder of her life.

Another progressive phase of Theresa's imagery is the presentation of a Castle where she is introduced to different aspects of herself. The sun continues to become brighter, a theme from one session to another. However, it is especially bright as she comes closer to the Castle. Just as the house is representative of one's own life or self in Theresa's case, the Castle may be symbolic of the place in which her soul dwells. The Castle is also the dwelling place of the king and queen who govern the kingdom. The Castle then is the symbol that informs one of his/her relationship to the Soul, the divine ruler. It is governed by the queen and king, the masculine and feminine.

One of the first images Theresa sees in the Castle is a green round table with a border below the table where she sees approximately 20 cups. Each cup seems to represent where a person sits. This is reminiscent of the Knights of the Round Table where the King calls the Knights together to decide upon matters of great importance. In this instance, each cup appears to represents a member of her Collective Consciousness who may be serving as a consultant to her Soul and to her as well.

While Theresa seems to be lacking in self-esteem given her limited life experiences, she is taken into a room where she looks at herself in a mirror. She sees herself as a Fairy God Mother with a magical wand in her hand. This description of her seems to represent her potential in life, the capacity to nurture and make things happen relative to the growth of herself and others, as if in a magical way. In addition, there are many plants shown in the area. Like the green grass, images of plants and blooming flowers are often indicative of growth to maturity and creativity. Further, in this imagery sequence the beautiful flowers appear to be symbolic of how each person is valued by God for their inherent beauty. It is difficult for Theresa to view herself in this way since she recalls experiences in her life that have tended to create guilt, remorse and inferiority.

Theresa is then taken to a room that looks like a planetarium with a ceiling that opens to the stars. She is told that she will be able to use this in the future. Moreover, she is told that like the flowers of the earth, the stars are part of nature and are natural. Perhaps stars represent the flowers of the Universe. At times "reaching for the stars" represents reaching for greater heights of creativity and action in one's life. This imagery sequence may represent a much broader perspective that will likely become useful in developing deeper insights into life and future difficult life circumstances.

It seems clear that each room in the Castle represents part of Theresa's life, or new insights or ideas which are presented in symbolic ways. For example, in one room, the floor is covered with green grass and with bright sun shining through the windows. She is told that this is the beauty of love, suggesting that the reciprocal relationships in nature are for the purpose of growth and creativity and which represent true love. Love is being defined as an act of being what one is created to be in relation to others. She is told that she is love and that she is capable of love, that which she is created to be and do.

Next, Theresa is taken deeper into the Castle where she comes to a place where there are "all sorts of people," an apparent reference to her Collective Consciousness who dwell in the Castle. She comments that they know her but she doesn't know them. This is a typical description of one's own Collective Consciousness. Further, it becomes apparent that some of them including the old woman have places at the round green table which she saw earlier.

Then Theresa comes to a room where there are stripes of colors over the door. This room, thus presented, may indicate that by dealing with the contents of each room she is performing the work necessary for a reconciliation with the divine forces of her own unconscious. Another interpretation might be that the colors over the door may be symbolic of the patterns of life and related issues being process in the many rooms of the Castle.

Finally, it might be noted that Theresa meets what she describes as a middle-aged man who makes her feel uncomfortable. She says that she does not like men of this age. However, he tells her that he *"is no one to be afraid of."* This may be an introduction to facing her fear of middle-aged men. More importantly, it may be an initial meeting with someone who will become a significant part of her imagery.

In a subsequent session Theresa comes to a big round tunnel, perhaps another symbolic presentation of the birth cannel. It appears that there is dark green moss growing on the walls on the inside of the tunnel. My clinical experience suggests that the moss-covered walls may represent jealousy and possessiveness. She later discussed this trait as one of her real difficulties with regards to men.

Theresa continues to experience images representing unresolved issues in her life, including ironing clothes. For example, she finds herself using an ironing board. However, she states that *I hate to iron clothes*. It seems that this image represents her resentments over her duties as a housewife and mother. Most likely it is a symbol of her feelings over being tied down, while her husband seems exempt from such duties and can come and go in the world as he pleases. As we have seen during the first stages of her marriage, she had a good deal of difficulty with her feelings of being *tied to a ball and chain*.

It appears that Theresa progresses from being guided by her Collective Consciousness to an archetypal entity who has blond hair who she begins to follow. He is wearing a white robe and he puts his arm around her. She begins to feel *this love when I am with him*. He tells her that he is going to take her to where she began. As they proceed she feels like they are going down the stairs to a basement where she sees a lot of people sitting around who seem transparent and they seem to be holding candles. The man in the white robe tells her that they are all her friends.

Generally, in imagery therapy, a basements suggests the place in the psyche where repressed material has been stored. This is to say material in the unconscious that is unacceptable and threatening to the conscious mind and is therefore hidden from consciousness. In Theresa's case, it appears that she is experiencing her own Collective Consciousness. It seems that she is being oriented to her Collective Consciousness without tapping into the specific content of the individual identities.

While in the basement, Theresa and the blond-haired man stand in a light beam coming through a window. It is at this point that she refers to the man as seeming like Jesus because he is warm and loving. Soon they go into another room in the basement where the man seems to turn on a movie projector which shows pictures of her as a child. Then there are pictures of her as an adult. She soon acknowledges that she feels embarrassed about that side of herself who she feels is an immature child. However, she is reassured that there is nothing to be ashamed of that it is all about growth. We can only speculate that the beam of light represents the divine light from which her own spark of life came. This combined with the human side of herself, the Collective Consciousness, and her spiritual inheritance seems to constitute the beginnings of her own identity. The transparent people holding candles appear to be symbolic of this combination of humanity and the divine light/fire or substance of life.

The theme of life needing light for its own substance and growth continues in Theresa's imagery as sunlight passes through the windowpanes onto the plants. Interestingly, some of the panes are colored green, red, blue, and yellow. Presumably these colors represent archetypal patterns which are transferred to the plants as patterns of life in the plants.

During another imagery sequence, the man (Jesus) pushes a button and the walls start to revolve. As the walls revolve, they reveal certain parts of herself. He says that she is "pink and lacy" suggesting femininity. He also says that this is heart shaped, representing her capacity to love. These are all descriptions of Theresa that seem to be describing given archetypal patterns (the colored lights shining on her) that are influencing her own life, such as femininity and the capacity to love.

Theresa's encounter with the "Light" continues with greater intensity and brightness. The light informs her about herself. In particular, a hand forms with little children on each fingertip and the color green seems to be prevalent. Theresa is told that the children belong to her. It is likely that this image refers to five "child" parts of herself who need to grow up. She is told that she needs to take a position in the middle of the hand. It is assumed that she is being told to take a central position of responsibility regarding the growth of her own self as symbolized by the undeveloped child parts of herself. Moreover, the hand seems to emerge from the green grass suggesting that the earth is a necessary ingredient of all growth, the ground of her own being.

Theresa finds a bridge that goes from the beach out over the ocean. Generally, a bridge is a symbolic image with a number of possible meanings. A bridge connects or unites two separated elements such as land separated by water. It is often meant to represent a crossing from one form of consciousness to a new more comprehensive level of consciousness. In her case it seems to suggest a bridge from her own physical consciousness or human awareness toward a divine awareness represented by the ocean. It is interesting to note that she is presented as a baby just starting to walk. This may be indicative of her level of spiritual awareness from which she is growing toward greater spiritual growth and consciousness.

It is noted that the sides of the bridge are high, and the bridge seems to be made of cobble stones and its color is brown. It would seem that the bridge has been symbolically constructed from individual stones of the earth or perhaps the individual parts of Theresa's own Collective Consciousness. The high sides may represent a protection against falling into the spiritual waters before she is ready. After all, her spiritual development is that of a baby just starting to walk and yet unsteady in her development.

Soon, Theresa is being held like a baby and she is told that all the things of nature are hers. The one holding her takes the form of a person with *"arms stretched like around the world"* and he says, *"it's all yours and you need nothing."* This suggests that she comes from nature and is nature itself. All that she needs she already contains.

Theresa and "Jesus," as she describes him return to the tunnel which appears to be a maze or labyrinth. They go very deep into the earth and go through a narrow passageway *like a pencil*, and come out to brilliant colors, a rainbow. As they pass through the tunnel the area behind them becomes white. Perhaps this imagery represents the process that Theresa will have to go through in order to come to full spiritual growth and reconciliation as symbolized by the rainbow. The maze or labyrinth is believed to represent the journey that one takes to discover the center of one's own being. (18) Then there is an ascent from the darkness to the light of increased consciousness. In her case the maze seems to represent the many experiences of self-discovery through which she must pass. As she and her guide, Jesus, successfully encounter each adventure of learning, the passage becomes purified and brighter with light as represented by the color white.

Finally, little animals and a black cloud appears. These images seem to represent Theresa's fears and doubts that tend to block her progress and ability to grow through growth producing experiences. Despite her doubts and fears she is surrounded by warmth and a great white light that she describes as the *Master*.

Consistently, the light continues to become brighter and whiter. Theresa starts flying unassisted. It is assumed that she may have accomplished a sense of new psychological and spiritual freedom. We take this event to represent a breakthrough for her. Further, this experience of independence and freedom may be preparation for facing some of the distorted concepts of herself having been developed from a rigid conditioning of the past.

Theresa returns to the Castle. She feels that she is going to be confronting her unhealthy view of men. Soon she comes to a room in the castle where *bunches of grapes* are hanging from the ceiling. She hears a voice that says, *"fruit of the vine and works of human hands."* It appears that one concept that she holds of men is that they are laborers, that they go into the place of work and return home with the fruits of their labor.

Then Jesus points out a door midway up the wall of the room and he says that it is *"very important."* The door is wooden and is square. This may suggest that Theresa's concept of men is that they are rigid, conservative (square) and difficult to reach or access (halfway up the wall). She continues through the door into a tunnel that is *square in shape* and the walls are of hot metal. The theme of conventionality is continued in this imagery. The tunnel is narrow suggesting that men tend to be narrow minded. The walls of hot metal would appear to indicate that men are critical/judgmental (hot) and thick skinned-hard to get through to or penetrate (metal).

Then Theresa sees five wooden beams going down the wall. At the top of the beams is a shelf with three little blue birds on it. Jesus says that they are babies and they appear to her to be sort of *ceramic looking*. It might be noted that the number of five in Islamic culture is symbolic of the pillars of piety. In Christian tradition there is reference to the five wounds of Christ. (19) Perhaps to Theresa the five beams may unconsciously represent false piety with regards to men. This image may be symbolic of the father holding up and supporting the children and family (baby birds) who are vulnerable and easily shattered (ceramic). Of significance may be the fact that the mother bird does not appear with the babies. Possibly, she does not see the role of the father as being supportive of the wife and mother.

Theresa and Jesus walk down a tunnel that has walls that have *like (brown) animal fur*. Apparently, Theresa views men as having a primitive, animalistic side to their nature. Perhaps this also refers to her concept of male sexuality.

I believe this to be a significant moment in Theresa's imagery. The primitive brown bear image seems to be something that is deeply embedded within the female psyche and may surface in their dreams during puberty. My thinking is that this image goes back to prehistorical times when men often wore animal skins to protect them from the elements. Hence, during a female's first sexual experience she is likely to be confused by what was happening to her. One sensation might have been the feeling of brown fur or a bear skin that might have been commonly worn by men during the cave dwelling era of humanity. Deep within the psyche of women is the concept of male sexuality as being primitive and animalistic.

Theresa then sees a round table with lights crisscrossing its surface from above. The table has black and white checks on top. This image seems to represent her concept of men as being black/white in their thinking. It may also represent her view of men as having the need to get together to play games of chance (poker) since they have a need for a "man's night out," to express their masculinity. It is likely that she may have some resentments toward men because they seem able to go out and have fun, while the housewife's duty is to stay home confined to the never-ending task of taking care of the home and children.

Theresa's concept of men appears to be that they are hard and "square," conservative and conventional in their thinking and behavior. Moreover, she tends to have a concept of men as being primitive and animalistic with regards to their sexuality. Finally, she is brought to a dark, round room that starts spinning her around. She is told that *"men are people too."* It seems clear that the round spinning room represents the need for her concept of men to be turned completely around.

It appears that Theresa has accomplished a great deal with regards to her distorted view of men as many translucent people of her Collective Consciousness are clapping their hands in celebration on her behalf. This suggests that what is accomplished at the level of ego consciousness also becomes of benefit to those of her Collective Consciousness who had struggled with the same issues in their lives.

It was further suggested that her distorted view of men had also been negatively affecting her attitude toward Jesus who is also male. A healthy concept of men may become helpful as she begins to work more closely with the male, archetypal Jesus in subsequent imagery sessions.

The theme of increasing brightness of white light continues. When Theresa opens the door, the light seems much brighter and more encompassing and she refers to the light as the *Father*. This may suggest a more dynamic and even more growth-oriented tone to future sessions. Her former concept of men may have been influenced by her relationship with her father. Hence, changing her concept of men to a much more healthy and positive view may have helped to open her to establish a closer relationship with the archetypal "Father" and certainly the archetypal "Christ."

On the way to the castle Theresa sees flowers of different colors, mostly a deep red which is the color of warmth and love. The flowers seem to be tulips which are flowers of early spring. We assume they represent a continual reference to new growth that is taking place within her.

During this imagery sequence, as Theresa comes to the castle, the castle door falls in front of her with chains being used to lower it. Apparently, her unconscious is opening to her, rather than her having to take the initiative to open the door to it. Upon entering the castle she sees the color brown, an earth color. Perhaps she is entering the earth where her resources for new growth is located. Symbolically, having been grounded firmly in the earth, her Collective Consciousness begins to seek growth toward the light.

This presents an interesting imagery sequence. Again, we find symbols of growth (green), spring flowers, the earth (brown), and wholeness/infinity (wheel) emerging as constant themes. She experiences intense sun light through the windows at a very high point in the castle. Part of the experience is the Father's distinct voice saying that he loves her. We see a progression in her imagery in which she experiences the higher, more spiritual levels of her unconscious.

Theresa soon arrives to a room where there is a green roulette wheel appearing with a brown center. Sitting in a high position in the room is a person with whom she starts to pass a big ball back and forth. It is suspected that the act of passing the ball back and forth is meant to suggest a cooperative relationship with the "higher self" as she enters into the game of life with chance factors involved.

As the floor of the room sinks Theresa goes down with the ball, indicating that she is like the ball, subject to the process and possible chance aspects of life. At the bottom, having fallen into the earth, she comes to an open porch area that is circular where she finds more translucent people of her Collective Consciousness people who will likely be part of her future. She is told that these are people who need help with their fears. Typically, she senses that these translucent people are actually her although she does not know them. This segment of her imagery would appear to be a continuation of the theme of healing and wholeness (circular porch). The way to wholeness appears to be related to future work with those of her Collective Consciousness who are dealing with issues of fear. We assume she will be dealing with future experiences related to processing and healing her fears and anxiety.

Theresa and the people of the Collective Consciousness descend a narrow stairway to a flower garden with white flowers. The whole garden seems to turn into open mouths trying to tell her something. She seems unable to hear what is being said. Since white is sometimes related to light, spirituality, purity, etc., (20) we assume that the message has something to do with such matters. Also combined with this is the concept that the garden may be symbolically related to "heavenly paradise and of the cosmic order." (21) Consistent with such themes is the message that comes from her white flower garden that *"life is beautiful, life is nothing to fear and life is forever."*

Theresa is told that she is very tired and needs to see "the blue light." The blue light appears to be coming from the "Father." This color seems to be related to peace and serenity. Apparently, this is the color and energy she needs as she begins to deal with her fears and apprehensions. White doves appear on both sides of the cubicle in which she is experiencing the blue light. They lift the cubicle upward with her in it. Further, they are also shining white light within the cubicle. The cubicle seems to be floating upwards to the "Father." It is a touching moment for her as He holds her like a baby. She feels as though he is giving her energy for facing her many burdens at this time of her life.

Apparently, this imagery experience is designed to be supportive and to help Theresa rise above her daily, burdensome life. We assume the blue and white light surrounding her (peace and serenity) is meant to help her rise above her fears and see them more for what they really are. Moreover, being lifted to the "Father" and into a transcendent experience may help her feel supported and involved in something more meaningful, inspiring and much bigger than her personal self.

The theme of dealing with Theresa's fears and apprehensions continues in subsequent sessions. Some of her fears involve her concept of the unconscious and the repressed material that it contains.

As Theresa walks down the beach toward the castle, she notices an area where there are ugly black trees. They do not frighten her, and she continues toward the castle. It would appear that this represents the dark and negative side of her unconscious. Clinical experience suggests that trees or a wooded area tend to be symbolic of the Collective Consciousness. A dark forest may suggest negative material to be faced in the Collective Consciousness. When she enters the Castle and goes down some stone steps, she finds murky water. This is the first time she descends into the castle and hears a voice that says, *"ugliness and dirt,'* which causes her to run back up the stairs. While she does not feel afraid, she does not want to deal with the ugliness as it repels her. Her lack of fear may be related to knowing that she can always go to the upper levels of the castle where she can find positive and supportive things such as love, peace and a sense of infinity. This may well be a symbolic introduction to what she will have to face in the future, that which is the basis of her fears and apprehension and which was also represented by the image of the ugly black trees.

When she gets to the upper level of the castle, Theresa sees a red and white triangle flag flying in the breeze. She feels that she is in the presence of a divine being where she is safe and loved. It is suspected that the triangle flag represents the divine trinity. The colors of red and white may represent a more positive spiritual, life giving quality. While the flag is triangular, the top of the Castle, the floor, appears rectangular in shape. A rectangle has four sides, a quaternity, and as such may be associated with the various interpretations of the number four. As indicated earlier, it may be related to the stages of her life: childhood, youth, adulthood and old age.

Theresa is told to go down some wrought iron steps. She is told to go down these steps to see what she is so fearful about. Then she comes to a room that has ceilings that are very low, such that she has to *crouch way down to walk in it*. She is told to go to the "other side" that is totally open with no sides or ceilings with very bright sun light. She feels fearful of falling while she is descending the stairs. This suggests that the stairs are meant to show her that she has a fear of falling, most likely psychologically and spiritually. The room with very low ceilings may be indicative of her fear of the world pressing in upon her. Those with high anxiety sometimes have a sensation of walls pressing in on them. Her difficulties with her husband's illness and the responsibilities of being a caretaker and head of the house would appear to offer sufficient cause for such fears. She is told that she tends to focus on the immediate and is fearful of thinking about the future. Such fears are likely based on her perception of the future as being full of difficulties, including the potential death of her husband. Further, she must face a potential future of being alone as a responsible adult with a young child to raise. Her imagery suggests that after facing her fears of falling and dealing with a world pressing down upon her, she will come to a wide-open life, full of bright sunshine.

After being held and comforted by the "Father," Theresa is put down into the Castle in a room with a carpet of many different colors such as green, pink and yellow to name a few. Again, we experience the theme of colors that appears to represent the colors of the rainbow. This would suggest a promise of a much better future once she faces the trials of her immediate life.

Later in the imagery, Theresa finds herself facing a drinking fountain which she is too small to reach. It is suggested that she project herself as a big person who is able to drink from the fountain. She discovers that the water of the fountain is actually wine. This may be reminiscent of the "blood of Christ" that one drinks during the act of Communion. It would also appear that she will need to grow beyond her spiritual childhood state to maturity in order to drink from the fountain.

Theresa is told to come into a room with snow white walls. Everything is sparkling white and *fluffy looking*. She is told that these are all things that she is afraid of. She is told that while she loves to grow, she is the very person who gets in her way. It would seem that the white room represents purity and perfection, something she is afraid she will never be able to achieve. It is as if she is afraid to grow beyond the innocence and purity of childhood and into the "ugliness" of adulthood. On the other hand, what she actually fears, growth and change, is something really beautiful much like a flower coming to bloom coming to creative maturity.

Finally, Theresa is taken to a place that she "does not like." It is a wall with *prickly things sticking out*. She is told that the wall represents the "bristly" side of her personality which suggests that she can become angry, defensive and "too sharp." Then she is shown rooms that are smooth, suggesting that she appears to fluctuates between being sharp and smooth.

As Theresa approaches the door to her unconscious the light becomes brighter, a bright white light that *disintegrates* the door, a theme that has been progressing from one session to another. It seems to be another magical day with the ocean deep blue with *white sparkles in it*. She is encouraged to swim despite the fact that she is unable to swim. She starts to swim, and she jumps in and out of the water like a dolphin. This segment seems to represent a new sense of freedom and the ability to do things that she would otherwise be unable to do.

Then Theresa returns to the castle and goes to the roof where she hears two voices calling to her. She feels frightened by one of the voices and the other voice says, "*don't be scared of him, he's just a jerk.*" This brief imagery while humorous, is significant. For the first time she seems to be confronted with two opposing forces, both calling to her. The significance is that she is able to differentiate between the two as she senses fear relative to one of the voices. In a certain sense she has developed the ability to differentiate between what is true and what is false, which may be important as we continue to later imagery sessions. Clinical experience suggests that this apparent test of differentiation is common during the later stages of imagery therapy.

Next, Jesus puts her on his back which she feels is reminiscent of the time when he was carrying the cross on his back. He tells her that it is all right because he is not that way anymore. Perhaps this imagery experience indicates that Theresa's concept of Jesus, quite possibly from her religious background, is of one who suffers and that she is one of the burdens that he has to carry. This seems to be an attempt to change this idea to one of a more loving relationship in which she is not a burden, but rather like a child being carried on her father's back. There appears to be a consistent theme from one session to another which is that we are all one: the sun, the sky, you and me, everyone.

Theresa meets an oriental old man with a long white beard. It is not known why this imagery emerged spontaneously at this time. The old man seems to represent oriental wisdom. As we shall see later, she appears to hold some fear of Oriental and Eastern religions and ideas. It appears that this issue may be surfacing at this time.

In a subsequent session as expected, the light has become so bright that there is no longer a door. The light is shining on several adults passing a ball. They seem very friendly and start passing the ball to Theresa such that they form a triangle. It would seem of interest to note that the triangle increases in size, perhaps to incorporate more area of thought and ideas. As we observe, the triangle appears to be an important theme in her imagery. In Christian theology it represents "God in three persons" (Father, Son and Holy Spirit). The image of three persons passing the ball in a triangle appears to represent the flow of communication and mutual cooperation across each part of the triad.

As the imagery continues, Theresa is again taken to the Castle. The outside of the castle seems to be gold instead of stone. She is told that it is 14K gold and that it represents something precious and beautiful and that it is her. It is obvious that this image is meant to represent her worth and beauty in the eyes of the divine.

When Theresa goes into the castle, she finds a kneeling angel with big white wings and blond hair. She is told that she does not need to be afraid because she is being protected. This imagery may represent the Guardian Angel who is kneeling to indicate his role of devotion, service and protection on her behalf. It seems important to note that this imagery may be in preparation for facing the darkness or negative part of herself. Although she feels alone she does not appear to falter in her strength and courage to face what is there, even though the angel seems to change into an ugly form. It appears that this experience is like a test of her growing ability to face and deal with her fears. Perhaps the feeling of being of great worth to the divine forces at hand can help her have a greater faith in being protected and cared for in the face of negative forces.

Then, Jesus turns into a King with a crown on his head. It would seem that Theresa's experience with facing her fear and confronting her dark side is a way of saying that she is in the service of "Jesus." This is to say that he is assuming the appearance of a King, the role that she has assigned him in her own religious life. It might be noted that the King is sometimes considered the embodiment of God, the mediator between heaven and earth. It was a common idea during the middle ages that kings ruled by divine right and were often followed blindly by their knights. The king in mythology has also been associated with ego development and maturity. (22)

Prior to this session Theresa had been in the process of learning about herself with little responsibility except that she participates in the imagery experiences that have unfolded before her. However, this session appears to suggest that she has some responsibility toward reflecting the light that she has been receiving from others.

Theresa walks into the Castle and the room appears to be "barren" and empty. At first, she appears to project herself as an ugly monster like *Frankenstein*. This seems to be an interesting image which for the first time, she projects herself as something negative. She feels no fear in this role of monster and it seems to be mostly created in jest. It is difficult to understand why she would create this projection, but it might have something to do with overcompensating for her own fear of such perceived monsters in her unconscious.

Once again, the theme of the king continues in Theresa's imagery. She enters into a room where there is a king sitting on a throne with a scepter in his hand. According to her imagery this is a king of power, the power to heal. He appears to be a mediator between Christ (the great healer) and humanity which needs healing. Healing in this case seems to have to do with understanding others and learning how other's feel, a spiritual or psychological kind of healing. It might also be noted that the room in which the king resides is gold, which is a second reference to gold. In the Christian tradition Gold is symbolic of love and the highest of virtues. (23)

Theresa sees an image of Mary and Joseph and a donkey. She sees the contrast between the gold and the "plainness" of this vision. It seems that this represents how what is plain and humble in appearance may actually be like gold, something of beauty. This is to say that something of great value and beauty may actually be something that appears plain and simple.

Theresa also sees a man with a long beard, a wise man in a very plain room. It might be recalled that she previously encountered an old oriental man with a long beard. This imagery seems to represent another form of gold - the beauty of wisdom gained from many years of life experience.

Theresa is told that her imagery of the king, along with the images of Mary, Joseph and the old wise oriental man, represents the beauty of love and friendship, a "beauty of this world." It is indicated that she needs to know the beauty of letting someone know you, really know you, and accepting you for the whole person that you really are.

Theresa later experiences her castle being presented as black. She indicates that she feels that black represents something *not good*. Hence, the black castle seems to represent her distorted concept that black is associated with something evil. She reveals that she does not like night or the blackness of night. She is informed that black is also beautiful.

Theresa enters a white room with white fur on the walls. We have already seen a number of images of white rooms that seem to represent spirituality, purity, light, love and friendship, beauty, etc. In this case the white room appears to be symbolic of her black vs. white polarization.

Then a white fluffy kitten appears in the room. This image also seems to be symbolic of Theresa's concept of white in contrast with black. The white kitten appears to suggest a soft, innocent and benign concept associated with white, which may also be in keeping with the soft fluffy white fur on the walls.

Another image appears of two oriental or Asian people sitting in a meditative position. Apparently, Theresa has developed another duality between Christianity and Eastern religions. She seems fearful of Eastern Religious thought because it appears to her to be in direct conflict with her Christian beliefs and values. She is told that although Eastern knowledge is different from what she knows, it is not necessarily wrong. The important thing appears to be that Eastern wisdom is based on love and that is similar to what is the most important aspect of Christianity. Interestingly, it is noted that Theresa is told that when something seems different from what she believes, she feels she has to make a choice. Her imagery suggests that this is not true. It would seem enough to acknowledge that one does not understand what appears to be different. It is important to approach such differences with a sense of openness and acceptance. One does not have to fear such differences. They may be neither right nor wrong. She is told that one can learn from everyone without regard to differences and that Jesus studied such philosophies and *"integrated them within his philosophy and teaching."*

Next, Theresa enters a canary yellow room. The room is blank. She is told that this room represents her intelligence. She is also told that she has a lot of intelligence which she does not apply enough. It is suggested that the room may be blank because she has not used her intellectual capacity to its fullest.

Then Theresa is taken to a room where everything is old with antique furnishings. She is told that this room is related to her obsession with getting old. The question seems to be, how can she have such a love of antiques, something old which has such beauty for her, yet think that growing old is ugly and distasteful? This room appears to represent a potential basis for accepting her own aging and seeing the real beauty of old age.

She is taken to the top of the castle where there is a garden of vegetables. The vegetable garden seems to represent growth that is occurring within her. The vegetable garden is also presented to show the relationship between the light of the sun and the earth which are two very important factors necessary for life and growth. We have already observed that one's unconscious symbolically contains the earth, the ground of being from which the Collective Consciousness springs forth, while the sun represents the nurturing light of the divine soul which is also a primary part of the unconscious.

The vegetable garden represents more of a relationship between humanity and plants. This is to say that the garden is planted and cultivated (nurtured) such that it produces its fruit, which becomes a source of nurturing for the gardener. Hence, like all things in nature the relationship is reciprocal.

It is interesting to note that Theresa seems to have difficulty with the idea that everything that grows starts small and become larger according to its own natural development. This seems to bring her to the unpleasant awareness of her own level of psychological maturity that she must also start small and grow in accordance with her own natural growth and development. To be sure, one's psychological growth does not always coincide with chronological age.

Suddenly Theresa has the image of Jesus knocking at a door, but the door does not open. This image seems to represent the spiritual help and nurturing that is being offered to her from her unconscious, but she does not open to it and respond to it. She is told that she keeps *"expecting things in this world to help and they can't."* This indicates that she needs to break with her external orientation to life and turn inward, where all that is needed to nurture her own growth resides.

Theresa is told that God the Father is in a supernatural state that will never be perceived directly and will never be completely understood because He remains in a supernatural state. The Christ (Jesus) as one of the three aspects of the "ONE" is the Father and Holy Spirit in a human state. By becoming human he takes on a concrete embodiment of God, and to some degree becomes comprehensible to humanity. Jesus represents the Father in a state that can be understood. In any case, the theme that the Trinity and that we are all "ONE" continues to permeate Theresa's imagery sessions.

Next, Theresa sees a white bird over Jesus' head. It is very white, whiter than she has ever seen, and it seems to want to land on his head. The White Bird is a very significant Archetypal symbol. It is not uncommon in the imagery work at certain stages of an unfolding process. It seems to represent the soul. Theresa seems to feel that she belongs there, presumably with Jesus. This would seem to suggest that the White Bird may be symbolic of her own Soul wishing to sit (be with) on the head of Christ.

Later in Theresa's imagery work she appears to see light that is coming from an eye. The single eye is another common image that emerges during certain stages of the imagery process. In some cases, it seems to represent the eye of the Soul that it is always observant and perceives spiritual matters. The eye appears to be symbolic of spiritual and mental perception. In Biblical times the eye seemed to represent the omnipresence of God. In Christian symbolism, God's creative wisdom is representative of the eye, while the eye in a triangle is symbolic of the Father in the Trinity. (24) Theresa is told that it is the eye of the world which can" *burn as well as do good.*"

Theresa asked the light if it is Jesus. This prompts a discussion regarding the relationship between Jesus and Christ. The discussion seems to suggest that Jesus was one of the human manifestations of the Christ. It is assumed that Christ is an Archetype that is manifested and embodied in human form during significant times in history and in given cultures. For example, it might be assumed that Jesus or the Buddha would be examples of those embodiments.

Theresa briefly sees herself as a football player. She is told that this represents her inner strength. Perhaps it suggests that she needs to become more aggressive, like a football player, when certain situations in her life would require it.

Then Theresa sees the stripes of a rainbow followed by an altar such that one might find in a church setting. As discussed above, the rainbow may represent a reconciliation with God and which may represent her own relationship with the divine. The altar often represents, in Christian tradition, the holy table of the Last Supper. (25) Given her imagery and Christian background it would seem clear that this is what the altar represents to her. She sees a Chalice sitting on the altar (26). The Chalice seems to be associated with communion. We assume that this is the cup in the Christian tradition that contains the blood of Christ. When one drinks of this cup, he/she is being nourished by God and receiving eternal salvation. Moreover, it is symbolic of the union with Christ (come-union).

Finally, it is suggested that religion can actually blind one to having a genuine relationship with God. Theresa is told that religion can be a good guide, but not to let it get to the point that it blinds one from a closeness to God. She is told not to let anything get between her and God, not even religion.

A subsequent session starts with a discussion about the Trinity, which has been a theme during the last few sessions. Consistent with Christian Tradition, the Trinity represents God in three forms the Father, Son and Holy Spirit. The emphasis of this image for her is that the Trinity is really "ONE," such that each individual manifestation is actually an expression of the ONE identity, God. This was represented in her imagery of three figures standing back to back, forming one beam of light. This beam was in the shape similar to the Washington Monument, an Obelisk, which is considered to be symbolic of the relationship between the earth, sun and sky (heavens). (27)

Theresa sees a field of different kinds of flowers. Each individual flower seems to represent a given person who presumably is considered special in the eyes of God. She is told by the Light that she is his flower. However, it is all beyond what she is able to understand.

This was Theresa's last imagery session. She is told to have patience and that all will unfold before her. The main thing is for her to continue to maintain her closeness with the Light, with him, presumably Jesus or Christ, and especially to love unconditionally.

A Follow-up of Theresa's Life

Following Theresa's imagery work, she became deeply involved in the care of her husband as his illness became more debilitating. She also had to assume responsibility for all of the household duties and decisions. Her life was full of frustration and she often felt like she was a robot doing what had to be done without thinking. All of her dependency needs had to be set aside, and she was forced into a position of mature responsible adulthood, one of the consistent themes of her imagery.

The death of her husband was somewhat of a relief for Theresa. However, she soon found that there were many life issues yet to face. Dealing with the financial problems caused by Bill's illness was the first to confront. This was followed by an adjustment to facing life alone and recovering psychologically from the difficult years of being the primary support and care for her husband.

Dating was one of the first problems facing Theresa. Being an intelligent and attractive woman, she had no difficulty with men wanting to date her. At first, she dated men who were "macho" and athletic, but who were lacking in maturity. Having grown in her own life and maturity, she soon lost interest in these men. Soon she realized that she preferred more mature and sensitive men who were warm, caring and gentle. At the time of my last visit with her, she was very comfortable in an apparent enduring relationship with such a man. Her growth seemed to be taking her toward the development of a deeper sense of warmth and intimacy in her life.

Theresa feels that she is now a "grown up person" having come through some very dynamic growth producing times. She appears to have no bitterness or resentments over her husband's illness and death. Her experience seems to have led her toward a deeper appreciation and love for life.

In retrospect, it would seem important to note that the imagery process is not a technique that relieves one from the experience of their life problems, as would also be true with all therapeutic modalities. Rather, it appears that Theresa's case is a good example of how coming into contact with her inner life and resources helped to form the basis for accepting and facing her difficulties and emerging from them with a deeper sense of herself and her own growth and development. The use of a more non-directive approach to imagery seems to have worked well with her, as it provided an opportunity for her unconscious to project a process with specific images that fit her background, life issues and perceptual frame of reference. The content of the imagery sessions clearly demonstrates that this was Theresa's journey and not one which I devised for her. It was a most interesting journey that prepared her well for the future and released her potentialities for facing an uncertain future and life. It was a meaningful journey for me, as well.

CASE STUDY IV
THE CASE OF CONNIE

Connie, a woman in her mid-thirties, came to me for help while in the midst of a number of life events which were creating emotional upheavals in her life. She had just left her husband after many years of an unhappy and abusive marriage. She was feeling guilt and remorse over leaving her two children with him. This created intense anxiety over their welfare, since both children were becoming more troubled as they grew toward adolescence. Her daughter in particular had elected to remain with her husband, leaving Connie with feelings of rejection and failure as a mother. She felt powerless to influence her husband and children in any positive way. Finally, she recognized that she would have to start working on putting her own life together before she could be of any help to her children. In addition to facing so many life changes, she was forced to confront her own intense rage, deep depression, free floating anxiety and panic attacks. She endured all of this while maintaining herself with subsistence employment and trying to improve her life with additional graduate education.

Connie came from a working-class Protestant background. Her father, a steel mill worker, was a warm and gentle man who provided modestly for his family, and Connie had enjoyed being "daddy's girl." However, her mother appeared cold and distant and seemed unable to handle conflict or respond to the suffering of those around her. Denial was her primary defense mechanism against life's difficult problems. During times when Connie was in conflict with her mother, her father seemed to linger on the sidelines and never intervened on her behalf. Neither parent seemed to be there when she needed them the most, although her father appeared accepting of her when she got into trouble during her adolescent years.

Connie's childhood experiences within a dysfunctional family disrupted her natural developmental patterns. Developmentally, she was unable to resolve the independence vs. dependence duality and having become polarized, the antecedents for her dependent personality became established. She came to idealize her older brother and projected her dependent need for attention, security, love and affection upon him. He unwittingly reinforced the dependence of his adoring younger sister. However, as he grew older with his own developmental needs, he began to develop friendships in his school and community. Hence, Connie's dependent clinging became more difficult for him to manage. Finally, he began to push her aside which led to feelings of hurt, rejection, abandonment, loneliness and worthlessness with festering anger and resentments. To make matters worse, she came to realize that her mother favored her brother over her. This caused deeper feelings of anger and resentments toward him. Then Connie experienced a traumatic sexual encounter with an older neighbor boy which had lasting and devasting effects on her life. This experience led to feelings of confusion, shame, guilt, worthlessness, ugliness and insecurity. She felt she had done something awful and felt responsible for what had happened to her. However, there were also deep feelings of hurt and rage over this and other childhood experiences that would surface later in life. Moreover, such childhood experiences made her vulnerable to future abusive relationships with men which tended to reinforce her feelings of shame and worthlessness.

When Connie attempted to express her traumatic sexual experience to her mother, her mother became angry and rejecting over being asked to face such uncomfortable issues. At the moment when Connie most needed the love, compassion and understanding of her mother, she felt rejected and abandoned by her.

Since there was little that Connie could do to express her feelings and her childhood sexual encounter, she was forced to suppress it at a terrible cost. She began to deal with her emotional suffering by taking aspirin, sometimes in large quantities. Soon she began to sneak into her grandfather's liquor supply and drank to get "high." Her subsequent inability to concentrate on her schoolwork yielded failing grades. Consequently, she began to resort to cheating to keep up.

During Connie's late grade school years her family moved, and she was forced to change schools. This change became emotionally devastating for her. Being unable to form new friendships, she became deeply depressed and turned to more self-destructive activities in an attempt to alleviate her suffering. At times she would resort to almost anything to numb the pain, including cutting herself with razor blades. She came to discover that physical pain could temporarily override the emotional pain.

Connie's feelings of depression, worthlessness and inadequacy increased, and she began to spend her lunch periods drinking. She was expelled after returning to school intoxicated a number of times. After she failed high school, it would be over a decade later before she returned to earn a high school diploma and begin her college education.

During Connie's late teenage years, she began to indulge in all-night episodes of drinking and sexual promiscuity. Sometimes she became abused both physically and psychologically by men who humiliated her. They also projected responsibility for their own bizarre behavior onto her.

Connie married, hoping to turn her life around and find some stability over the chaotic existence she had been living. However, her marriage led to further despair and unhappiness. Her belief that her husband would take care of her and free her from worry and responsibility was merely an extension of her already dependent and addictive personality. Her husband soon became abusive and unfaithful, while giving a good appearance to the world outside of their home. The couple seemed to thrive on attacking one another which produced an unhealthy atmosphere for their children.

Connie appeared caught in this abusive relationship with no apparent way out. In part, she stayed in the marriage to provide a stable home for her children. She discovered that because of her own personal problems she was unable to give anything of substance to them. Feelings of inadequacy and unworthiness as a mother surfaced in combination with other emotional upheavals linked to her past.

During Connie's early twenties she was seriously injured in a traumatic automobile accident. She was hospitalized for a number of months. During this time she became addicted to morphine, which was not readily available outside the medical setting.

Meanwhile, she learned that her husband had been unfaithful during her hospital stay. This further intensified her emotional suffering. Following her hospitalization, she began to abuse alcohol and other drugs, such as valium and PCP; virtually anything to alleviate her emotional and physical pain. This was cause for further humiliation in her life because it was easy for her husband to place blame upon her for the difficulties in their relationship and the troublesome behavior of the children.

Connie's addiction continued for about seven years. During her late twenties, she came to realize that she had become completely dependent on alcohol and drugs to deal with her feelings of rejection, worthlessness, depression, panic attacks and unhappiness. Feeling that she was dying psychologically if not physically, she checked into a drug and alcohol rehabilitation hospital. Following hospitalization, she entered a half-way house and started her long journey to recovery. This process took about two years of courageous and disciplined work.

After leaving her home and marriage and dealing with addiction issues, Connie was able to complete her high school education. Subsequently, she entered college and completed a bachelor's and master's degree. During her college years she pursued several self-development activities such as yoga, meditation and relaxation practices to help deal with her emotions. This self-development work brought her to new and more wholesome friendships that helped to support her through some of her most difficult times. Finding herself successful in higher education and professional work, she was emotionally ready to divorce her abusive husband and assume an independent life.

The divorce brought forth many of Connie's old symptoms of depression, rage, panic attacks, free-floating anxiety, social phobias and agoraphobia. These symptoms were a reminder that she needed to face her past. Her old addictive compulsions which she struggled to overcome also returned during this period. At this point she volunteered for my experimental therapy program, as means to deal with her destructive past experiences.

It soon became clear that Connie was going to be a good candidate for my research work since she had already been engaged in meditation experiences and yoga practices. She had little difficulty adjusting to the imagery process. She was able to create vivid and meaningful images. More importantly, she had the desire and courage to face her life issues and bring them to resolution.

My work with Connie covered a period of about one and one-half years. Her intense depth work included nearly 50 weekly imagery/counseling sessions, of which 39 selected sessions are presented below. Such sessions took approximately one to two hours each with about 45 minutes being devoted to imagery work. Data for this case study came from tape recorded imagery and counseling sessions. Moreover, some of the interpretative material was revised based on Connie's subsequent review of the imagery transcripts and the initial draft of her case study. The presentation of her case study data and interpretative discussions given below describe her very intense therapeutic journey.

PART 1
Cutting Dependent Relationships

This session presents a clear image of what needs to occur in Connie's life. She has spent her life as a very dependent person. Now it is time for letting go of all addictions including dependent relationships. One attachment that needs to be cut away is her marriage and relationship with her husband, Ted.

This session begins with imagery of an old lady, a wise woman who seems to be helping Connie's divorce lawyer prosecute her case. With regards to her lawyer she keeps seeing his face and feels more trusting because he seems to be getting help or guidance from *another plane or something. I just keep feeling that or hearing this word "trust" and to let go, let go of Ted and to decide what to do. Now Ted is in front of me. I don't feel any pain in my gut, and he is with that woman.* This is the woman Ted has been seeing and she feels she is being shown this image to prepare her for seeing them together. It is as though her unconscious is attempting to provide her with a solid basis in terms that fit her own belief system for trusting her lawyer and letting go of her relationship with her husband.

Moreover, it is time for Connie to release all her dependent relationships. She is shown an orange robe *like that worn by Buddhist Monks* which she quickly recognizes as representing *giving up* of all worldly possessions. In her case it seems to represent giving up all of her dependent relationships. The next person presented to her is her mother. *My mom is here. (Begins to cry) I've really been holding onto her. But I have to let her go, too. I don't think I've ever felt so much love from her. It has been good for what I've been going through, but now it's time to let go. I have to let go for her sake too, so she can move on and be ok.*

Additional relationships are presented to her. She is given a pair of scissors as symbolic of the need to cut the dependent ties between herself and others. *I feel like I'm letting go of so many people in my life and one more person comes up to let go of. I feel so good with her now. She even hugs me on her own. She has never done that. The scissors are there again. I think I'm afraid with her that if I use the scissors that I'll have to let go like I did with Ted. But that's not true, because I'll still have her. Every time I do this the image comes to me, my angel shows me my inner light and I feel all this energy coming back to me. My kids are here too. When I let go of their love, then there is more like little fragments left. I've been sort of afraid that if I let go, that will be the last contact and there's a part of me that has to panic and hang on. They are so sweet. I wish you could see them. My grandmother is here. It's like all the generations of women are together.*

Letting go is a struggle for Connie. Not having had mutual, trusting relationships in the past, it is difficult for her to conceptualize having friends without a needy, dependent attachment being involved. It is another area of trust that she faces in this imagery session as she expresses her fear and panic over the possibility of losing contact with those on whom she has come to depend. However, she seems to realize that breaking dependent attachments does not mean losing contact with others.

As would be expected, Connie had developed friendships that are unhealthy and parasitic. She also needs to change the dependence she has developed with some of her healthier friends. Moreover, she must make a complete break with other relationships that have dragged her down and kept her from growing toward health and self-sufficiency. She recalls a dream in which a fire seems to be burning off unwanted attachments. Fire can be harmful and consuming, but within the imagery process it can be a transforming agent for growth. Interestingly, she was able to rise up out of the fire despite those who are trying to hold her back. *In the dream there was immense heat that was coming through the walls of this place. This fire and there were people all over, and they were really afraid of the heat. They couldn't get away. But I could fly and people were pulling at my feet and trying to pull me down, but they couldn't touch me. That's what this freedom feels like. They're still trying to pull me down and drain the energy out of me, but I'm free of that. They can't touch the energy, my energy, and I guess the feeling of comfort I've been having of being held is just within myself, that being free of attachments. It is being okay with being alone and being with God. I feel like I'm back in the womb. And now there's this light that's radiating within me.*

This imagery seems to represent a transformation from the negativity of her life to a more positive and transcendent view of herself and the world. The idea that she feels like she is back in the womb is a symbolic reference to a rebirth of her life and personality. It seems clear that the theme of this imagery is informing her of what she needs to do to grow and develop toward a more independent and self-sufficient person. She must break her dependent relationships with friends and family. Moreover, she must cut the ties with those unhealthy relationships of her past, those who try to drag her down and drain her energy, those who were part of her addictive past.

PART 2
Expressing Childhood Loneliness and Hurt

The previous session suggested that Connie needs to cut the ties that bind her to dependent relationships. This session appears to start the process of dealing with some of the factors that created her dependent and addictive life.

This imagery session emphasizes the complexities of Connie's dysfunctional family. Even in her childhood she assumed responsibility for her parent's emotional welfare. She says, *yes, I'm afraid I'll hurt them if I show them the pain. I can tell them how much I was hurting, but I can't show them at this time. I'm afraid to because I'm afraid my mom will get mad at me. I don't think she's angry with me, she gets angry because she can't cope with my pain. I don't think she could when I was little either. If she couldn't cope with it, I guess I would feel responsible for hurting her.* Connie finally admits to her suppressed anger over having to be responsible for her mother's emotional states. While an intense emotional outpouring at a self-development workshop had helped to resolve her anger, her fear of hurting her mother keeps her unable to express her anger. Hence, we see the depth and intensity of this childhood pattern continuing into adulthood.

I attempted to have Connie look at her mother more realistically, in terms of a parent's responsibilities regarding the emotional development of a child. I was hoping to help her face the anger and resentments she had long suppressed for fear of harming her mother and losing her love. However, she confides that, *when I feel, or I lose it, or I cry, then she gets angry and then I feel guilty because she's hurting and because I'm afraid something will happen to her if I tell her what's wrong with me. I am afraid she couldn't make it. It doesn't matter what happens to me though. I am afraid she couldn't make it. I just don't want her to hurt. It's okay if I do.*

Then during an imagery sequence, Connie re-experiences a time in her childhood when she tried to tell her mother how badly she was feeling. She says, *I can just see my mom hanging clothes on the line. I was out there with her. I can see my father, he was young. I wanted to tell my mom something. She was depressed. She didn't want me to bother her, and I can feel it.* Next, she recalls another experience. *Yes, and now I'm seeing when I was sick and she took care of me. Those were the most special times when I could feel her love. Yes, when I was sick was the only time when she really showed me any affection, and I was sick a lot. It was okay to be sick but it wasn't okay to have something emotionally wrong.*

It seems clear that Connie's feelings of responsibility for her mother's emotional states created the conditions for suppressing her own feelings of pain, combined with feelings of guilt when her mother responded with anger. Because of her mother's inability to deal with emotional pain, Connie felt alone and isolated with no one she could turn to for help. She discovered that the only time she could feel her mother's love and affection was when she was ill. This seems to have reinforced her feelings of dependence. This is to say that when she became ill and dependent her mother would take care of her, and she could feel her mother's love and affection. I might note that my work with cancer patients and chronically ill persons revealed a tendency toward some of the patients believing that the only way they could feel loved and nurtured was when they are ill.

When asked about her father and whether she might have been able to express her pain to him, Connie responded, *he was very loving when I did see him. He worked a couple of jobs. My mom was angry if I would get too close to my father. So, I stayed away from him to make my mom happy. I think she was jealous* of her relationship with her father. Moreover, she indicated that she was jealous of her mother's relationship with her brother. *It seemed like she wouldn't get mad at him like she would get mad at me.* Hence, her mother's affection toward her brother was likely another difficulty in her relationship with her mother.

Connie expresses her complicated relationship with her father which continues into the present. *I can see my father and I can feel his love, and it's very comforting and still is. But, I'm still cautious of the love of my father around my mom because I am afraid she'll get mad about that, too. Why am I so afraid of my mom, I don't know? What I'm afraid will happen is that she won't love me if.* It was suggested that she was never really able to earn her mother's love unless she was ill. She responds, *and I've been sick a lot until the last couple of years.* However, she seems to have come to the point at which she wants to be well and become more independent. *Yes, just that I wanted to take care of myself.*

I offered a summation of Connie's perception of her relationship with her mother, brother and father based on her need for love from each one of them. "So you wanted the love of your mother, and you wanted the love of your brother, but you had to get sick to get the love of your mother. And you had the love of your father but you couldn't receive it, because to do so would make your mother jealous and upset with you."

I attempted to have Connie look at her mother more realistically in order to help her face the anger and resentments she has long suppressed for fear of harming her mother and losing her love. I tried to help her see that she was not responsible for her mother's emotional responses and well-being. During this sequence I am fairly directive. It seemed to me that she needed to start viewing her mother as an adult, one who can take care of herself and might actually be able to respond to her pain. It appeared that Connie's mother was changing and trying to be the mother that she was unable to be when she was a child. Connie seemed to be changing her perception of her mother and exploring a different kind of relationship with her. She says, *she just started hugging me. Since I've been teaching yoga, she would come into my yoga class and at first it was like she would hug me and push me away at the same time. Now she started to hold on for a little bit longer. So, there's this beauty inside of her that I don't want to make her sound like an awful person because she is not. She's got a lot. She wants to give to people and the only way she knows how to give is materially. She gives clothes. She gives furniture, money.*

On the other hand, it was felt that Connie was at this time in her life projecting onto her mother the image of the ideal mother that she had never had, in an attempt to develop a new relationship. The concern was that she may be attempting to develop a new relationship with her mother that would reinforce her dependent needs. In any case, Connie and her mother were evidently coming together to relive and heal their relationship. Healing would require breaking with old patterns of protecting her mother from an awareness of her suffering.

It is suggested that she does not need to defend her mother or make excuses for her. Connie started to cry, *it's so painful*. I continue, "you cannot be a mother to your mother. You tried to do that as a child, a little girl. You just couldn't do it and you are still trying to look after her." Connie responds, *what would happen if I didn't? I guess I always thought it would be my fault if something happened to her. Rationally, I know she can* (take care of herself). *But I guess I never thought rationally about it. I just had this thing in the back of my head that gnawed at me that she wouldn't be able to make it if I really exposed my pain to her. I guess I want to tell her how bad I hurt.*

Then, I presented a viewpoint that Connie seems not to have considered consciously, which is that she had been betrayed by her mother. It was suggested that, "you were somehow tricked into believing that you were always the one at fault, you were the one to blame." Further, it was pointed out that her mother's jealousy had denied her access to her father's love. She reacted by saying, *I feel really depressed when you say that. It's like I don't want to believe it.* I continued by reminding her that "those were really terrible years, and I do not understand why you're not angry about this."

Connie responded by saying, *I don't know, maybe I am but I'm just not aware of it.* Then she confided that, *I felt the anger when I was at this workshop. We had intensive. I felt anger when I wanted to tell my mom what happened with the neighbor boy and I felt like I couldn't. I had to protect my mom. I was so angry at her because I couldn't tell her and I had to be alone and I started screaming and just screaming and I lay on my side and cried. I never cried when I was little. I never let it out. Now when I think about it I don't feel angry. I cry sometimes but I don't feel what I did that day at the intensive. I don't know whether that was the release.* However, it was pointed out that she continues to have difficulty telling her mother how badly she feels. *Yes, because I would feel guilty if she hurt, and I don't know how to stop that except to tell myself that I'm not to blame and it's not my fault.* Moreover, she expressed a sense of growth by saying that, *first thing I thought of is that I have to take a pill before I tell her. I would have to take something before I could tell her how bad I was feeling so that I would have the nerve to tell her, and I wouldn't care about how she hurt that would take the guilt away. I'm not going to do that, but that was my first thought.* This statement may explain some of the reasons why Connie resorted to drugs and alcohol. It was to mask her pain, but also to numb her feelings such that she could express her pain. She has developed some insight into her addictive behavior and has developed the strength to stop this kind of behavior. Connie recalled a few episodes during her relationship with her husband that reinforced her insights and need to change her behavior. She confided, *When I was drinking and I would have a bad night, a bad drunk, a few times my husband called my parents over. I cried and screamed then but I guess it didn't matter because I was like a blubbering idiot. It wasn't really dealing with anything. The next day I felt bad because I had made a scene. That was the only time I ever did anything like that in front of my parents.*

Next it was suggested to Connie that she locate the child within herself who tried to protect her mother from her own suffering and who had to absorb the loneliness and hurt of her childhood. *I can see her again*, she said. *She is, she's on my lap. I forgot to hold her this past week because I've been so miserable. I did for a couple of days but I stopped doing that. But I was holding her just like I am holding her now. I felt so good to just. It was like really, right now, it's peaceful to hold her. It like takes the shaking away inside.*

It is noted that such feelings of inner shaking and pain may be coming from this child. Connie indicates that, *I never realized that before. I used to wonder why I was so nervous. I pretended like she wasn't there and pretended like the pain wasn't there and the anger wasn't there. I've been afraid to even think negative thoughts about mom.* Accessing these inner children are important in the healing process in order to objectify her emotions and separate such child elements from the adult mind.

Repressed material from childhood experiences often takes the form of inner children. The suggestion to seek the children within oneself is often helpful since it allows one to access the childhood material and re-experience the related pain. Since the child mind cannot comprehend a given traumatic experience, it is vital to bring both the experience and related emotional suffering into consciousness where they can then be processed and resolved by the adult mind. The adult mind offers a much larger framework and cognitive development by which the repressed material can be comprehended. When Connie visualizes holding and nurturing the inner-child, her damaged self, she achieves a sense of peace that helps her accept her feelings and overcome denial. Denial is one of the primary defense mechanisms of the dependent, addictive personality. (1) Becoming a loving mother to her own damaged inner-child helped to remove the necessity to seek such affection from her own physical mother.

Differentiating the child-self from the adult-self makes it possible to shift the discussion toward examining the beliefs and thought patterns surrounding her relationship with her mother and other family members. Then Connie would be able to review childhood response patterns more objectively. The direction that seemed to emerge in the imagery work was to resolve internally the issues surrounding her child/parent relationship so as to form the emotional base and cognitive development to create a healthier relationship with her parents. Her present family situation seemed ripe for this to occur.

Next, Connie feels that an angel is *taking me to my brother now. He's grown up now. (Crying) I want him to hold me again. Am I never going to let go of that? I want him to take the pain away. Well, I can feel him hold me. I think he feels acceptance.* Connie is asked what she might want to tell her brother. She responds that she wants to *tell him how bad it hurts. It's like he wanted to protect me before when I was hurt.* This was in reference to a time when her brother brought her to his home in an attempt to help her deal with her alcohol and drug addiction. However, his wife became angry over her being there. Connie felt she acted toward her like her mother did when she was a child. Hence, this did not end well for her. In any case it was an instance when her brother, as an adult, tried to help her.

The first session indicated that Connie needed to sever all of her dependency ties, especially with her parents. She was given a pair of scissors to cut these ties. This session was symbolic rather than actual. The second session seems to be taking Connie into the process of resolving her dependent issues with her mother. This requires that she acknowledge and accept her childhood loneliness and pain in the form of the inner-child. Part of the healing process includes loving her inner child in ways that she needed to have been loved during her own childhood. (2)

    The last part of this imagery session indicates that Connie also needs to face her relationship with her brother. Her dependence on him is represented by her needing him to hold her and take the hurt away. Since he unwittingly participated in creating the suffering of her childhood, she is looking to him to take this pain away.

PART 3
Facing Ugliness, Developing a New Concept of Men, and Healing her Relationship with her Mother

Session three is an extension of the previous imagery sessions with the theme of healing Connie's relationship with her mother. Further, this session seems to start the process of facing the "ugly" dark side of herself that has had a negative impact on her sense of self-esteem and worth. As the session begins, she speaks of an Angel who acts as her guide.

We're by a lake, just feels so good to be there with him. (The Angel) It is very serene. He wants me to feel this right now because I haven't been feeling it. We're going to rest for a while. He wants me to know that he is taking care of me. Yes, and even though I feel really bad and really alone, I still have him. I don't know why he loves me though. But it's okay.

One of the issues of this session is being loved and loving oneself. It is suggested that if Connie were able to see herself as her angel views her, she might have ample reasons for loving herself. She responded to this by saying, *when you say that, I felt a lot of fear. It's a panic fear that comes up for me a lot that has in the past. My heart is beating real fast.* I say, "Well, I'm wondering what's behind this panic, this fear."

It is interesting that her panic/fear seems to be related to the suggestion that she is loved and has reason to love herself. The reason for this will become apparent as the session progresses. In preparation for the work to be accomplished in this session her angel wants her to feel loved, calm and relaxed. Soon she is taken to her apartment where she meets with what appears to be an Animus figure. (3) *I'm just back in my apartment and alone and he's (Angel) putting my hand in someone else's, but I don't know who it is. It's a, I don't know. I've never seen him before. It's a man and I just don't know who it is. He's dark but I have never seen him before. He's got dark hair and sort of dark skinned and he's very warm, kind, like a friend.*

Actually, Connie describes an image of a man who generally fits her therapist. This may indicate an element of transference with significant therapeutic consequences. To Connie, I may have been one of the few men in her life who actually cares about her and treats her kindly, thus presenting an image that is a drastic change from her previous perception of men. Perhaps the intent is for this image to become internalized and integrated as a new concept of men and possibly her animus image. That she does not recognize the man in her imagery may indicate that she is not ready to entertain the idea that the male image might be related to her perception of her therapist. More importantly is that she has experienced a more positive male image that may become her image of men in the future. That is, it will be functioning at unconscious levels to draw her away from abusive men and toward men who might offer her a much healthier relationship.

Connie is also shown an image of a more positive man in her life, her father. *Now, I can see my father's face. It's when he was younger. His face has been coming up a lot lately. He was sort of always in the background, not ever intrusive just there. And I feel a lot of warmth and love from him, too. And it flashes back and forth from my father's face and that man who's in my apartment. The man I have never met. Maybe it's some aspect of my father that I have never known before.* It appears that the similarity between the image of the man in her apartment and her father is that both love her and project a lot of warmth toward her. Her father has the potential of being part of her animus, a positive image and perception by which to identify more positive men in the world. However, there appears to be something that she needs to resolve with him.

Connie says, *I know I don't want my father to be angry with me because I left my husband. I know he's upset about it, and I want him to understand that, that I couldn't live like that anymore. Cause, he was fond of my husband. He saw the good side of my husband, all the time. And now I am seeing my husband's face.* It is suggested that her father and husband are significant men in her life, who have come together to form her concept of men and her ambivalence toward men. Perhaps it is time to let go of her negative concept of men to make possible a more positive concept of men. She indicates that, *it feels really weird letting go, the male relationship. It feels good too. It feels like a freedom that's not complete yet.* With regards to a different concept and experience with men, she refers to the man in her apartment as one who *has a lot of warmth and love. There's no negativity there. I think the angel is saying it's in the future.* I suggest that, "so you leave your husband and you leave your father behind and the neighbor boy, and then you have the conditions by which this kind of man can come into your life." *Yes, there's a lot of warmth and love. There's no negativity there, and I think the angel is saying it's in the future.*

Connie's angel then takes her to the light. *The angel is taking me to the light again, to this light and we are kneeling together to get the light. This light is God, but it is dim.* Apparently, God is perceived in the same context as the warm, loving, beautiful and healing image of the "male" angel. However, God's light is dim which suggests that her own feelings of dark ugliness are dimming the light. On the other hand, it appears that her angel is taking her to the light and its love and warmth as preparation for facing this darkness within herself. While with her angel and the light she asked, *why do I feel obsessed with taking aspirin, with taking pills, especially when I don't feel good?* Suddenly, she sees an ugly monster in front of her. She is told not to be frightened and to love it.

Typically, in such situations there is often an attempt to persuade one to care for and feel sorry for such monsters and ugliness. It is important to counter this kind of suggestion as these types of monsters are not part of the self. However, they have become part of the self because of abusive experiences that generate guilt and severe loss of self-esteem. In Connie's case she is about to face the ugly side of herself as represented by the monster. Because of abuse and mental neglect, she incorporated the monster within her unconscious. While denying it consciously, she created an unconscious projection of herself as one who is ugly, worthless, unwanted or unlovable. It took on an autonomous life in the dark side of her psyche and became threatened by any feelings that she might develop about being worthy of love. Connie says that the monster is the part that *no one else, no one else could stand it and love it.* It is suggested that, "so you took it in and then it causes you trouble." She responds, *yes, it's like I pretend that it's not there, this ugliness. It has something to do with my pelvic area because I can feel it there.* She continues that it is *there just because of what I did was wrong and it was ugly. I am ugly because no one would want me.*

Interestingly, Connie identifies with the monster because it is too ugly for anyone to love. Since she feels she is too ugly to love, she identifies with the ugly monster. Since it resides in her genital area it becomes clear that it developed when she, as a young girl, blamed herself for engaging in sexual activity with the neighbor boy. Further, we see her absorbing all of the "ugliness" of the experience and projecting it out into the world as a feeling that no one could love her, not even her mother. In this session we can observe the process by which the inner monster is faced and expelled. This is what I sometimes refer to as the process of facing one's own demons. Connie had to face the experience by which she came to feel herself ugly and totally unlovable, even by her parents. She has to resolve the experience by realizing that as a child she was not responsible for what had happened to her.

Part of the process is to bring the innocent child forward into consciousness. Connie has difficulty loving the child because *it's like she was ruined. She's not that (innocent) anymore. It's that part that was taken away from her, the innocence and beauty. I love her but I feel like I could never get her back again.* It is suggested that this is true because the monster is there. Connie responds, *right the monster is like taking over. It overpowers that little girl. I think that is why I'm sick right now too, it just feels like it's so, it's taken over.* It is suggested that, "it's time now. You don't have to have this. You don't have to care of it, want it, love it. It's time now to see it for what it is. The little girl doesn't have to be overpowered anymore. You don't want it anymore. See, there comes a time when it's time to say, 'I don't want what this monster represents.'"

Next Connie says, *it's just that I've believed that I couldn't. But the angel just handed her to me. I'm feeling a lot of love again. Whenever I get the child back, I do.* With regards to her feelings of panic she indicates that, *the feelings have always made me hyperventilate too, and I have never understood why. It would just happen, sometimes without any reason.* She began to realize that such feelings of panic often came when she was feeling more positive about herself and thinking of love, caring and all the beautiful things of life. Feelings of panic would emerge when someone would display feelings of love and care toward her, suggesting that she is worthy of such love and care. Connie suddenly became aware that during such times, *it was afraid I'd throw it out and I just did. Oh, it feels so good to get that done. I've been praying for years about that panic. Now I can see my mom again and she and I are hugging and it's today, it's the way she is today. I feel like I have broken through a big barrier with her. It (monster) was always in the way. I talked to her last weekend and she told me she thought I was always against her, and I think she realized that I wasn't against her, that I wanted to protect her. I feel like I've really resolved something with her as the angel takes me to her. There isn't that resistance in me to be around her anymore. It's just a good feeling.* We observe a breakthrough for Connie in this session. During her imagery the abused child is brought to her. She represents that part of herself that is innocent, pure, and beautiful. This is the opposite of what she has been projecting of herself for most of her life. She realized that she was so possessed by her negative identity that whenever she began to move in a direction of more loving and positive thoughts and relationships, she would begin to have panic attacks as the negative side of herself became deeply threatened. Being negative and ugly was what she believed herself to be. To lose her identity, however ugly, was like losing herself. Connie develops an insight into what has been creating her panic attacks over the years. Once Connie let go of this negative belief about herself, the monster, or perhaps a demonic presence, is led away by her angel. The act of accepting the innocent, beautiful child seems to represent a turning away from the negative side of life and laying claim to a more positive and loving perception of herself and others.

It becomes evident that with Connie's new perspective she is able to view her mother differently and more objectively. Interestingly, she had just had an actual telephone conversation with her mother in which they had been able to express their true feelings and come to an understanding. This reconciliation demonstrates a significant relationship between the internal imagery work and the flow of external life. We find that there remains a thread of healing her relationship with her mother that runs through sessions one through three.

PART 4
Giving up Her House and Centering Within Herself

Connie continues with the theme of letting go of people and things of the past. This imagery session contributes to breaking away from the negativity of her past by presenting the house of her marriage. It seems clear that she is to let go of this house and put it behind her such that she can move forward in her new life. She says, *it's like you're on one side of me and the angel is on the other side. I am going back to my house. It's so hard to go back there. I'm standing outside looking at the house and it's like a part of me. It has my energy in it. So, I am to take it (energy) and leave the house. (Crying)I feel like it's breathing with me. I think it's mourning, too. I see my dog there. I think it's everything that I was and I'm not that anymore, but I don't know who I am.*

Connie's visualization of being flanked on both sides by her angel and me indicates that she is going to need both internal and external support to help in dealing with what is to come. I represent an external orientation and her angel is an internal support. She assumes a position in the center, perhaps to symbolize the need to assume a position of transcendence between two opposites, internal and external help. Having moved to this position she is able to view these fields of action as resources for the resolution of her life issues.

As the session progresses, Connie realizes that she is going to have to face giving up her house, a part of her not easily set aside. At the present time her identity is centered on people and things outside herself. She even personifies objects of the world and gives them emotion as if her perceptual system is geared to attach itself emotionally. Perhaps she has been able to survive her agonies by projecting her emotions into objects, people and animals.

Next, Connie focuses on her concerns about going back to school. She says, *now the worries come back about school. It's like that's what I thought I was too. (A student) It's my identity, the only thing I have left.* It is suggested that this is something that is outside of herself and she is asked about those things within herself. She responds, *I am beginning to see it again. (The inner light) It gets brighter and as it gets brighter it pulls the energy out of the house and back into me.* Then she is encouraged to move to the center of the light that is doing that such that she feels as though she is doing it herself. She indicates *it feels good to do that. It's like it draws my power back into me. It centers me. I feel more calm and the pain is gone.* It is again suggested that she is addressing the light as if it were something apart from herself, rather then also being who she is. It is noted that while her schoolwork and being a student is very important, they need to be seen for what they are, things that she does. Also, being a student is the means to something else, like a career, independence and self-sufficiency. Connie replies, *yes, it's like I'm this energy. I guess I want to say love. It's formless. I think I wanted it to be something tangible, like the house, the dog and school, but it won't be that.* However, *my house was a place of comfort. It's a friend. It's like I feel like I'm leaving a friend.* It is difficult to demonstrate to Connie that her house is what she made it to be. It was comfortable because she made it that way for herself and her family. While it seems like a friend, it is a friend because she made it a friend, which is to say she projected friend upon it. Her projections are the energy that she has invested in such objects. She responds, *yes, and I have that part of myself there to protect it and it doesn't need that. I did the same thing with my car, this last car I had. I was afraid that it would miss me. And it was real hard to let go of that car, too. It was probably hard for it, the way I was holding on to it. And I wanted someone to take care of it. They're not. I've got to say goodbye to the house and I feel myself saying goodbye to it.*

Then Connie finds herself back at her apartment. I ask her, "is this your apartment or an apartment with you in it?" She says, t*here's light in it. Maybe that light is me. It's brilliant and it's flashing. It's like my mind always wants to hold onto my body. I'd say, "but it is supposed to look like this (the light)." The light is supposed to look like my body. The light doesn't look like that.* The idea being examined is the possibility that her house and body are containers of the light and the manifestation of the light, but not the light itself. She acknowledges, *yes, it is just like a container to hold the light while it's there. A lot of containers, yes, I have. It's hard to let go of them just like it is the house. It does feel good to sort of melt inside the light and just. It's all I have, isn't it. It's all that I am.*

In session four there is an attempt to lead Connie toward a more internal focus. Likewise, there seems to be an attempt on the part of her unconscious to help her shift to a more internal orientation to the self. Being a dependent personality, she has become possessive of all her attachments including unhealthy relationships. In this regard, what she owns is also what owns her. By letting go of her attachments in the external world she can realize greater freedom for the Self. The center of herself, perhaps the Self, is represented by a beautiful light. Connie's last task of this session seems to be to identify with the light as a manifestation of her inner self. Finally, she continues to have some difficulty perceiving herself as precious and beautiful.

PART 5
Further "Letting Go" and Centering the Self

This session took place at the time when Connie was concerned that her children, especially her daughter Sherry, who had chosen to stay with Ted, her husband, who she fears will abuse her. However, Sherry's wish to take care of her father helped to soften the hurt, since the decision was not merely a rejection of Connie.

Her first encounter is with her husband. She says, *it's like fading in and out. I thought I was resisting him (Ted), but I think he's resisting me. I feel the angel's presence right away, but Ted keeps fading in and out. I think the fading in and out is because he's not real strong in my life right now. That feels good. I feel real stable right now, and that there are just glimpses of him instead of him all the time, and that feels good. It feels like I've moved through. It seems like he doesn't have the control over me, because I'm more stable now. But I haven't thought that I was stable until right now when I see him fading in and out. It's like he doesn't have the power to stay here real strong now.*

Connie's relationship with her husband had been difficult and abusive. She had resorted to drugs and alcohol to minimize the pain, but which only made things worse. It made her appear as the one who was creating all the problems. Hence, she decided to leave her husband because she felt it was the only way to start the process of healing her life. However, leaving was also very painful because she had to leave her home and children. Especially painful was leaving her youngest child, Sherry. The imagery below suggests that as she begins to heal her life and become more stable, her relationship with her husband and his influence on her life begins to fade away.

Next, Connie encounters her daughters. She says, *I see Terry and Sherry, my daughters. Terry is sort of fading in and out too, but Sherry is not. (*Terry is the oldest child and is likely on her own*) Sherry is staying there with him, (husband). I guess I am wondering if it seems like I should still hang onto Sherry because I'm still afraid of what will happen to her if I let her go, because she is younger. But it doesn't feel painful right now. It feels more of a protection thing. More like sending her love and being there for her.* Connie seems to be going through the process of letting go of her youngest daughter, except for loving her and being there for her when she needs contact or help.

Connie is then taken to her grandmother. She seems to resist going to see her grandmother. Seeing her grandmother seems to remind her of some of the most painful times of her life that she experienced in her childhood. Apparently, her grandmother tried to help her but had not the capacity to know what to do for her. Further, her grandmother, having died a number of years ago has been coming to her in her meditation, suggesting something unresolved in her relationship with her grandmother.

Connie reveals that during meditation her grandmother keeps coming to her, and *I don't know how to handle her. It's like, I guess I'm afraid of her being earthbound, and I want to let go of her. I just don't want her around.* She continues, *I'm asking her what she wants and now she is taking me somewhere. Okay, I'm back in my teenage years and*

Grandma lives with us. I was like in such a fog all the time and that's what it feels like right now. It's like I couldn't think clearly and grandma used to ask me to do stuff and she would pay me for it, but I wouldn't move. I was just lethargic. I just didn't want to do anything. I was so depressed and that's the way I felt before she came just now. I remember I didn't know what was happening to me. And I think grandma was trying to help me in her own way and I didn't know that. I always liked her, though. She was pretty neat. I don't know. I guess what keeps coming to me is that she wants me to do something with my life.

It was suggested that perhaps grandma needs some reassurance from Connie that she does intend to do something with her life and that she is in the process of doing that right now. Connie tells her grandma that, *I'm going to be all right now, that it's finally over with, and I'm not going to wait for life to do something for me. I'm going to do it. I am asking her why she always comes around when I'm with my mom and my aunt and my cousins in the yoga class. She says she wants to be with us. She wants to do for us what she never did when she was alive.*

It is suggested that Connie tell her grandma that she can take care of herself and that there is a better place for her, but that she can come back and check on her when she wants to. *She's like a child. The angel is giving me scissors again to cut grandma loose, the cord that holds us together. Grandma has gone to the light. It's strange how I feel so centered after I cut someone loose.*

It is apparent that Connie has resisted confronting her relationship with her grandmother because her grandmother represents a very difficult time in her childhood and adolescence. During that time, she was deeply depressed and could barely function. To be sure this was a very painful time in her life and she did not want to revisit that time. However, it was necessary to face this time of her life and let her grandmother go in order to move on with her life and continue with her efforts to improve her life and become a fully independent and self-sufficient person.

Then a beautiful bright light appears in front of Connie. She describes it as *supreme love*, and it appears to be getting brighter indicating that she is becoming more accepting of it as part of herself. The sensation of *melting* into this light suggests that she is becoming the light. This is to say that she is becoming aware of her potential for loving others in an unconditional rather than a possessive way. Connie refers to the light, *now there is that light that's in front of me again. At first, I thought it was the angel because it is so bright. But it is not, because it is in front of me and it's not at my side. It's very powerful. It's hard to talk when I'm feeling the light.* I comment that she is feeling what it's like to be herself. She responds, *when you said that it got even brighter. I was thinking that I should tell you what it is like. If I can put it into words, it's so much easier for me to write than to talk about what the light is. It's not still. It flashes but it's in different degrees. You know how ice cream melts in your mouth? I feel like I'm melting into the light. It's supreme love. It would be nice to love others like this. I wish that I could give them this love that I feel within. But it is hard to be in this state and be with others at the same time. It's like, it's not like what I ever felt love was. It's just impossible to put into words.* Connie continues, *it's like what I went into last Friday when I was meditating. There are no boundaries. I've been wanting so much to be held all the time, especially when I'm hurting, and it like holds me and it holds me like no human could.*

My response to Connie's experience of being held by the light is that having had such an experience, "how better you can hold others when you do not need to be held yourself. How better you can be held when needing to be held is not a deprivation, but an expression of the love of that light within."

Connie's imagery has been observed in a number of cases when Imagery Therapy has been used. It seems to be a process by which one is led into the light and experiences its healing quality, which is felt as intense unconditional love. It is assumed that this inner light is a projection of the Supra Consciousness.

Next, Connie's imagery switches to an ocean scene reminiscent of the beach where Connie had walked with her father. She finally feels free to be close to him without fear of making her mother angry. Moreover, this session continues to emphasize letting go of people and experiences of the past. Indeed, it appears that both mother and father have been newly integrated into a loving family. Her ability to love and to be loved appears to be related to her capacity to be centered within that loving core of herself. It appears also that by accepting this potential of herself she is beginning to change her perception of herself as worthless, ugly and unlovable.

PART 6
Facing a Love-Hate Relationship with Husband and Saying Goodbye to Parents

During this imagery session Connie examines her abusive relationship with her husband. To fully resolve this relationship, it appears that she needs to face the love/hate bind that has her wanting to cling to him while at the same time feeling intense anger and bitterness toward him. To this end, she begins to admit her feelings of anger and rage that she has been trying to suppress, since leaving her marriage. Connie says, *I can see Ted now, my husband. (Crying) I guess the first thing that I wanted to ask him was why he treated me like that. But the question turned into, "why did you let him treat you like that?" I think it was a denial over the way he was treating me. And the denial was the hope that it was going to change and never, never just facing up to the fact that he wasn't ever going to change. And that's the basis of a lot of my anger. It's funny how I can still care about him and hate him at the same time.*

It might be noted that Connie's abusive relationship with her husband follows a common pattern. First, her deeper feelings of ugliness and inferiority contributes to her belief that she deserves to be treated badly. Another factor common in espousal abuse cases was her inability to face the fact that her marriage was not going to change. Like many women in abusive situations she believed that if she could find the key to pleasing her husband, she would be able to receive the love and care that she longed for. Often when such women threaten to leave the relationship the abuser will promise to change and express their undying love. This feeds into the hopefulness and dependent needs of the abused person. Connie's hopefulness, which was continually being frustrated, became the source of much of her anger which she also denied throughout her marriage. Her frustrated hopes, combined with constant abuse, most likely created her ambivalent feelings of love and hate.

Realizing that her husband was not going to change, Connie had to change herself. She had to give up her hope and a sense of responsibility for pleasing him. As indicated above, she also had to come to the awareness that she had contributed to the abuse by letting her husband abuse her. However, up until now, she had not developed this awareness and she had not the strength and capacity to stop the abuse herself. Having achieved this level of growth makes it possible to let go of her past relationship with her husband.

Finally, after Connie acknowledges her feelings of bitterness toward her ex-husband that have been festering for many years, she seems open to letting go of such feelings. She shares some of her most recent healing experiences. *I've had these images lately; the last few days and they are coming back to me again. It happens right after feeling intense anger toward him. I see a flower in my heart and there's this orange-golden sun that's almost like a sunrise. I can see it peeking, coming up over the earth and then just radiating this intense heat. I think this flower is like me blossoming. It would be love blossoming. I think I am having a relationship with myself that I have never had before, and to have that is to let go of all relationships. But it's sort of scary. Whenever I would reach within before, it was just empty and now it's the flowers are there and the sun.*

It comes time for Connie to say goodbye to her mother and father as they are moving south for retirement. *I can see my father's face. I think the angel wants me to see them, to start allowing them into my consciousness so that I can separate myself from them. That fearful question is, "what will happen to me when they leave?" I don't know. I just don't understand yet. That pity poor me, why does it have to be everyone at once, why couldn't it be a couple this year and a couple next year? But I know there's a part of me that knows it's happening. And now mom and dad are there together. They're saying goodbye and they are walking away. As they walk away, I can feel the energy coming into me again. I've been hanging onto them and it takes a lot of energy to do that.*

The time approaches when she must say goodbye to her parents who are moving south for retirement. Rather than develop her usual feelings of abandonment I suggest that she integrate her parents within herself such that she can carry them with her wherever she goes.

PART 7
Dealing with Anger

This session begins with the suggestion to seek the "angry one" in Connie's unconscious, since we had already discussed the possible dissociative aspects of her anger and rage. She responds, *I see my angel. He's pulling me by the arm. I keep going back to myself when I was younger. I can see me, and it's mostly, there's different times in my life but mostly it's when I was drinking. I see this woman who is afraid of her anger and who is drinking. I'm starting to feel the anger, too. I keep seeing this woman who is like a zombie.*

It seems that the first time she recalls feeling deep bouts of anger was over the abandonment and rejection of her brother. Connie says, *I can see myself when I was little. I had a nervous habit of cracking my bones and I never realized it. I was just obsessed to do it and I was only in the fourth or fifth grade and it was because I had so much anger in me. I just didn't know how to express it. It was right before I started drinking. Now I see myself in Islay's drinking Coke and aspirin in the fifth grade. It made me feel different and there is like this fire inside.*

It appears that Connie's anger had been repressed as it was something that she was unable to face until this time in her life. She continues, *I don't think I ever realized it was there until now. I mean, I never saw it before. My brother is there when he was a teenager. There's a lot of times when I just wanted to hurt him. I wanted to and I did. I would try to. I would go up behind him and attack or pull his hair, sort of the way I feel about Dr. Baker.* (Baker is one of her professors who reminds her of her brother. Apparently, he became a trigger that made her aware of her anger and rage). *I see this little girl with this fire on her just screaming and being devoured by the fire.*

To be sure this little girl was the one who absorbed all the anger when Connie was a child, since she was too young at the time to face it herself. She rejected it as it seemed something ugly and hideous. Repression became her defense against her anger and which enabled her to keep from being overwhelmed by it. However, she seems to have developed the growth and maturity to return to her childhood anger, the angry child, and seek the means by which to resolve it.

At first Connie vacillates between seeing the child as being ugly and feeling compassion for her and all the suffering she has experienced. Then she sees fire that seems to be absorbing all the anger. She says, *I can visualize myself holding the fire in my hands. I feel the energy in my hands as I do it, the healing energy. Now I'm hugging myself. (The child). It's like that angry part of myself and me have merged into a oneness. I don't have to push it away anymore. Now I can see Jesus on the cross again and he has that same fire within. I think that's even better than worrying about expressing it, or even how I can express it, is to accept that anger. And so I can visualize that other me and me hugging and merging together when I feel angry.*

It might be noted that a process is being set in motion in Connie's imagery by which she is able to resolve her anger. First, she differentiates the angry aspects of herself from her present self. Second, she comes to understand them by learning how they came to be so angry and how they came into being. The third task is to develop love, compassion and acceptance of them. Fourth, the resolved angry self becomes integrated within the greater system. This is actually a process of growth of "increasing differentiations with increasing integrations" a definition I owe to the late Ross L. Mooney and which is consistent with the definition of biological growth.

Connie is taken to another younger professor for whom she had developed an infatuation. She says, *it seems like the anger wants to take me to where he is now. I'm just looking in his face and I can see a lot of hurt in his face. I have and I feel a lot of compassion for him. I guess my heart feels like it's aching. Yes, it's like longing to be near him, and I couldn't be because he was married and I was too. There was something there between us. It was really unhealthy, I guess. It was an attachment. I used to be so drawn to his office to be near him. And a lot of my anger toward him. I mean I loved him but I felt a lot of anger too, because we fed each other. It was like he fed me and I fed him.*

It is suggested that it was time for Connie to break the attachment with her professor and release herself and him from a co-dependent, unhealthy relationship. She indicated that, *it seems to be okay with him now. I just get a little twinge of heartache when I think of him, but it's not anything like it was before. It was real intense. I am cutting away the cords between us, the strings that hold us together. He was like, the first time that I ever looked at my anger, he was a big part of that. And I guess that's why my angel is taking me back there again.* It seems that her projection of anger onto the professor may have been related to her dependent relationship with her brother.

Connie continues to face her anger regarding relationships with others. She begins to have flashbacks of people with whom she has been angry. Soon her angel takes her to her mother in law. She says, *it's like face to face. I've avoided her because I've been so angry with her, and I'm angry with myself, too. I have let her treat me terrible since I've known her. She used to take my baby away from me. She used to take her and I was afraid to go get her. So my parents would come over and go get the baby and give the baby to me. And, my husband would let her do it. It was like he wanted his mom to have the baby. And she would tell me that I didn't know how to take care of him (husband) right. My husband would give her money and we didn't have enough to live on. It's like I never told that woman how I felt. I always let her scream at me, belittle me, take advantage of me, until a few years ago and then I got away from her. I just wouldn't go over to her house anymore. I started college. But I've never dealt with the anger. I've just been avoiding it. I have a lot of forgiving to do in order to save my own self.*

Connie asked how she might be able to forgive, especially with regards to her mother in law and her husband. It is suggested that she will need to grow to the point that she is no longer vulnerable to being imposed upon by others. When she can stand up and say no and not let people treat her badly, she will be able to forgive, especially forgive herself. She says, *I don't like being around them, my kids yes, but not Ted and his mom. And what I'm feeling now is a blossoming in my heart again. It happened the last time when I let go of a lot of anger. So, I think the angel is showing what's on the other side.*

Hence, Connie had been projecting anger upon others and upon herself because of her rejection of her own anger. To her, the "angry one" was part of her ugliness which was unacceptable to her and which she did not want to face. During this imagery session she was strongly urged to confront and accept her anger and even love that part of herself. As she hugs herself, the fire of rage is transformed to a fire of love and healing as her angry self merges with her conscious self.

Connie's image of Jesus on the cross is an archetypal image of love and human sacrifice on behalf of others through suffering. This seems to represent her angry selves whose intense suffering on her behalf helped her survive her abusive past.

During this session Connie saw an image of a dragon which seems to represent the primitive aspects of her anger, which often occurs when one's basic needs are not being fulfilled. (4) Becoming friends with the dragon appears to mean becoming aware of and accepting one's basic needs which she had rejected as base and animalistic rather than human. Acceptance of this part of one's self can be a humbling experience, but it is also a critical part of being human and growing toward responsible adulthood.

PART 8
The Child of Love

This is a significant session for Connie because something new is emerging in her life, as represented in the newborn child that she sees in her imagery. It appears that her capacity to love herself and others unconditionally has just been born. This seems to be one of the primary factors in letting go of the dependent relationships of her past.

After the way becomes clearer, an infant appears. Connie reveals, *the infant is there. It's really sweet and soft. I ask it who it is and what it is. It's the birth of love in my heart. It's telling me that I have been through the pain, the labor pain, suffering what I've been through. Yes, that's what it's been. The painful part of birth is over and the beauty is there, the reward of the birth. And it's more powerful than my mind. The child is there, the infant to love me, when I start, when my mind starts to be the tyrant. It's to love others, too. Then I'm having images of the times that my mind does tyrannize. And the child is there to erase that part. It feels like my heart is blossoming, it's real warm. And, I'm holding that infant now. It's the good part of me that I haven't been able to contact in the past.*

In imagery work the appearance of a newly born child is not uncommon. This child is often referred to as the "Divine Child" (5) who is not damaged from past experiences. The child often brings a new perspective to life based on love and caring for others. Moreover, the child having been born from the Supra Consciousness, often grows rapidly compared to the birth of a physical child.

Next, Connie sees her husband's face and feels an acceptance of him that she has not felt before. As she sees her husband's face she says, *but the child is there too, the love within me, only it's different. It's a different kind of love than what I had for him before.* She begins to feel acceptance and compassion for him. She continues, *I feel really free. It's like I have been set loose, set free from a web. I feel like I can breathe again. And your face is there now. I'm feeling that love for you, too. It's just real genuine love. It's like the child is telling me that it's okay to love you like that, that's the right kind of love. I'm thinking that it's so good to have a friend like you. You're such a gentle soul. My angel is real bright. It's like, it's agreeing. Your angel is here too. It feels like the room is so bright.*

During the last session Connie expressed a desire to forgive those who had abused her. Perhaps the birth of this infant is symbolic of the growth needed to carry her toward this goal. In the presence of the child she feels acceptance and compassion for her husband, which proves to be a freeing experience. In her expression of love for me her therapist, she is able to feel a deep love for a man without confusing love with sexual involvement. It might be noted that Carl Rogers used the terminology of needing to have "unconditional positive regard" for the client, which he believed helped to develop a therapeutic atmosphere that was conducive to healing. I have also found this to be true in my therapeutic work with others. However, I have also discovered that when the client can develop such feelings of unconditional love and warmth toward the therapist, the conditions for healing are significantly increased. It is noted that these feelings need to be clearly differentiated from sexual feelings. In addition, the client referred to me as a *good friend*. This seems to help her differentiate me from someone with whom she might have a sexual relationship, to one who was there to listen and help her process the many negative experiences of her life. It has been my experience that the client will sometimes assign a role to the therapist, such as friend, because that is what the client needs at a particular time.

When one is having a spiritual experience there is often a feeling of there being no boundaries, such that there seems to be no break anywhere between oneself and others. Connie reports such a feeling. *My heart feels so open. It's like it's boundless. I guess I'm thinking that there's no separation and it doesn't end with just me, with my heart, that it's everyone's heart. And my mom and dad are here. Our hearts are still together, too, even though they are gone. And I'm seeing the child again, that infant. It's like giving birth. It was complete with my parents gone. The last of the labor. The child makes me feel real secure.* She continues, *I really feel okay with my parents gone now and this is the first I've felt like that.* It appears that Connie is in the process of letting go of her dependent attachment with her parents. Hence, this is another dependent relationship that she has faced and progressed toward increased independence and self-sufficiency. It is to be noted that severing the bond of dependent relationships does not mean the end of the relationships. It means a more open and loving relationship with others in which there is a great deal of personal freedom involved.

Connie reports that one of her friends is coming to her in her imagery. This friend is apparently an alcoholic and is going through a bad time. Connie indicates that, *she's a person who I love very much. I want to help her. It seems like she's going through a bad time. She does that when she's going through a bad time. I have been concerned with her drinking again. She's an alcoholic. I guess I've been holding on to her, the worry, the concern about her is like holding on. I'm seeing that her angel is there to help her.* This is the first reference to Connie being in a position of helping another person who is experiencing addiction problems. Up to this point she has been working on her own healing and development. Now she is showing deep concern toward another person and she seems to realize that she has been holding on to her friend in a co-dependent relationship. She appears to be catching on to a healing process whose condition requires extending her friend the freedom that comes from unconditional love, acceptance and compassion.

PART 9
Saying No to Negative Men

This imagery session seems to suggest that it is time for Connie to begin to relate to men again after a period of separation from them. During this time, she has worked on healing certain aspects of her life and growing in increased maturity regarding relationships with men. Her work has been important in understanding the negative aspects of dependent relationships and she may be ready to turn away from abusive men in her life. Hence, this would lead to gravitating toward more positive, non-abusive men. Interestingly, a serpent appears in her imagery as a healing symbol that draws such negativity from her.

It appears that Connie's relationships with abusive men may have begun with her encounter with the neighbor boy. She says, *what's coming to me is that I was thinking over the last couple of days about going to see my brother and his wife. I have not thought about that for a long time. What the angel wants me to see is that that is all connected to what has been happening with other men.* It is suggested that saying no to abusive men is also saying no to the neighbor boy. She responds, *yes. There is an apple there, too. It is symbolic of whether or not I take the apple means whether or not I decide to see these men. There is also this image that has been coming to me. It's there now. It is of myself being caught in a spider's web, and I'm struggling with it and pushing the web away and tearing parts of it off me.* It appears that in order for Connie to break away from the web that has entangled her in the past, she needs to say no to negative, abusive men. Of course, the apple is clearly a Christian symbol of the "fall" in which one yields to earthly desires and temptations. Connie is shown that when she takes the apple she becomes caught in "a spider web" which takes away her sense of freedom and she falls into a web of addiction and dependence. (6)

Connie continues, *each time I get a little bit, or get more loose, get more of the web away from me, it gets clearer. The picture becomes clearer. I am back in my apartment now. The angel is telling me to be with myself there and that it won't be that much longer. My brother's face is there again but he's smiling. What's coming is that he feels the freedom, too.* She is beginning to be able to see more clearly what has entangled her life. She is being shown that she is not entirely a victim, but rather a participant in painful relationships, since her clinging to others drains them of their life energy. As she develops a greater sense of personal freedom it releases others such that they can also feel a new sense of freedom in their lives. She says, *I'm beginning to see what my clinging has done to these other men in my life, too. What it has done to my husband, my brother, and whoever else I've done it to, my parents, how much it has drained them. The way that I'm being shown is that there is a woman in grad school who is very dependent and when I walk away from her, I feel drained. It's the way they have felt from being around me, although, it was at a more subtle level. And Dr. Baker is there. I have felt so angry with him and didn't realize why. So intense. It's been the lost anger that I've had for my brother. Yes, the anger about never being good enough for my brother and his criticizing me. I felt like that around Dr. Baker. What I did in his class wasn't good enough and he was very critical of me. I reacted to it so strongly that I realize that it can't be him. The image of my brother. I think the anger must fit the way I interact with men.*

It seems clear that Connie has been drawn to men who remind her of her brother. Not being able to resolve her dependent relationship with her brother, she has transferred her anger and dependence onto other men. In part, it may have been her unresolved dependent childhood relationship with her brother that has caused her to become entangled in a web of addiction and dependence regarding men. It might also be noted that her brother, now a grown man, is likely to have grown well beyond his adolescence. Such growth Connie may not have been able to see, since she has not been able to let go of her negative, dependent relationship with him.

Connie reveals one reason why she is unable to relate to men who are not abusive and who are positive in their attitudes and lives. She indicates that, *I think it's positive men that I get really angry with because I don't feel good enough. I feel less than. I push them away with my anger.* It is suggested that if she says "no" to negative men then she will become open to saying "yes" to more positive men. She responds that, *it's beginning to come together now.*

Next, Connie becomes aware of her anger toward her children and how that anger is getting in the way of her relationship with them. She realizes that it is her anger that is repelling them. She sees an image of her children and says, *my children are here now. I've been feeling really angry at them too, because they just don't want any connection, too busy. They're supposed to come over tonight. My anger has interfered with how I relate to them when we do talk. The anger is a set up I do, to let go. I become angry and then I don't call. It's a painful process, but it's how I've let go in the past. They faded out, it's nothing right now. I'm just having different images of faces that come by, and they fade out.*

Then Connie's angel brings a serpent to her. She says, *the angel is back and he has a serpent. He put the serpent on me. It's me again. It's the inner light that I saw before when the angel put the serpent on me. It got brighter. It seems like it drew more negativity out and as the negativity is drawn out then I become brighter. The serpent is to heal. It heals me. I feel like the energy is, I don't know how to explain it. I can really feel it in my right hand. It's like this bright light. It's in my right hand. I wish I could describe it. The energy might be, maybe it's me. It's that I'm not confined to this body and it's shifting around. But it doesn't go too far away and it goes in different shapes and still at the same time there's a glow in my right hand. And now the energy is coming back to the center. I am with the angel again and the angel is reassuring me that it has been there and it will always be there with me.*

An important insight in this imagery session is that Connie is shown that she is a participant in the development of negative relationships in her life. Realizing this, she can see that she also has control over what happens to her through the choices she makes; whether to choose the apple of desire and dependence and fall into the web of entanglement, or to make choices leading to more healthy mutual relationships.

Connie is also coming to understand that her projected anger repels others, though it often protected her against potentially negative people by repulsing them when she is feeling too vulnerable. However, her anger seems no longer needed as she seeks to make contact with others, especially those in her family, specifically her children, who are close to her.

We might at first consider the serpent to be a negative symbol since is it often associated with evil in the Judeo-Christian tradition. But in other cultures, the serpent is associated with wisdom and healing. (7) In Connie's case it seems to play a healing role by drawing out Connie's negativity. To be sure, the serpent may represent male sexuality which has caused a good deal of anger and negativity. Hence, the serpent, male sexuality, comes to withdraw the poison that it had once injected within her. This is the essence of its healing capacity for her.

We had a discussion following this session in which Connie shared with me more of her experience with the serpent. She felt embarrassed about telling me about it during the session. The serpent in her imagery entered her vagina and went up through her spinal column and through each Chakra to the top of her head. Then it came back down her spinal column and exited through her vagina. This is in keeping with the idea that what wounds us is that which also heals us. The snake, a phallic symbol, represents male masculinity. Connie had been wounded and damaged so many times in her life by male masculinity and sexuality. It seems fitting that the serpent would come to heal her by entering her vagina and drawing out all of the male poison and venom that had accumulated over the years. This also resulted in the healing of a certain aspect of her anger and negativity toward the neighbor boy, her husband and men in general.

It might be noted that Connie has experienced three archetypal images in the last few imagery sessions. The first image was of Jesus on the cross, a symbol of self-sacrifice through suffering. This seems to be related to a part of herself that has absorbed the anger and rage created by her negative sexual childhood experiences. Second was the image of the "Divine Child of Love," or a new birth of life within herself, representing pure love needed for the acceptance and forgiveness of herself and others. Third, we find the introduction of the serpent, which appears to represent healing and the drawing from her the negative emotions that have blocked her vital energy from flowing into consciousness.

PART 10
Releasing the Child to the Divine Mother

In this session Connie is dealing with her relationship with her children which was introduced in the previous session. It seems that she needs to break with the old patterns of "negative games" with her children, such that she can view them in a more adult and loving way. A significant event occurs during this imagery session which is the emergence of the "Divine Mother" archetype. (8) The Mother seems to be related to her need to learn what it means to be a loving mother to her children. She appears to be involved in the release of one of her own frightened inner children.

Connie says, *I feel so powerless over the anger and what is always happening. My kids, the angel brought them to me. I feel like I'm going through labor with them again. Before, even now, I was in negative games with them and letting myself be dragged down. I still have a connection, a thread to them. And now, it's even more empty because I want to sever that. It's that in severing this connection that I'll be able to love again in a deeper way. It was only my ego that was holding onto them before because I was afraid of what they would think or say about me or what other people would. I feel now that they're here. I feel love for them again. The anger is gone, and I can see that they really don't know what they're doing. They're really messed up and confused. It's time to quit blaming them.*

Connie continues to examine her relationship with her children, seeing how she enters into "negative games" with them. There appears to be a pattern in which she and her children strike out at each other in an escalating cycle without being able to see the negativity that binds them. In this session she comes to realize that her children really do not know what they are doing. They are actually very confused children, similar to what would be expected of children who have been raised in dysfunctional alcoholic homes. (9) Hence, she realizes that she must sever her unhealthy connection with her children by viewing them and loving them as they really are. Her ego involvement blocks this process, such that she takes personally their contrary reactions to her. She is concerned that if she turns away her children would say incriminating things about her to others.

Perhaps the most difficult truth for Connie to face is her inability to be the nurturing mother that her children really need. In response to this underlying concern she received an image of the "Divine Mother," an archetypal image, the one who is nurturing and unconditionally loving. Both she and her children need such nurturing and mother's love.

Connie indicates that, *severing this negative connection with them is for them, too. It's not just for me but it's for them. Now there's this image of a divine mother. She's a bright light that has the form of a woman. What I'm getting is that she's not only taking care of me, but she is taking care of my kids, too. I'm thinking of the divine mother in me that takes care of me. But she's just an image that comes like a symbol of what I have within.*

It is suggested that there is a difference between being taken care of and being the mother that is within her. This is to say that it might be better to express the loving, caring mother archetype within her to her children and to others who need mothering. It is

175

suggested that part of her growth would include becoming a loving and caring mother, wife and woman. Then she is asked to locate the child in past imagery sessions, who had been abused.

Connie responds, *why do I feel that I need to be attached? She* (the child) *looks sad. It's different from before but she's sad because it's time to let go of people taking care of her.*

It is suggested that Connie take the abused child to the "Mother" and to tell her that she can take care of herself. The child does not need to feel any more responsibility for any further abuse.

Connie says, *that's what I've been doing hanging onto that child again, and she is very frightened, just like panicky because of being alone. She goes into depression. That's what she did when she was, when I was her, when I was little and it was really painful. I was just thinking, separation anxiety.*

Connie is encouraged to tell the child that she does not have to worry about her anymore, that she has everything under control. The child can go to the "Mother" to the light. *She'll go, yes. She doesn't want to but she's going*, Connie says. *At the same time, I'm doing this with my kids. Yes, I feel, I feel empty again. It feels like a piece is missing, not only with her but with the kids. But there's nobody but me in the end. At least, I don't have to worry about a man taking care of me.*

Perhaps the most difficult truth for Connie to face is her inability to be the nurturing mother her children really need. In response to this underlying concern she receives the image of the "Great Mother," an archetypal image (10) that is also involved with nurturing her children and herself at unconscious levels. My experience indicates that the "Archetypal Mother," or what I refer to as the Divine Mother, represents the ground of being out of which all life emerges. Other terms such as motherland, mother church, earth mother and mother nature describe the archetypal patterns of the "Mother." Connie defined nurturing in terms of dependence, such as having all of one's deprived needs fulfilled. She is now learning how to be a strong, loving, caring mother who helps children develop their own strengths, security, and self-sufficiency with feelings of being loved and valued.

In this imagery session I am trying to set the stage for Connie to let go of her inner, damaged child. Clinical experience suggests that the inner child or children are there to absorb the abuses of childhood. Such children stay until they are convinced that they are no longer needed and are released to go, at which time they become integrated within the greater system. Sometimes this process is referred to as going to the light. Sometimes the presence of the Divine Mother becomes an avenue for releasing the inner child to the healing and nurturing qualities of the Supra Consciousness.

During this session it was suggested that Connie locate the frightened child within who appeared earlier in her imagery. She was prompted to give the child over to the "Mother" so she can be nurtured and develop a sense of security, happiness, and freedom from fear. Presumably, this "child" is the part of her that clings to anyone who might take care of her. As she gives this inner child over to the mother she feels as though she is doing the same with her own children. Although this may be more symbolic than real, it is nonetheless a real experience for her as she feels the loss of these inner and outer relationships, however unhealthy they might have been. Connie has come to discover her own inner Archetypal Mother and her capacity to be the strong, loving, caring and a nurturing mother. Having discovered her potential for nurturing and unconditional motherly love, she may develop her capacity to express this to her children. This seemed to be the case as her relationships with her children began to change in ways that seem much healthier for all.

PART 11
The Sick Baby

This session seems to contain a birth experience in which Connie becomes a newborn infant. Apparently, she re-experiences her early childhood of loneliness and emptiness. Connie begins, *it's a she* (angel) *and she has wings. I ask her to take me back to the core. I keep seeing the core. It's the image of the core and it's very deep. It's almost like there's a tunnel and at the end of the tunnel, there's a core. The angel is taking me through the tunnel to the core. I can feel her pulling me. I can see myself as a child, as an infant. This child was beautiful, a very good baby, never cried, but no one came around her. She started like that, all alone.*

Next, Connie says, *I can see my father coming home, picking up the child and holding her. That took the loneliness away. There are a lot of sensations around my throat. I can see myself being sick a lot and not liking it because it was like I was going to be with that loneliness. That's what happened this weekend with being sick again.*

Apparently, being ill over the weekend and feeling loneliness triggered this imagery of when she was a sickly child. It seemed to bring forward the imagery of the deep core that perhaps is symbolic of the womb of her birth. Connie continues, *I think that is part of me that I have to face. The worst thing that could have happened to me was to get sick and have to be alone in the apartment. There's such an emptiness about being sick and I keep going back to it. I think, too, that when I take aspirin and antihistamines, I try to push away that empty feeling of being sick. It keeps coming back, so now it's time to face it in the core. I can see my mom taking care of me when I was sick, when I was little. Even though she was there, there was this terrible fear of being alone. I was afraid of going to sleep because I would get a high fever. I would go out of my head, like I would hallucinate when I woke up. I would see things that weren't there and I would throw up. No one could take that away. It's like no one can take away the emptiness and there's no one that can nurture me. I see the core and it's in flames. The core is burning.*

After expressing some concerns about the fire, it is suggested that the flame is life and healing. Connie is encouraged to take the child into the flames and let the emptiness, the loneliness, and the fear that's associated with it to be burnt away. She indicates that *the flame is in my throat. First, it is outside and then it's in my throat and my chest. It's in the flames. Yes, I can see the flames around her* (the child), *and she's still there. It's turning into a light in my head. Now the child is back again, and I see her mother taking the bottle from her. How depressing that was, that depressed feeling inside.* It is suggested that such negative feelings, having been consumed in the flames can release the child to grow and develop and be integrated again within the whole, without loneliness and without emptiness. Connie ends the session with, *I'm seeing the core turning into light.*

There are several archetypal images and experiences of transformation in this imagery session. First is the image of moving down the tunnel toward the core. The tunnel most likely represents the birth canal and the core is apparently symbolic of the womb. It seems that Connie is re-experiencing her birth and infancy when she felt depressed, lonely and empty. Next is the presence of the fire, the fire that heals but does not consume. It is an agent of transformation that, in this case, becomes the means by which the human psyche transforms a negative element into one that is positive. (11) Moreover, the transformative and healing fire moves into her throat and chest, presumably the physical areas where her childhood infections often occurred.

In a previous imagery session Connie felt her mother's hand placed lovingly on her throat. This small bit of imagery seemed to go without notice at the time. However, it may have been more significant than otherwise considered. Also, it is recalled that she had much difficulty expressing herself as a child. What seems to be a constant reference to the throat area may be indicative of the psyche trying to remove such unconscious obstructions to verbal expression. Perhaps her mother's love in the present, as represented by her hand on Connie's throat, is a healing process and an encouragement for her to communicate with her mother.

Finally, it seems clear that the flames are serving a healing function by burning away all the negative and diseased parts of the tunnel, the birth canal and the core, the womb. Following this healing process Connie experiences light in her head and later she sees the core turning into light. This would suggest that the healing process had been completed and the birth canal and womb are healthy and without disease.

PART 12
Growing Up and facing Shame and Guilt

Before this session, Connie and I had a discussion concerning the possibility that there may be some "demonic" or dark side activity going on within her. The specifics of this discussion have been lost from memory, but I suggested that she try to confront what she sensed might be there.

Connie starts the session with, *I'm bringing someone to me and I think it's Socrates. It's an older man and he has sneakers on. And he's real pleasant. My mom is here, too. Socrates is taking me over to my mom. I'm supposed to tell her that I want to grow up. And I want her to believe that I can do it that I can take care of myself.*

It is suggested that her mother seems to be holding on to her, as well. Connie, responds, *yes, and I want her to feel my strength. I want her to see it. I started to feel guilty for doing that and then I let it go. It's like I feel a lot of strength. My child is here, the child within me. She's afraid for me to tell my mom that, but I'm telling her that I'll take care of her now.*

By assuming responsibility for her own life, the inner child is free to play and be a child and be released to return to the light from whence she came. Connie says, *and now I do feel the strength inside of me. It's been starting to come. It's like something that's emerging, but I can see it more clearly now. There's a knowingness that I can take care of myself.*

Since Connie is feeling a great deal of strength it is suggested that it might be time to confront the demon she thinks might be there. She responds, *it's funny, because right before you said that I felt a sensation in my pelvic area. I feel a lot of emotion starting to come up. I have visions that I, I don't know, I guess I'm ashamed to say what they are. Of the ugliness that's there. It's visions of sores and pus and, and it's a lot of shame, too. Okay, what I'm feeling is that the angel is pulling it from me. I've suffered a long time with it. I was worried that it would harm the angel, but the angel grows brighter as it pulls it away from me.*

Connie continues, *the angel is telling me that I don't have to do anything, just sit here. My knees feel like they're cleansed. There's like a burst of fresh air through my knees, and there is in my pelvic area, too. I feel like it's being replaced with light. The light even goes up to my throat. The angel said not to let it trick me into thinking it was back or that it could come back. It might try to do that.*

In such situations the process of getting rid of demons is first to become aware that they are there. Secondly, is the feeling that one does not want it there and that this feeling or position is sincere and insistent. There is nothing more one needs to do as one has a choice in such matters. Then the demon will be "pulled out" usually by the angel or by some divine source. When she realizes what her angel has done for her, Connie reacts with emotion and appreciation, *it makes me feel like crying. It brings tears to my eyes.*

This imagery session begins with Socrates, who we assume represents the archetypal image of "the wise man."(12) It seems important to Connie that her mother understand her need to grow up and to break her co-dependent relationship with her. It is a turning point in Connie's work, since she feels the need to start assuming responsibility for her own life and grow toward increasing independence and self-sufficiency.

The "demon" likely represents the ugliness of the sexual experiences with the neighbor boy and other abusive men. Connie seems to experience dynamic healing sensations, when the angel pulls the demon from her. She feels a sensation that her knees and pelvic area are being cleansed. From her description of the experience we get the idea that the contaminated area is a source of her guilt and shame. The focus then goes up to her throat, which we suspect may be related to her inability to speak of her childhood sexual experience, which symbolically got stuck in her throat.

Hence, it seems that growing up for Connie depends on a release of the shame and guilt related to her unfortunate childhood sexual experience, which seems to have been absorbed by the little girl in her imagery. By facing such "ugly" experiences she is able to relieve the shame and guild associated with them. Having faced this, another emotional block to her growth to full responsible adulthood has been released.

PART 13
Letting go of Another Child

Another child emerges in Connie's imagery. It is the child who absorbed all of the loneliness and depression due to having been uprooted and sent to another school where she was unable to develop new friendships. This seems to be the time in her life when her addiction to drugs and alcohol began.

Connie begins the imagery with, *now I feel the presence of the angel. What I'm seeing is myself when we changed schools when I was in the fifth grade. It was a traumatic experience for me. I felt all alone when I moved to this school, this new school. And I was real shy, and I had been depressed anyhow but my depression was a lot worse, because I had to leave all my friends and I didn't know how to make new ones. The kids were real standoffish there, they weren't friendly.*

Connie continues, *I felt like no one liked me. I started slipping in and out again really, a lot more mentally. I was scared to death of the depression and yet I kept going into it. That's when my school grades got bad. I didn't understand anything. I missed the basics of math and English, and I started cheating to get through because I didn't know how to get caught up. School wasn't fun anymore. I didn't like it. The angel is taking me to a store where we used to hang out. We would buy Cokes. I started putting aspirin in my Coke. It took me out of that daze that I was always in, stimulated me a little bit. Now I'm back at home stealing Grandpa's beer, sixth grade. I think whenever I start to go into a daze or depression, I take aspirin to stimulate me. I think that it will stimulate me, but it doesn't.*

To be sure Connie suffered from bouts of deep depression when she was a child, especially when she started in the sixth grade in a new school where she did not know anyone. Further, she was very shy and was unable to reach out to her fellow students and develop friendships. She says, *now I'm still at the new school. Those were really terrible years. I started getting into trouble, and I started writing on myself with razor blades.* Typically, she began to become self-destructive and cutting herself to create pain that would override the psychological pain that she felt. It temporarily brought her out of a state of depression. However, she did not think of it in those terms. *I told myself it was a fad. I was writing my boyfriend's name in my leg but it took me out of the daze. My mother and I grew even further apart in these years, too. We were always fighting. I took a lot of aspirin, a lot of it. I sometimes took ten aspirin before I would go to school, and my ears would ring. I drank every time I got a chance to. And then one time I tried to kill myself with aspirin. I took a whole bottle. I got scared and told my mom and she kept me up all night. She was afraid to let me go to sleep. My boyfriend broke up with me, and I couldn't handle it. It was more of the depression. It felt like it did when my brother wouldn't talk to me. He didn't want anything to do with me.*

It seems apparent that Connie's addictions began in an attempt to treat her childhood depression, which started with taking aspirin to numb her psychological pain. She continues, *what I'm seeing now is the angel standing over that girl who was depressed and afraid. It seems weird because she's older now. I'm so used to seeing a child or infant*. What this likely means is that she is going through an age progression with varying degrees of confusion, depression and anxiety that at times became overwhelming. Connie feels that she wants to let go of this older girl and is trying to *do it mentally, but I won't know who I am*. It appears that her identity is tied to this girl and it is difficult for her to let go of a part of her life that has been a part of her for so long, even though it represents such a painful part of her life. Connie recognizes that this part of her represents her painful past and it is important for her to move into the present and future. She acknowledges that *she has suffered so much. It's time. I want her to get better. I want her to go with the angel*.

Connie's desire to give the girl over to the angel so that she can heal and grow is a step toward learning how to stand up for herself and learning to love herself. Indeed, caring about this girl and not wanting her to suffer anymore is loving herself, since she is part of herself.

Unfortunately, given Connie's dependent personality, she was unable to reorient and restructure her life after moving to a new school. The result was intense loneliness, deep depression and self-destructiveness. Her inability to establish new friendships further increased the intensity of her emotional turmoil.

Connie's behavior during this time of her life, as relived in an adult state while in imagery therapy may give some insight into why children perform such self-destructive acts. The pain that she felt was not as problematic as her inability to perceive a way out of her suffering. During childhood, the adult world, (parents, grandparents, aunts and uncles and teachers etc.), is the primary resource by which the child is able to face the world with a sense of security. For Connie, the adult world did not seem available to her and she was left to her own inadequate child perspective and resources. Since the school friends she had depended on were no longer there she was unable to find a way to escape her painful circumstances except by means of artificial stimulation. Hence, the pattern of addictive behavior started, first with aspirin and Cokes, followed by alcohol and self-mutilation combined with destructive co-dependent relationships.

When Connie lets go of the inner child who absorbed a good deal of her suffering during this time of her life, she feels a loss of identity. However, as we are coming to see, the process of imagery therapy helped her heal this part of her life and achieve sufficient growth to differentiate her unresolved past in the form of inner children. Next, with the adult mind, the past becomes understood and incorporated within the present. Then the past becomes resolved and integrated within the self. This follows the archetypal process of growth which was earlier defined as "increasing differentiations with increasing integrations."

PART 14
The Angry Child

As expected, the theme of working with Connie's inner children continues in this imagery session. So far, her inner children have been associated with fear, anger, depression, shame and guilt. Now she finds a child who is particularly enraged with her brother. This is the one of her inner children who absorbed the anger and rage toward her brother that she had repressed.

At first Connie resists going with the angel who is pulling her arm. She feels it is because she keeps seeing her brother's face. She says, *I've seen him a lot today even before I came here. Consciously I'm saying, "I'm done with you," but what the angel is saying is that it's time to look at him again, instead of pushing him away because I want to detach. He seems happy. It's when he was younger, too. It's not now. I have released the child in him since I have released my child. Now I don't feel the anger, but I see myself being angry at him. I see my child being really angry at him and wanting to beat him up.*

Apparently, this is part of Connie who she has repressed and who is the one who absorbed her anger over her brother's rejection of her dependent clinging. Connie says, *she's almost insane with rage.* It is suggested that Connie differentiate herself from this child and become an observer in the process. She continues, *it helps because I feel okay with the anger when I allow her to do that, and I don't feel ashamed of it or anything. I'm not fighting it. It's like she always was, what she did to the cats was what she wanted to do to him. Now she can leave the cats alone because she always loved the cats, but she was hurting them just like she wanted to hurt her brother. Yes, she just gets out of control with it and that's how I get when I feel the rage, that I'm just going to lose it. Now she is exhausted from attacking her brother. She's released all the rage.*

Suggesting that one separate oneself from one's inner child and become an observer of the child is often a helpful approach. It is especially true when dealing with difficult to control emotions such as anger and rage. In this case it was very helpful and made it possible for Connie to observe the behavior of the angry child without having to feel out of control emotions. After the child becomes exhausted, it is suggested that she make contact with her in a loving and compassionate way. In the past her approach to the child was one of rejection and repression. In fact, Connie expressed that she has not really liked this child and has been afraid of her because of her out of control anger and rage. At times the child has turned on her because of the rejection, which has caused tremendous inner tension and conflict.

Connie is encouraged to approach the child and acknowledge what she has done for her. She represents all of her repressed anger and rage over feeling rejected by her brother. Without this child, she would not have been able to carry or express such rage by herself. It is suggested that it is time to love this child and not be afraid of her. "It is time, tell her it is over now and that no one is going to reject her anymore." Connie says, *I'm realizing that she can't hurt me either. As she tries to, I just, all I have to do is say stop. And what I'm*

184

feeling as I say that is an emptiness inside of me. This is a typical feeling when releasing an inner child who represents aspects of one's unresolved past. The child is released back into the light to be healed and released for further growth. It is important to note that letting go of pathological anger and rage does not mean that one loses potential for anger when circumstances require it. Rather, the expression of anger will fit the situation and be healthy in its substance.

Connie realizes that, *maybe now I won't be so afraid of my anger. She just spotted the angel. What I'm smiling about is that the angel gets so bright when it's time for (taking a child home). She's going with the angel. My emptiness is getting lesser. It's not so intense as it was at first. And the light in me gets brighter again as I release her. The light in me is so bright that my eyes are hurting. Can you see it?*

These are touching moments of celebration when something within oneself becomes resolved. Actually, in response to her question, "yes" the room did become more illuminated, while not as bright as she was experiencing it. During the days of my research with such cases, the room would become, at times, visibly brighter. I recall one particular moment of brightness with another person. It was as if there were thousands of volts of electricity dancing about the room.

During this moment of celebration, I say to Connie, "you had to give yourself over to the process. You had to walk over to her to accept her and reassure her. She is what you've been fighting in yourself for quite some time. Now what makes it possible for her to go is that you are growing in strength. You can stand up for yourself, so she doesn't have to do that now. So now she is free to go with the angel, to be healed of her anger and rage and become free to grow. When she is healthy and growing, you will also be growing and healing your life."

Connie responds, *and my brother is more free too because he doesn't have that child that's angry at him all the time. I see my inner guru, and he's touching me on the head. His presence is so strong and loving. I feel him blessing me. I guess there is more of a oneness feeling within me. I don't feel so scattered. I feel real present right here and now, not off somewhere else.*

This imagery session seems to be a continuation of Connie facing her inner children, a process that began a number of sessions ago. The angry child that she finds this time in her unconscious appears to be directing her rage toward her brother. The child represents one of her responses to her difficult dependent relationship with her brother. For most of her life Connie has been afraid that the rage and anger she was feeling would cause her to lose control. She was afraid that the anger might be turned against her. The inner tension and conflict must have been overwhelming at times. She realizes that this child, having been faced and differentiated, cannot harm her and is able to accept her as a meaningful part of herself. As she releases the child, she again feels a temporary emptiness that she has felt with the release of other children within her. With this release, she sees a light of increasing brightness which comes to fill the negative void left by the absence of the angry child.

After the experience with the light Connie realizes that her relationship with her brother may have a chance to move toward resolution, since she no longer feels anger toward him. No doubt, her anger and rage repelled him in the past as it has repelled many others in her life. She seems to have accomplished much toward dealing with her repressed anger. The next session appears to be a celebration of what she has accomplished regarding her negative relationship with men. There appears to be a feeling of openness to the divine world and what it has to offer by way of love, compassion, growth and healing.

PART 15
Going down a Pathway of Saints and a Change in Connie's Attraction to Men

This session begins with a celebration where Connie walks down a path lined with saints. The path leads to a light which appears to represent a light of transformation or a new light of consciousness. It seems that this path also leads to new relationships with non-abusive men.

Connie indicates, *Saint Rose is here, too. She's been here a lot lately. It seems like many times during the day she's there bringing me a rose a lot of the times. I feel very comforted by her and this pathway is lined with saints on both sides, and I'm walking up the center of it. At the end of the path there's a light. The saints are helping me walk.*

It appears that there is a celebration going on with Connie being at the center of it. She continues, *I feel a lot of emotions and it's not, you know, real. It's like my heart feels enlarged or something. I guess what I keep thinking is that finally, the peacefulness comes again. And finally, the integration and the light that I'm walking through is really within me. It's God. It's almost like I'm afraid to walk up the path because I feel like I don't deserve it. The saints are telling me to come on. I don't know, I'm just there. I'm walking up the path. They're standing. They're lined on both sides of the path. The saints are helping me. They're helping me walk up the path towards the light.*

After encouraging her to continue down the pathway she notices that *the light gets brighter as I walk towards it. Now, it's really over top of my head. And the light is streaming from over top of my head down through my arm. And there's a tingling sensation. I've had that happen a lot in my right arm. I see an oil painting in front of me. I am supposed to be working on it.*

Apparently, the painting is Connie's painting that she is working on at an unconscious level. Moreover, the painting appears to have something to do with her relationship with men, a change in the kind of men to whom she is attracted. She says, *there is a man who I know here. I'm trying to figure out what it is that, why I feel so attracted to him. He's here right now. The angel likes him. I guess I need to give myself permission to be okay with it. Yes, he's really a sweet person, and I can feel his sweetness. I feel very drawn to him.*

It is suggested that she tell this man, in her imagery, that she is fond of him and that she is drawn to him. She says, *it's like the angel arranged it because it's getting real bright. I don't know what to say to him. I'll ask him why he's there. He says, because I'm thinking of him. It's sort of nice to do this imagery because it's what I've been wanting to say anyhow.*

Next it is pointed out that there has been a change in her relationships with men. This man in her imagery represents this change. She is drawn to a man who is kind and gentle and who would not abuse her. He is different from the negative men to whom she used to be attracted. The idea is that there are men in the world who are not abusive, and that she has grown in her ability to differentiate between such men and men who are negative.

Then Connie makes the observation, *now I'm going back to the energy in me. It's in my throat. It's the throat Chakra. There's been a lot of new energy there that I have not felt before. It's like a heat and a coolness at the same time. That man's face is back. I've been wanting to ask him to go to lunch or something, and I have not done it. I don't know whether it would be right or maybe.* It might be noted that the throat Chakra represents the spiritual area of verbal expression. According to Hindu thought the Chakras refer to energy centers of the psyche and the throat Chakra is related to verbal expression. (13) Connie has had a very difficult time expressing her thoughts and feelings since childhood. It appears that this deficiency is being healed, and she is considering the possibility of expressing her desire to ask this man who she recently met, to lunch. It is suggested that she does not need to think of this man as a potential romantic relationship but rather as a possible friend. Perhaps she could establish a friendship with him and get to know him before developing any romantic aspirations. She responds, *I keep thinking the angel wants me to ask him too, and he gets real bright all the time when he's around.* It is pointed out that the worst that might happen is that he might say "no," but she will have put forth the effort to offer friendship. Connie indicates that she feels that that is the scary thing about it and that she might feel rejected. On the other hand, she realizes *that, it won't be the end of the world.*

Perhaps the path lined with saints represents the path or journey which Connie is presently taking in her therapy and personal growth work. She is heading toward a light that seems to symbolize an increasingly healthy life of creativity and new insight. The picture which appears before her most likely represents her efforts to paint a picture of a new and more constructive life for herself. This imagery session, whatever our specific interpretation, appears to indicate a transcendent experience by which Connie's negative beliefs and thought patterns are being transformed.

The next part of Connie's imagery session suggests growth in her relationships with men as she is presented with the face of a man who she knows to be kind, gentle and positive and to whom she has recently felt attracted. Having dealt with her anger toward her brother during previous sessions, combined with previous releases of negative emotions, she seems to have broken with the cycle of her past that caused her to be attracted to abusive men. Her imagery strongly suggests that she try to develop a friendship with this gentleman. No doubt it would put her own feelings of unworthiness and inadequacy to a fearful test.

It should be noted that Connie did approach this man during the following week, and he responded favorably to her. It was a positive and affirming step toward changing her attitude regarding men. Without the need to project her deprived past upon men, she was able to make a healthier choice concerning possible male friendships.

We finish this discussion with one final note. There is a brief reference to Connie's throat Chakra. This reference to her throat is a recurring theme which refers back to her childhood when *words got stuck in my throat*, and she was unable to express her psychic pain and suffering. Hence, it appeared to be the place where words got stuck and where physical illness often occurred. Now it seems related to preparing her for expressing something she wants or needs from another person.

At this point I am omitting a number of imagery sessions which seem to be a kind of "cleaning up" or psychological severing of minor dependent situations. Having resolved most of the dependent relationships in her life, Connie was entering a new phase of imagery work. During the time of these omitted sessions she was basically without emotional symptoms. She felt herself to be healing and appeared balanced and more centered.

The next set of imagery sessions marks a shift in the therapeutic process in which Connie is being taken into the Collective Consciousness. This is to say that she will be experiencing images that are not part of her personal history, but rather seem more focused on the broader suffering embedded in the history of humanity.

PART 16
The Indian and Egyptian Girl

It was surprising when Connie began to receive spontaneous images that seemed unrelated to what she had previously been experiencing. Although the emergence of the Collective Consciousness is not uncommon in imagery work, it was unexpected in her case at this stage of the therapeutic process. This would suggest that the Collective Consciousness is directly related to the resolution of her present life circumstances. In any case, the following session is a good example of how the Collective Consciousness emerges spontaneously during imagery therapy.

This session begins with Connie reporting on being a Native American in an Indian community. She says, *I am in an Indian Community. I can see the teepees. It's quiet and there's no one around. I think it's quiet because everyone is eating around the fire, and I'm back where the tepees are. I'm just having flashes of being on the stake. It seems to me what's coming to me is that I was behind, sneaking behind the teepees to meet some man or something that I wasn't supposed to see.* It appears that she had been caught and was now facing punishment. She continues, *it wasn't from my people. It was some other people. Another group of people and I don't know who they are. There are people there but I can't see who they are. I'm in a lot of pain, like in shock.* It seems that she had been seeing this man for some time. She suggests that, *I would go out whenever I had the chance to be with him, when the people were eating or if they were sleeping, I would meet this man.*

Apparently, she was discovered, and she described a man who she was hoping might help her. *I see a man there too. I see him there and not for any special reason. He is like a warrior with white feathers on. I think I was looking to him to help me and he couldn't.*

Next it seems that the man who Connie, the Indian girl, was seeking to meet in the Indian community was related to a close friend named Paul. She says, *I keep seeing Paul's face too, and I guess I just want to pretend like he's not there. I keep wanting to cry when I'm around Paul.* It is suggested that perhaps the man she had been meeting was now the man she knows as Paul. She responds, *that's what I was thinking. It's like he is a person that means a lot to me. I guess it was. I've been feeling that.*

Connie's focus changes to an Egyptian woman who represents another part of her Collective Consciousness. She says that she is seeing this woman and indicates that *she is beautiful but a tyrant. She has like a catty look on her face. I think that she was really a cruel person. She wants me to release her.* It was suggested that perhaps some of Connie's suffering is related to her and the negativity of her life. Connie responds that, *yes, I think so. She has the same eyes that I do.* Perhaps it is time to release this Egyptian woman and let go of the suffering that has resulted from the cruelties of her life. Suddenly, Connie sees the angel who is *real bright.* Connie continues, *she's looking at the angel too. It seems like a lot of my karma is from her. She's in chains, and I don't know if it's because of them or?* It is suggested that the chains represent being bound by what she had been and how she had acted toward others, perhaps imprisoning others. *I'm going to give her over to the angel..*

190

She just merged with the angel. She was hanging onto me because I think she thought that through me she could learn a lot. Yes, it is me who was learning to love. The light is brighter within again.

Connie's attention turns back to the Indian girl. She says, *yes, she suffered terribly. What I keep seeing is they gutted her and she was still alive. I just keep seeing Paul's face again. I think I'm confused about how I feel about him.* She is asked to examine her emotions related to Paul. At times she feels like crying when she is with him. She says that she has a *longing for him, to be with him but yet a fear that I don't want that. So it's ambivalent feelings. I guess from not understanding why I feel the way I do about him or maybe it's just because I'm in a vulnerable place.* However, Connie's imagery of the Indian girl and how she suffered relative to the Indian man may help her develop insight into her feelings toward her friend, Paul.

Of course, we have no way to verify the possible historical events that Connie experienced in her imagery therapy. However, this is not necessary for therapeutic purposes. The significant question is whether it feels like a valid experience for her and that it fits within the context of her belief system. As a therapist, I believe that no judgment should be offered and that the appropriate response is to attend to the images that emerge spontaneously as they are perceived by the client. It is important to help her establish a relationship between such images and what is going on in her life in the present.

What is important is that Connie's imagery stories give her a way to explain her own suffering. To the degree that her imagery experiences ring true for her is the degree to which she can bring some meaning to the anguish that she has experienced in her own life. In this way, her imagery makes it possible for her to resolve her life of suffering and to begin life in a new way. For example, the release of the Egyptian woman may be the way that her psyche has chosen to release her from the feelings of guilt, shame, worthlessness and perhaps some deeper need to be abused or punished by others.

Moreover, Connie's imagery gives her an explanation for her ambivalent feelings toward her friend, Paul. She realizes that there may be no need to change her present friendship. Therefore, she may be able to avoid yet another emotional entanglement that could interfere with her sense of peace and happiness.

Finally, it might be noted that following this imagery session Connie sensed strong feelings of being loved. Her *opening up* seems to indicate therapeutic progress, especially since this session is related to those preceding it, such that she is learning to love more unconditionally.

PART 17
Meeting of the Indian Lovers

Connie continues in this imagery session to visualize the story of the Indian girl and her lover which first appeared in the previous session. The session begins with her being with them. She says, *I'm going back and forth between them feeling what she is feeling and then letting go of that and being able to observe.* It seems that he is waiting for her beside a rock. Connie is encouraged to go with the Indian girl to meet with her lover. *Okay, I'm going with her* she says. *I want to ask him why he let them do that to me. I think it is most confusing why he didn't save her. I can see her vividly. They're just looking at each other. She is really a meek person and she wants to tell him know sorry she is that it all happened. She has been taking the blame for what happened, but yet she has been blaming him for not rescuing her. She does feel real safe with him though, even though the painful part has happened. What they're realizing is even though they had to say goodbye in that other lifetime that it's not forever. She's still suffering though, physically.*

Connie is told that the Indian girl will probably continue to suffer until she releases herself from the blame that she carries. It was suggested that Connie encourage her to let go of all that she is carrying. "She went through the punishment of her day so she doesn't need to hold herself accountable anymore." Connie says that *she feels a great deal of relief from what you have just said. She didn't know she could be released. The angel is telling her that it's going to move into a higher love, and that she needs to let go of that to be with him today. She hasn't let the angel take care of her, heal her because she doesn't feel that she has deserved it. Okay, they're hugging and saying goodbye for that lifetime. She's ready to go with the angel now. The angel is getting bright. I feel a light in my abdominal area where she was tortured. I'm seeing now that other person, that Egyptian queen or whatever. She's being taken care of. She's smiling a lot more now.*

It should be noted that what is left unresolved in the past, no matter how far in the past, remains in the present. Connie, who is on the front end of life, whose life it is, is in a position of authority to bring such elements of the Collective Consciousness into Ego consciousness for the purpose of healing and growth of the greater system. If necessary, once these collective parts of the self go to the light and become healed, they may be free to come back into consciousness to help guide oneself through certain life experiences to bring about a more growth producing outcome.

Connie confides that the Egyptian woman seems to have come back to help her during a visit with her parents. She says, *she helped during my trip to see mom and dad. I didn't know for sure if this was happening but I think now that she's come back again. It was all that love I was getting from my parents and she showed me that I was worthy of it, that I would not misuse it anymore. It made her happy that she had been set free so that I could be loved.*

Then Connie sees an image of her friend Paul. *I'm seeing Paul again. He's giving me another rose. He gave me a couple of roses again Sunday. I guess I don't feel the resistance right now that I usually do. And the angel is blessing us. It's real bright. I feel like my higher self and the angel are celebrating. And now I see you, and it's like your other self is beside me. He's real bright too, and he's also working with Paul and me.*

I had suggested to Connie that she separate herself from the Indian girl so that she would no longer feel the pain involved with her. More importantly from this perspective, she can assume a more objective role in helping to resolve issues that surface into consciousness from the Collective Consciousness. We have learned that healing and resolution depends on the ability to differentiate oneself from given aspects of the self in order to integrate such differentiated parts of the self within the greater whole.

Several themes that emerged in this session appear consistent with Connie's own feelings and thought patterns. One is confusion with regard to the behavior of men toward her. This confusion is combined with feelings of having been betrayed by the one she loves. There seems to be a parallel between the Indian woman's feelings about her lover not rescuing her and her feelings of rejection and abandonment regarding her relationship with abusive men. Another theme is blaming oneself for what goes wrong in the world which had been a consistent pattern since Connie's early childhood. In the imagery, the Indian girl blames herself for breaking with tribal law and feels that she deserved to be punished.

In the imagery process Connie brings together the two Indian lovers with her more comprehensive insight and different cultural perspective to their relationship. It seemed that they needed to understand what had happened to them. The Indian girl needed to know that because of social and cultural customs of the tribe there was nothing her lover could have done and that he loves her and regrets deeply what had happened. This combined with realizing that the Indian woman had already been punished enough, had suffered enough, seemed to release her from her cycle of suffering.

This pattern of acceptance and deeper insight that leads to releasing oneself from guilt, shame, and self-punishment served as a continued basis for Connie to set aside her own painful past. The wisdom needed to help the Indian woman transcend her suffering may be the insight needed for resolving her own suffering. Having faced and processed her own feelings of unworthiness, Connie opened herself to love from others and also to her own capacity to love at a much higher level than before possible.

The last part of the session finds the return of the Egyptian woman who seems to have undergone a dramatic change following her healing experiences with the light. Having been healed of her negative, cruel attitude she has reappeared to help Connie develop feelings of worth and of being loved. It appears that the Egyptian woman has paved the way for her to feel loved and valued by those around her, especially by her parents who she had recently visited.

Furthermore, Connie's relationship with Paul is progressing well and seems to be incorporating a higher form of love which is symbolized by him bringing her roses in her imagery sessions. With Paul she seems to be developing a warm and caring friendship with a man that does not involve sexual contact or dependence. Through this relationship Connie is discovering that she can have many loving male friendships in her life that focus on her as a worthy, valued person with much to offer others beyond her sexuality.

Connie's imagery of the past two sessions, when taken to represent a number of recurring themes in her life, appears to have significant therapeutic value. One important aspect of these sessions is that she became directly involved in the resolution of given elements in her Collective Consciousness. Once she was able to differentiate these elements from herself, she could take her newly developed insights and apply them to the life stories of the Indian and Egyptian women. The process of resolving one's past experiences of suffering may well become the means by which one gains the freedom to begin life anew in the present and future.

It needs to be noted that it is of little interest therapeutically whether Connie's imagery demonstrates the validity of past lives. What does matter is that the life issues involved, such as feelings of betrayal, guilt, shame, and unworthiness are resolved and brought to a favorable conclusion. Also, it is important that these imagery stories become metaphors available to Connie as models for her in confronting her own past. Her friendship with Paul is one example of the relationship between her internal imagery and external events.

PART 18
Seeking Love, Approval and Affection from Husband

After spending several sessions with what appears to have been Connie's Collective Consciousness, she returns to another facet of her relationship with her husband. There seems to be something that she is avoiding, as indicated by a dream that she had just had and the details of which she had forgotten. It appears that the dream might be an indication that she is resisting or holding back on something that she may need to face. She is encouraged to seek what is behind the resistance. Connie responds that *what keeps coming is that it's something that I'm running from*. It is further suggested that it may be time to stop running and turn to face what she is running from. Then she says, *I'm seeing Ted's face, my husband, and as his face appeared my higher self got bright. There's like another little fragment that I thought I had let go of, of anger and love. His image came to me quite often last week, and when it does I start crying. I think I want it to be like it was in another lifetime. Maybe it was just a hope. I don't know. It was, maybe it has been a couple of lifetimes of wanting that love from him that I've never gotten. I've just never resolved it yet.* This would seem to explain why she had been drawn to him to seek his affection, approval and love.

Connie continues, *yes, I can see him physically abusing me before*. Apparently, the more she would try to gain his love and approval *the more angry he got. What I'm seeing is his higher self, the light within him. It helps me see past all the abusiveness, the anger and hate*. It was observed that in a certain way she became punished for doing the very thing she thought she should be doing. She responded, *yes, I'm feeling a lot of negativity from him right now. I mean, that just came in front of me. It was like I feel a lot of compassion for him. It's real confusing kind of stuff. I can see this little boy within him, how damaged he is. That's where my compassion comes in. I see my mother in law's face, too.* (The reader might recall that Connie's mother in law had also treated her badly during her marriage with Ted).

Connie feels she needs to resolve the negative relationship with her husband and move on with her life. Having seen the damaged child within him she begins to feel a sense of compassion toward him. She says, *I think it is time to turn him over to the angel. I see his damaged child looking at me. I feel a release inside too, as I do that. And again, there is the connection with the higher self. What I'm getting from my higher self is to take the time to be with me, with the "I am," and the connection will be there. I see Don, a dear friend of mine. It's very comforting to be around him, very nurturing, I feel close to him.* It appears that her image of Don would suggest that he represents moving on with her life and developing more positive nurturing relationships.

Connie's dream led me to believe that she was avoiding something that she needed to face. Her imagery suggested that the problem was related to seeking love and approval from her husband. She believes that her desire for her husband's love and acceptance goes back beyond this life. This belief appears to gain support from seeing images of him abusing her from before. To be sure, this had been a constant theme in her marriage and one of the patterns that she has had to fight in order to go through with the divorce. It seems impossible for her to bring her marriage to some completion without first resolving her divided feelings of anger and love for her husband. Hence, there are many facets to this love/hate web that binds her to her husband.

Once again Connie's unconscious leads her to a perspective from which she might come to feel love and compassion for her husband. From this position she was able to see that there was no way she could have gained his love and affection because of his own distortions of life. It is likely that his anger toward her, when she attempted to gain his love and approval, was related to being asked to do something that he, given his own inadequacies, was unable to give.

To be sure, part of Connie's new insight into her husband's behavior was being able to see the damaged little boy within him. Further, she is able to see her mother in law's destructive influence over her husband. Realizing that there is nothing she can do to help her husband or gain the love and affection that she had desperately sought from him, she was able to let go of her relationship with him and turn him over to divine forces as she had done in the past with her own inner children and collective selves. Having accomplished this, she feels a release from her husband with an increased openness toward the world and others.

It should be noted that Connie's release from her negative relationship with her husband seems to represent a healthy theme in her therapy. That is, with issues to be resolved there is: (1) a phase of transcending the situation or problem, (2) a phase of developing a full understanding of the problem and removing it from a personal perspective and differentiating it from the self. For example, (I am not responsible for what has happened, but I am responsible for helping to resolve it), (3) a third phase is of developing a more transcending love and compassion toward the person or persons involved, and (4) releasing one from being negatively bound to the person or persons or situation involved. Having released her negative relationship with her husband she is able to move on with her life and develop more positive, non-abusive relationships with others.

PART 19
Writing of Her Experiences
and Exploring Her Perceptions of Men

The session begins with Connie feeling *a lot of light around me again. I can see a lot of light. I feel like my right arm is turning into light again. That's been happening more lately. I've been asking what it's for*. It was suggested that it might have to do with writing. She responds, *yes, there's this, a lot of light energy, just energy around me and it extends to others, too. It's like everything is energy. It's like I just melt into it. I go back and forth between what is him and what is me, what is my higher self. For one instant I see him and then in another instant, I'm that light.* She is asked if perhaps the light that is her and the higher self are actually one and the same. She continues that, *yes, it is. I didn't realize that. I have, I'm seeing it now. I have this angel above my head. It's different than, than sunshine, my guardian angel. I keep thinking it's the angel of wisdom. That light is in my arm, too. I think I need to sit down and write instead of thinking about needing to know what I'm writing about, just do it. The angel got real bright when I said that. It's pretty neat how they have their ways of agreeing with us.*

Connie then begins to explore her feelings and the validity of those feelings toward men, especially when she first meets them. She expresses an image, *I'm seeing a face of a person who I have been in close contact with, who's only, I guess I've been asking for guidance. It's a male and his name is Adam. Always with men, especially in the beginning, I feel a little confused about my feelings toward them.* It appears that she is never sure of what she is feeling towards men and the validity of those feelings. She continues, *the angel is getting real bright again. It's like it's telling me it's okay to feel, and that I take things too seriously. I have noticed the illusion of relationships. I keep noticing that. It keeps coming back to me how I think they're always one way and they're not. I just observe myself going through those phases.* Apparently, Connie has become aware that her own need for love and approval can alter the perception she may have when relating to men.

Then the angel brings Ted to Connie. When in his presence she continues to experience feelings of hurt and resentments, although they are not as intense as they have been in the past. She says, *I've been questioning what happened and why. Yet, on the other hand, I'm real happy that it did happen, that I'm out of that mess.* Then she indicates that, *I see you there, you're standing between Ted and me. I think it's because in my dreams I don't know that he can't hurt me. In my waking state, I know that I'll be alright. But when I'm dreaming, I don't know that. That's why you're there with me in my dreams, because there's that other dimension that I need reassurance in.* It is suggested that when Connie feels at a deeper level that her husband cannot hurt her, she can start letting go of her resentments. She responds, *yes, that makes a lot of sense. It's almost like we're working on another dimension together, another plane. We're doing other work I'm not consciously aware of. Yes, it does go deep, deeper than what I can comprehend because a lot of it is still being worked out.*

Connie is advised that during this inner process that she keep away from her husband as much as possible. While she has made great strides in resolving her relationship with her husband, there appears to be some resentments that seem to be at a deeper level. She is cautioned that she could be drawn to other men who could present similar problems. She is warned not to get involved with other men, at least intimately, until such deeper issues become resolved. She expressed her own concerns saying that *I think that's what's happening with Paul, too. I don't want any kind of relationship. I don't mean any kind, just not an intimate one with him. I want to be able to work this out with him differently than I have before with other men. I don't want to have a real intimate relationship either. It's like I just want to be friends with him. The angel will help us with it. It's like the angel is telling me that, and to talk to him again about it.* The session ends with Connie expressing, *what I'm seeing now is that my angel, Christ and my higher self are all coming together. The light is so bright when that happens.*

Connie typically begins this imagery session immersed in what appears to be divine or transcendent images. Up to this point her reference to the divine side of herself focused on her relationship with the angel. Then her "higher self" emerged and now there is mention of "Christ." Perhaps this progression of Connie's concept of her inner Self as divine combined with her human consciousness is related to the biblical idea of being made in "God's image," an image of light consciousness. The idea of being "Christ" but not Christ, seems to be similar to Collective Consciousness perceived as "me but not me." At any rate, similar to Theresa, Connie's imagery sessions tend to begin with transcendent images in keeping with the theme of viewing issues of life from a much broader perspective than could be possible when immersed within them. It seems that such transcendent images help to provide her with support and strength to face the difficult issues of her life.

It appears that Connie's relationship with her husband represents a major source of misconceptions regarding relationships with men. In her recent dreams I am standing between her and her husband. It has been my clinical experience that so long as there are no sexual or manipulative overtones, the projection of the therapist into dreams and imagery is a positive indication of the integration of the supportive function of the therapist within the unconscious. This can also be helpful between therapy sessions in dreams and meditation. It appears that Connie is not sure whether her husband can hurt her in her dream world. Hence, she has inserted the therapist to help protect and guide her. She is getting the idea that she and her husband are continuing to work together at deeper unconscious levels to bring their relationship to a positive resolution. In any case, the impression is formed in this imagery session that Connie is being prepared for dealing with another aspect of the love/hate relationship with her husband.

Finally, Connie continues to work toward developing closer and more positive relationships with men. Ordinarily, when she enters another phase of resolving issues with her husband she becomes unsure of herself in other relationships and withdraws. However, this time she wants to maintain her friendships with other men like Paul, without becoming intimately involved with them. With her deprived need for love and affection during these times, she seems to become vulnerable to being drawn into unhealthy situations with men. She is encouraged to talk with Paul about her dilemma rather than withdraw from him.

PART 20
Connie Returns to the Collective Consciousness

In the next session Connie expresses her feelings toward her husband, Ted, in the context of images that do not seem part of her own personal experiences with him. That is, her relationship with Ted seems to have its roots deep within the Collective Consciousness. The angel takes her to stand in front of Ted. She says, *I think I was getting tied up in feeling responsible for him the way he feels. I was feeling like I owed him something. It was the same old crap. Another way I see him is on a horse. I don't know why but that keeps coming up in front of me.* This suggests that her relationship with him may go deep within the Collective Consciousness. She continues, *I see him with like a cape on and boots. It almost feels like I was tied up with him before. Maybe that's why I feel so drawn to him. I can see myself getting up on the horse with him riding. I feel like I do now. It's like depressed around him, for lack of better words. But it's like I owe him something.*

With that, the question is what does Connie feel that she owes him that keeps her drawn to him and having to experience the negativity of their relationship. She indicates that, *I guess I really feel now, I wasn't seeing it before, is the emotionally abusive part of him. That may not be showing through now, but it's there. I see it with him on the horse, too. It's like he was really powerful and abusive. It's almost like this is something left undone from before and needs to be broken off. Maybe that's why the feelings were there so quick, because they were always there.*

Connie is asked to separate herself from the one on the horse and to try to get the one in her Collective Consciousness to come to her so that they might talk about what happened between her and the man on the horse. It is suggested that she be kind and gentle with her, but firm, as well. Connie responds that she is asking her to come to her. *Okay, I'm holding out my hand to her. She's coming towards me now. She's getting off the horse, separating from him and coming to me.* Connie puts her arm around the woman and asked her how she came to be with this man. She indicates that the relationship had to do with her father. She says, *I don't know. What keeps coming is that it's through her father.* It appears that there was an arrangement between this man and her father to pay a dept. This arrangement was very unpleasant for her and she now wants to be released. Then Connie shows her the angel and says, *I wish I could tell her how good it feels to be able to do this each time* (when one of her collective becomes released to the light) *and go through it. It's like a clarity.* Hence, it appears that the attraction to her husband goes back to a relationship that was part of her Collective Consciousness. The intention of her present relationship with him is to resolve the negative and unhealthy relationship she had with him in the past. Connie watches as the woman goes with the angel. *She's gone with the angel. I can see them merging into one. I can see freedom with him too. Upon his face. He's smiling. He looked real stern before. It's vacillating back and forth between then and now. I feel a lot of strength that I was not feeling and did not realize it. I guess what's happening is that I'm aware of my own strength again.* She asserts, *I think it would be best if I don't see him at all. I just need to break it off completely. I'm getting again that it will free him too, to deal with some things in his life that he needs to deal with.*

Then Connie says, *I see my child again. Yes, the one who was abused. She is agonizing again.* She reassures the child that she does not need to be involved in separating from her husband. *It's like an opening to the whole world again*, she says. *I see Roberts face now. He's holding his hand out to me, and we're walking towards the light. It's like it's a higher path. It's just happening again going on to the higher. The light feels brighter again.*

As was suspected from Connie's last imagery session, her relationship with her husband is brought forward again. This time it seems that she is taken into her Collective Consciousness in order to unravel the mystery surrounding their relationship. She seems to have been drawn to her husband because of something that appears to have roots which extend deep into her unconscious.

It was suggested that Connie separate herself from the woman riding on the horse and that she persuade her to come forward to meet with her. This separation of the woman from the horse and rider would seem to represent a break from the powerful abusive force in her life. Symbolically, what was needed was for Connie to get off the horse of masculine power and stop riding through life clinging to an abusive man. Differentiating herself from that part of herself in the Collective Consciousness makes possible an integration of that self into the greater whole.

For years Connie had felt indebted to her husband without knowing why she felt that way. As the story unfolds in her imagery, she finds the insight needed for breaking the bond with her husband and resolving the feelings that have kept her drawn to him. It might be noted, as is typically true, that her responsibility to her husband has nothing to do with her personally. Second, the debt was incurred by someone else, the father in the story. Nor was the woman of her Collective Consciousness responsible for acquiring this debt. Hence, there is no reason for Connie to feel any personal obligation toward her husband making it possible for her to break with this negative, abusive relationship. Once she realizes this she can release that part of her collective to the light.

Another theme that has emerged in Connie's imagery is that letting go of her husband, as represented by letting go of the rider on the horse appears to have a freeing effect on her husband. That is, when she resolves her own dependent needs regarding Ted he is free from an entanglement in his own life. Having been freed from her clinging to him, he may be in a better position to deal with the deficiencies of his own life.

Then Connie's damaged inner-child appears in her imagery. It seems that the child is somehow linked to the issue of pleasing her husband as represented by the woman in the Collective Consciousness. Perhaps a release of this part of herself may also pave the way for the release of the inner child.

Finally, we see another recurring theme when the face of a very positive man who Connie has recently met appears in her imagery. As indicated above, when she resolves her many life issues surrounding her marital relationship, she becomes less drawn to abusive men and more attracted to strong but gentle, non-abusive men. This appears to represent her growth toward a more positive and healthy life.

PART 21
The Accident

In this session Connie finds herself reliving an auto accident in which she had been seriously injured. It appears that she had come close to death. The session begins with Connie saying, *the angel is taking me closer to the light. In the light there's another doorway. In the center of the light there's another doorway. I keep seeing Chuck in the doorway. It's like the angel and I hesitated and the angel said it was okay to let him be there. What I'm seeing is the night when I was in the car wreck. I was at the Inn drinking with my cousin and then this guy came over to the table to talk to us. I remember I wanted to be with him. I liked him. I can see us walking out and getting into the car. He was with us. I guess I'm feeling a little bit of fear.*

It seems apparent that Connie's fear is related to what she knows is coming in her imagery which is to relive her experience of the auto accident in which she came close to dying. She continues, *the pain was really, it was so bad that I had to leave my body. It was like I was riding over the ambulance watching them take me to the hospital. I watched my mom and all of them crying. I never remembered all this stuff. I had amnesia. My cousin was all right. The friend got hurt real bad too. He was in the emergency room too. His arm is paralyzed. I keep seeing blood in the catheter bag on the bed. My leg was all twisted. I had to have surgery on it a couple of operations. I think I've been wanting to protect my leg. I can remember when they couldn't operate on my leg. I just couldn't take another operation. And whenever I'd come back into my body the pain would start. I was unconscious for a while. I wanted to stay out of it. I didn't want to come back except for Terry, my son. I was afraid that he wouldn't be taken care of right. I remember the awful sound of the saws they used on my leg on the bones. I couldn't believe what they were doing to me and my leg. I could even see the doctor operating on it. I can feel a lot of sensation in my leg right now too, as I am remembering this. What I am thinking is that it needs me to accept it, to be okay with what has happened to it because I still feel appalled by it. I think there's a lot of depression that goes along with that accident.*

It seems clear that Connie is remembering what had been lost to memory because it had been too difficult for her to face until now. She indicates that, *I was thinking about what I should do with all this imagery? Then the angel appears brighter. I can see myself lying in bed, really, really suffering. I need to turn her over to the angel like I did the others. It was one of the most awful things that ever happened. I think she needs to be released too. The angel is taking over. She's going to the angel.*

This imagery session seems straight forward and self-explanatory. Chuck has been a positive influence in her life except for some suggested transference issue with him that was described in a previous session. We assume that his projection in her imagery is meant to suggest a supportive role or even a resolution of the transference issue of their relationship. However, it would be difficult to establish a relationship between her friendship with him and the auto accident presented in this session.

The reader might recall that during the period of the auto accident and recovery Connie's husband had been seeing other women while she was in the hospital. This left her with deep emotional pain combined with her physical suffering. It was also during this time when her addictive behavior became most pronounced.

The significant thing of this imagery session is that Connie relives the traumatic physical experience, much as she has relived many of her past painful emotional experiences. It is interesting that much of what she remembers is as if from an "out-of-body" point of view. Otherwise, she remained unconscious and with amnesia for quite a while. My impression is that many of her out-of-body memories were being recalled for the first time.

Typical of out-of-body experiences Connie showed no fear even though it appeared as if she were close to death. Her only disturbing memories were of her surgeries. Otherwise, she did not seem to want to return to her body. This is to say that it appeared that she had little desire to continue life in physical form. However, we assume that her only desire to continue with her life was to return to take care of her youngest child. This is also consistent with reports of others who have had near death experiences. (14)

Connie experienced deep depression related to the physical trauma of the auto accident. The tremendous suffering had deep emotional consequences. Viewing her suffering in her imagery gives her the feeling that another part of herself absorbed the physical and emotional suffering of the accident. Hence, as she has done in previous sessions, she turned this part of herself over to the angel, the light, representing a release of the experience for integration within the greater Self.

PART 22
The Inner-Child

It had been about a month since Connie had last come for imagery therapy. In the meantime, a former neighbor had insisted on telling her the details of her husband's many infidelities. It appeared that she believed the information would help Connie in her divorce proceedings. However, it soon became obvious that her neighbor's intentions were vindictive. Connie's first response was depression, followed by anger. This experience also initiated many of her old feelings of guilt and responsibility for not being able to please her husband. It brought back that part of her that felt that her husband sought the company of other women because she could not please him. Further, the feelings were so intense that she had difficulty responding to her neighbor as a mature adult. She had even phoned me in the interim for additional help, which was unlike her.

Connie tried to meditate on her difficulty with the former neighbor. During one of her meditations she received an image of one of her inner-children. The following imagery session is an attempt to visualize the child and work with her.

Connie indicates that she is feeling a lot of guilt that seems to be coming from an inner-child. She is encouraged to communicate with the child and reassure her that what happened regarding her husband, including his infidelity, was not her fault and that she is a child and not responsible for what adults do. The child is told to let Connie, an adult, handle things and for her to go and play and have fun and to do things that she was never able to do.

Connie says that, *she's looking at you now*. This suggests to me that the child is focusing on me and looking toward me for reassurance and support. Perhaps Connie has tried to repress her and keep her from coming forward in an attempt to avoid the emotional pain that she possessed regarding the betrayal of her husband. I ask Connie to step aside and let the child come forward and to let me work with her for a while. In essence, I am asking Connie to consciously and voluntarily dissociate. In this way it allows me to work directly with the child, while Connie can become a conscious observer in the process. Of course, her position as observer can assist me in working with the child to bring about a positive outcome. I ask her, "Why don't you step aside and let me talk to her directly? You can be off to the side, and you can listen to what's going on. Tell her it's all right, she can come on. I'm not going to hurt her."

Suddenly, the child, through Connie starts to cry and says, *I don't want to hurt anymore*. I say to her, "I don't want you to hurt anymore. I want you to go where the children are, to be with the children, to play and have fun and to be a child. These are all adult things now. These aren't child things. These are adult things and these are things for adults to take care of. You don't have to take care of these things anymore. Connie is not a child anymore. You're going to have to let her take care of things. It's going to be rough for her. It's going to be painful sometimes."

The child says, *I never trusted her. I haven't trusted her to take care of it*. I respond, "well, you'll just have to start trusting. She has lots of help. I'll help her. Her angel will help her and there's not much she has to do except just be confident in herself and believe in herself. That's all, and you have to believe in her too, you know." *Uh hum.* "You need to have fun now. That's what childhood is about when it is really right. You've been having some fun, haven't you?" *Yes* "Yes, you've been playing some. And I want you to do that and bring some of that fun back to Connie. She wants you to be all right too. And, it would help her to know that you're all right. And you can talk to me too, like you are now. If you need some help you can talk to me. I'd be happy to talk to you." *Okay* "And I won't hurt you," She responds, *I know, that's why I called you.*

It might be noted that Connie would rarely call me between imagery sessions. It appears that the emotional pain became so intense that she dissociated and the child came forward and contacted me. This child is estimated to be between 10 to 11 years old, the age at which she experienced a dependent relationship with her brother that included feelings of rejection and abandonment. I continue to be supportive and reassuring to Connie's child. I continue with a dialogue with her, "yes, you can do that (phone me). I won't hurt you. I might not always be able to help, but I'll do all that I can. Okay, you go back to the angel now. You go play and don't worry about this. Let Connie handle this, and I'll help her too."

At this point the child recedes and Connie comes forward. She says, *I'm giving her back to the angel now. Okay. She's really suffering.* I suggest that she continue to work with the child and to reassure her that these things will take care of themselves. She responds, *yes, I think this will be my chance to grow up some more.*

The child of Connie's imagery is one who we have encountered before, the part of her that represents her childhood pattern of trying to please others. She also holds herself responsible for everything that goes wrong in relationships. This pattern appears to create feelings of depression, rejection, guilt and shame; the core of which began during her dependent relationship with her brother and her encounter with the neighbor boy.

The strategy of this session was to help Connie's inner child understand that what has happened in the outer world is not her responsibility and that she needs to return to her child world, to play and to grow in a more positive way. I asked to talk with the child directly because I thought that it might be beneficial for her to have a more personal contact with a loving father figure who would love her and not hurt her.

The therapeutic principle involved is to relieve the inner-child from responsibility for absorbing any of the emotional or physical pain related to a given conflict. It is important to emphasize that the adult personality is strong enough to respond effectively to each life situation. Interestingly enough, certain life situations which bring to the surface vulnerabilities to anger, aggression, rejection, etc., such as Connie's encounter with her vindictive neighbor seem to draw given inner children forward to respond and absorb the related emotional upheavals. This is to say that each inner-child seems to be highly specialized in their response to given situations.

When Connie had called me to ask for an additional imagery session, it was apparently the child prompting her to call for help. Since Connie was consciously aware of having made the phone call it would not have been considered a full dissociation on her part. This suggests trusting in a man the child perceived as a helper rather than an abuser.

However, it also indicates a lack of confidence in the adult personality to handle a difficult emotional situation.

    The child is finally given over to the angel and is presumably returned to a protected and secure childhood state. Perhaps Connie's wish not to respond childishly to the stressful situation with her former neighbor will free her to explore more adult ways of facing the hurtful emotions and dealing with the gossiping woman.

PART 23
The Angry Child and the Little Baby

Connie had another imagery session the following day due to the intense emotions of depression and anger. During this session there appeared to be a different inner-child, a little girl who apparently was brought forward to help respond to and absorb Connie's anger toward the gossiping neighbor.

Interestingly, over a period of a few weeks, Connie has been seeing the image of a new-born baby. This baby has emerged several times in dreams and in her meditation. It is suggested that she look for this baby and explore what it might represent for her. It seems significant that this baby is healthy and undamaged.

Connie begins the session with, *I see that person I've been angry with, that one that I was just telling you about. I see her face. I get real confused with her. It's like getting mixed messages because one minute she's real nice and the next minute she's real arrogant. I think it's the child in me that gets real confused because the child responds with anger, wanting her to like me and then hating her the next minute.*

It is noted that this child is a different child than the one who surfaced during the last session with feelings of guilt, shame and in a depressed state. The primary emotion regarding this child is anger. Connie says, *I still have trouble with the anger while letting her, it's like I don't want to look at her or anything*. She is encouraged to face her anger, the anger within herself which emerges as a little child who is *really mean looking*. It is suggested that she approach the child and ask her why she is so angry. Connie indicates that *she is angry because she feels defenseless*.

Next, Connie is asked to enter into a dialogue with the angry child and tell her that she understands how she feels but that her anger makes it difficult for her to respond to people like the arrogant neighbor. She tells the child that she is an adult now and is developing the capacity to deal with such people. The strategy, similar to that in the previous session, is to convince this child that Connie is an adult who can handle difficult situations with others. She no longer needs the child's help with issues of anger. Rather it is time to go and play with other children and to have fun like children are supposed to have.

It appears that a child of the previous session comes with the angel to take the angry child away. Connie describes the imagery; *I see her coming with the angel. It's like she has one hand in the angel's hand and reaching out to the angry one. I feel like a light sensation here when she's going with the angel.*

Connie is then asked to locate the little baby who she has been seeing in her dreams and imagery of the past week. *I see it*, she says. It appears that this baby is healthy and without any damage. She is told that this beautiful little baby is her, a rebirth of herself, a part of herself who is healthy and will bring a more positive sense of growth to her life. As the baby grows, Connie will gain more psychological and emotional strength and will be able to view and relate to others in a more positive growth-oriented way. Connie responds, *hum, it's amazing that it's like this is all still happening. That baby is still alive. Do you know what I mean?* Apparently, she finds it difficult to understand that such a healthy, growing baby can exist within herself given all the inner and outer turmoil in her life. She continues, *there is nothing they can do to hurt me. It feels real comforting to hold her. Uh hum, she's not an infant anymore. She's really beautiful and innocent. To nurture her is like nurturing myself or nurturing the baby in me. I just got a flash too, of children with the angel, and they're waving goodbye.*

Connie's confrontation with her neighbor brought to the surface a second child, an angry child. The child's angry response, which threatened to overwhelm Connie at times, seems to be related to feeling defenseless when confronted with such negative, arrogant people. It seems that this child is related to the child of the previous session who had been released to the light. Hence, I suggested that the child of the light come with the angel to take the angry child to the healing light. It is sometimes helpful to have such children come and show the other, "damaged" child the way.

In this imagery session Connie refers to a newborn baby, who had appeared in her dreams and meditation during the past few weeks. Presumably, this represents the birth of a new aspect of herself and her growth, similar to the "divine child" (15) who symbolizes a higher level of love. The reader may recall that this particular child appeared during the time when she was trying to resolve her relationship with her parents and the issues surrounding her marriage and children. This birth seems to have led to a more transcendent perspective with regards to such relationships and a deeper understanding of the people involved. It is assumed then, that this new baby will serve a similar function in Connie's future.

It should be noted that the emergence of newborn babies in one's imagery suggests that progress is being made in the therapy process. These inner babies are not damaged from previous life experiences and represent a healthy change and development in the personality. Interestingly, newborn inner children are often observed progressing through normal developmental stages, but this progression is quite accelerated such that they often grow to mature adulthood in a matter of months. Further, it has been observed that damaged inner children may begin to regress and become infants who presumably return to the psychic womb to be reborn. This rebirth constitutes a transformation of the damaged aspects of the self through the process of rebirth. The child then begins its life anew, but within the context of a much healthier atmosphere. It is assumed that many of the newborn babies of the unconscious are the result of this phenomenon. However, the "divine child" is thought to be a result of a union between the "Supra-Consciousness" and the human side of the self. It often represents the introduction of new patterns, traits, ideas, and creative potentials into consciousness.

It is my impression that Connie's divine child may represent her ability to be a nurturing mother. It seems that she is being given the task of nurturing her newly emerging healthy, undamaged self as symbolized by the growing baby. It might also be assumed that as she learns how to nurture and mother herself, she will be able to apply this capacity to her own children. At any rate, since she has a brief image of her inner children saying goodbye to her, we sense that the healthy child is there to take the place of the inner children with whom we have been working during past imagery sessions. Presumably, they are in the process of healing and being integrated within the greater system since they will no longer be needed as mechanisms of defense.

PART 24
A Celebration - Transformation

Having integrated the inner children of the past few sessions, it appears that Connie is ready to make some specific decisions regarding a new direction in her life. She is still in the process of divorcing her husband and the door remains open for her to return to him. Her husband has been on his good behavior most of the time, and she is beginning to fall into hoping that he might have actually changed. This hope coupled with loneliness, has drawn her toward the love side of their love/hate relationship. However, it seems that she is able to see through her desire to return to her husband. Hence, she realizes that she would be, after all, returning to the same abusive situation of the past.

Connie begins the session saying, *I can feel my higher self above me, my head. It's pouring light into the crown of my head. It was doing that last night too, when I was doing Yoga. The presence of my angel. It feels good to feel the pure energy again because it's been gone for a while. It got lost in the pain.* Then she indicates that, *I see Ted's face, my husband. The anger is gone from between us. Although there is this feeling of love with him again that I thought would be gone forever, it sometimes hurts. My heart opens when I see his face. It's like warmth and a glow around my heart, but it feels sad too. It's like part of me wants to hold onto him again. My angel is telling me that I need to let him go with the angel, with the Light.*

It was suggested that Connie could feel love for her husband so long as she was not being dominated by him. This is to say that when she is free from her husband as the abuser, she can step back and see him in ways that she could not have seen him before. However, when her life was drained by an abusive situation, she had to fight for her existence. Hence, her perception was based on the narrow issues of survival and not on a broader view of the whole relationship.

Connie continues, *I don't think I've ever felt towards him like I feel now. It is a different kind of love. It's, there's this warmth, this energy that's different from him. When we are together when we're talking or whatever. It's hard to explain.*

Connie later experiences an interesting imagery. This imagery is consistent with her background with Eastern traditions, meditation and Yoga. She says, *I'm seeing images of Lord Shiva. He's an Indian symbol of God. An image keeps coming to me over the last couple of days. What's coming now is that I'm walking up to Lord Shiva with my aspirin and giving it to him, giving him the bottle. What's coming to me is that I just need to let that image happen and not worry about it. It's not punishing myself, just let myself go, even the part of me that takes aspirin. Now, I can see Lord Shiva touching your head and smiling at you. You know how you talked about a celebration, where there's like a transformation* (yes) *That's what I'm feeling now, of lights, of an energy change within me.*

It appears that Connie is coming to face a former pattern in which her husband begins to treat her nicely until her anger melts away and she feels love for him. His mixed signals are similar to those manifested by her neighbor which had upset her so much during previous sessions. Perhaps her encounter with this woman, along with subsequent imagery of two depressed and angry inner children, was good preparation for dealing with her husband and breaking the cycle of her self-defeating patterns.

Next, we find that Connie surprisingly shifts from imagery concerning her husband to an image of an Indian symbol of God, Lord Shiva. This imagery apparently emerged from her work with Yoga and meditation. Its introduction at this moment would seem to be a significant symbol to consider since Shiva may represent the destruction of her negative thought patterns, emotional responses, experiences, addictive behavior and abusive relationships of the past. Interestingly, Shiva's destruction always leads to transformation and rebirth which Connie evidently celebrates in this session. (16)

Whether our assumptions about the meaning of Connie's imagery of Shiva are actually true, she none the less had arrived to a point in therapy when a transformation of at least some of her negative childhood experiences has occurred. It will be interesting to observe whether such transformations might affect her behavior regarding her relationships with men.

PART 25
A Time for a Decision

This imagery session seems to be an extension of the previous one. It appears that Connie is coming to a critical decision regarding her relationship with her husband.

Connie experiences *a brilliant light again, but the light was, was also above my head. I can feel the presence of my angel. Is it OK if I ask if we can approach a certain issue or should I just let it happen?* She is told to go ahead and ask for what she wants and to "just let it happen, too." She continues, *there is nothing happening yet I'll tell you what the question was. It concerns Ted and me. It's that I have felt a different kind of hurt over the relationship lately. Before, I was real angry with him and it was easy to stay away from him. I avoided him. But now I'm not angry anymore, and I'm feeling a loss again. I think it is about craving to be with him, to have that part of my life filled, to have a relationship.*

I ask Connie if she thought it would become any different than it was before. She responds, *no, and I know that. So, I don't want to go back with him. Yet, I'm still having trouble letting go.* We explore the idea that she needs to let go of her husband, and that until she lets go of him, she will not be able to find other ways to fill the void that she feels. She responds that, *I was thinking that today. It reaffirms what the angel was telling me earlier. I guess the question to the angel then is how do I let go. It's like on a different level.*

I suggest that, "it is a matter of doing things on behalf of your own life. You see, it's a cooperative relationship with your own life. For a moment, take your life to be bigger than you are, to be the most important thing in the world to you. You love, you love life, you love your life, and you want to have it be the best that it can be, to be fulfilled in the best way that it can be. Try to want that very badly. Try to move into a position where you can fulfill your own life. You see, it's a different perspective now. So with Ted you know that if you go back with him things would probably not change. It would be the same thing. The necessity, it seems to me, is to walk away. You can be sad about it and wish it would be otherwise, but I don't think it would in any way fulfilling to your own life."

Connie responds, *yes, I definitely agree with that. I know intellectually that it would be more fulfilling to stay away from him. I know there is a decision lingering again. Well, I've been praying about it, but my prayers aren't, don't seem like they're manifesting anything.* It is suggested that she let her prayers be manifested in what she does. She says that, *I can feel the brightness of my angel right now, like it's agreeing with everything you're saying.* I continue to share my thoughts, "I have a funny notion of prayers. Every time you move on behalf of something or someone it's as if a prayer is lifted up. Living on behalf of your life is a prayer that carries direction." Connie wonders, *what could I do to speed up my process? It's like the answer comes as soon as I ask the question. It's just the answer is quit hanging on, just do it. And Ted is not going to make any headway in life in the relationship. In a sense I'm moving back in, in a real subtle way, to the same old crap I was in before. But when he starts treating me nice then I think, you know, I want to be around*

212

him again. Then I get mixed up with him again. It's the same nightmare over again. So, it's me that hasn't made the final decision.

Connie continues, *how to release Ted? I guess I've been hanging on to my mom and that's real subtle, too. I see myself and that image has been coming to me. It's like, you know, how I get images of a child all the time? This time it's an adult that's coming, and she's been coming to me for about, I don't know, five days, often. But it is who I am now. What I am moved to do when she comes around is just hold her and love her, and accept her no matter what.* It is suggested that she is dealing with the present now instead of the past which has been the focus of previous sessions. She concurs, *yes, that is, that must be why, that myself is coming to me as I am now. It's like right now needs attention.*

Connie came to this imagery session with a fairly clear question regarding her relationship with her husband. It would appear as though the direction of her life is now in her own hands and all that is left for her to do is to choose. The struggle seems to be centered on what she now knows, versus her old cycle of feelings and thoughts. Much therapeutic work has been completed as preparation for this moment of choice. Connie has developed the insight and knowledge needed to make healthy choices in her life. However, she must test the validity of her new insight and knowledge by taking action. This is to say, one must experience externally what one has learned internally or one cannot know its full validity. To take action in this case requires conscious choice, whereas Connie's past choices were governed by unconscious factors such as dependent needs and addictive compulsions. This gave the appearance that her life was totally controlled by outside forces.

Connie has come to realize that if she continues her dependent relationship with her husband she cannot move forward with her life. She needs to let go before the void she feels can be filled in more healthy ways. Typically, she experiences high anxiety during moments of change and growth, when she lets go of a particular belief or pattern without knowing what to expect. Hence, growth often becomes an act of faith. It is also an act of taking responsibility for one's own life and the direction of its growth. For one like Connie, who has spent her life in total dependence, responsible choice can be especially difficult and anxiety-ridden. It is for this reason that I suggest that Connie begin to think on behalf of her own life, as if it were a growing child for whom she is responsible.

Connie's realizes that returning to her marriage would be damaging not only for herself, but also for her husband. This suggests that she has developed beyond her own dependent needs. She is one who is now able to nurture herself and others rather than being absorbed in her own dependent issues.

The image of the adult self who has been appearing to Connie for the past week, seems significant. It seems that her remaining immature feelings of dependence are holding her back from a clear decision regarding her marriage. Perhaps by accepting this adult part of herself, she will be in a better position to make more responsible adult choices on her own behalf.

Connie's imagery of the past two sessions gives the strong impression that she is working through a decision concerning whether to return to her marriage or take charge of her own life and its direction. Whether an actual decision was made during this imagery session is not known. However, she finally completed the divorce proceedings and did not return to her husband. To be sure, she seems to be taking charge of her own life and starting in a direction that is more fitting to creating a new and more healthy life for herself.

PART 26
A Christ Experience

The reader will recall earlier that Connie had had an experience where she saw an image of "Christ," in which she seemed to melt into the Christ light. It was as if both of them were the same but "separate at the same time." In this imagery session she has a second experience with the Christ archetype.

Connie says, *I'm in front of the cross. It seems like the reason I'm in front of the cross is because I'm serving Christ at this time. It makes me have; it makes me feel like I have some kind of purpose in mind. I just realized that. If I'm looking for purpose then it's here. So, like I've always hated the word Jesus Christ because of the religion that I've had all of my life, bad experiences, and now it feels good to, to be connected with him, the Christ within. I can see him standing before me now and he's resurrected. He's taking me by the hand. You wouldn't believe the angels that are around him. He's taking me to a friend of mine. Actually, it's my Yoga teacher. I can see, it's like another part of me that's with her. It's like both of us are at odds. There's a part of me that I avoid, takes over. What I see is him bringing her out of hiding. She keeps trying to hide. He's taking her by the hand. She's burning up inside with pain, but I don't feel that in me right now. I'm watching her. I'm feeling now, a lot of light as Christ is nurturing her. Now, I'm touching her. There's a lot of light exploding in me. It's like releasing her, freeing myself. It's freeing me. I see her going with the angel. Christ is giving her to the angel right now and my heart feels like there's a lot of light and love in it.*

Having had some difficult experiences in her past with organized religion Connie had come to hate *the word "Jesus Christ,"* probably because she had felt condemned by those in the religious community. Now it appears that she is coming to a resolution of those past experiences. This is to say that she seems to be separating the essence of Christianity from organized religion and is presumably putting herself in the service of it.

It is interesting to note that it is the Resurrected Christ that Connie sees in her imagery. While the cross may represent suffering and death, the resurrection is a symbol of rebirth and a renewal of life.(17) (18) Perhaps the cross represents her own suffering and the death of her negative past, especially in terms of her abusive husband. Also, she may have unconsciously perceived her suffering as a form of atonement which allows her to return to Christ as a resurrected Soul. Such themes also seem consistent with her imagery of Shiva, the Hindu god of destruction and rebirth.

At any rate, we assume that Connie's Christian imagery is an indication that she has undergone significant growth. Her decision not to return to her husband means that she has chosen a new and more positive direction in her life. Thus, it seems that she has found herself worthy of Christ through suffering, which is a Christian concept. The Christ represents life and love, which she had once thought unattainable, as she had apparently felt unworthy of being loved even by God. To be sure, such feelings were undoubtedly reinforced by the religious community.

Christ taking Connie to her Yoga teacher seems to mean that having been rejected by the Christian community, she had sought other avenues to love and acceptance. However, there seems to have been conflict between her and her Yoga teacher. Perhaps there is a part of herself that has been hiding within the context of the Yoga tradition. This part of her is burning inside. We assume the burning relates to her feelings of anger over being condemned by the religious community. That Christ would come to get this part of her and nurture it is a symbol to her that such condemnation did not come from God, but rather from humanity.

This resolution of her past negative experiences with organized religion appeared to help Connie come to a turning point in her therapy. She seems to have turned away from the negative, self-destructive aspects of her past. We see this represented in the symbols of the cross and the resurrected Christ and previously in the image of the Hindu god, Shiva.

PART 27
A New Relationship

Connie, having shut the door to her abusive relationship with her husband, is now open to new and presumably more healthy relationships with men. In the session below we find that she has recently met a man who is appealing to her and who seems to be a kind and gentle man.

Connie says, *you're smiling. It looks like I'm going for a walk with you and the angel. You're taking me to my child. It's the one who's smiling and you put my hand in hers. It's like it's good to be with her in this way. She's smiling rather than hurting. I don't feel like I have to battle with her anymore. She's going to be OK. She is OK and this new man that I met is here. I'm like watching the child with him. I guess I'm feeling afraid, not the child but me.* When asked why she is afraid she responds, *I'm afraid of the sexual feelings that I have towards him.*

It is suggested that such feelings are natural especially if this man is attractive and is a nice man who is not abusive. Connie indicates that, *he treats me real good.* Further, she comments that *my child is sure excited.* She is asked why the child seems so excited and if she knows this man. She responds that, *yes, she knows him. She's real excited to see him again. What keeps coming is that he was her father in another life. I can see him and me. We are kneeling together at a fire but it was when I was not a child anymore.* Moreover, Connie begins to feel that this imagery seems to be telling her that it is all right to have a relationship with this man. She says, *I've been feeling like it's the go ahead or telling me it's OK. I still see, maybe it's not myself, it's like an older person who's with him and the Master is there, too. It was me when I was older in another lifetime, I think. I see Christ as like blessing us, and you're there again smiling.*

Connie's abusive relationship with her husband and other men has caused her to be cautious regarding relationships with men. However, she has met a man for whom she has developed feelings who she is not sure she can trust. It appears that she is about to enter into a new relationship which promises to go beyond friendship and this is frightening for her. It also appears that this relationship has roots in the Collective Consciousness. The problem for her appears to be that one of her inner children seems to want to jump into the relationship while Connie feels the need to be cautious and take things more slowly.

PART 28
Integration of the Affectionate Child

This imagery session seems to be an extension of the previous one. During the past week, Connie has had to "stifle" the excitement of the child in order to act appropriately toward her new friend.

With regards to the child Connie says, *I can see her. I feel like smiling too, but she's the one that smiles and gets all excited. I'm still feeling a lot of her you now, I have not separated myself from her. She's the one who is starved for affection, gets all excited. I've been trying to stifle her because when I feel that emerging in me, I get afraid of it, so I push it back down. I try to hide it. I don't want it to be obvious that I'm excited to see him. And she does not want to go. She doesn't want to. What's coming to me is that she's waited a long time for that kind of affection especially from someone who she thinks is so intelligent and someone who acts like her father. For me to tell her to go away and not be there is real hard for her.*

It is suggested that Connie explain to her that this is an adult relationship and the need for affection and attention needs to be minimized. She responds that the child is asking *where she can go to get it. She is looking up at the angel and now I see her getting excited with the angel.* It is further indicated that if the child goes with the angel she will be going to a place where the one who is her father can visit her. Connie asks, *you mean she can go with him in that time when he was her father, go with him and the angel? The angel is getting brighter. I think that means yes.* I also respond, "yes, just as she exists, he also exists. She just lost touch with her father, but I think he is there now." *She's willing to go. She and the angel are holding hands and the angel is taking her to him. Sunshine, the angel, I always say the angel. Now I just see the angel. It's bright and now it's time to come back.*

Connie's new friendship has created a struggle for her as she tries to respond in more adult ways, while having to stifle the excitement of her inner-child. Since the child has come from the Collective Consciousness in response to this new relationship, I suggested that she might return to where that part of the man, in the outer world, might exist internally. With this idea brought forward for consideration the child seemed willing to go with the angel, where she could meet with her actual father.

The only thing that seems to be standing in Connie's way to a closer relationship is her own feeling that there is more work to be done regarding other unresolved issues in her life. She feels that it is not fair to this man to burden him with her own emotional problems. As we shall see after a few weeks of absence from imagery therapy, Connie begins another round of work which seems directly related to her teenage years.

PART 29
The Adolescent

It has been almost a month since Connie has had an imagery session. During this time she has been dating her new friend, Doug. Recently she had decided that she needed a break from him since she was feeling some emotional upheavals from within. She felt that she had to face these issues before resuming her relationship with Doug. Now, Connie finds that she needs to confront the addictive aspect of her personality.

She begins the session by saying, *it's been coming to me a lot lately. It's been there especially when I've been feeling at my limit. I think it's whenever I get confused or I'm hurting inside. I have been on my knees trying to let things happen. I can see Doug's face and he's feeling real sad too. I feel like I, even though I've broken away on a physical level, that he's pulling me towards him on a psychic level. It's been tough and my angel is here again telling me to take charge of my life. It's reaffirming what it said to me yesterday. My higher self sort of takes care of the ache inside and I think the ache is also that teenager. She's been coming forth. I can see her. She's real sad.*

It appears that when Connie starts to become sad and confused, she is drawn to start taking large quantities of aspirin. This is what she did during her teenage years to help numb the pain. When I point this out to her she responds, *yes, it's sort of a feeling. I think she* (the inner teenager) *has been real confused about that because someone treated her real well and for me to push that person away hurts her. I can even see her with a bottle of aspirin in her hands. It shuts off some of the energy and it also hurts her. It's like a way of punishing herself. Maybe it's because she doesn't like herself. She blames everything on herself. She started beating herself mentally and physically, taking pills or drugs or whatever.*

It is suggested that it may be time to change this way of thinking to which Connie says, *I'd like to. She's looking at the angel and the higher self both. I can see the higher self in her, too. It's the love in her and she's looking down. She sees the light within. She's going to let this light just absorb all the hurt. She looks better. She's smiling. To know that she has a lot of strength without the addictions is to be able to let go of them. I can feel a lot of light inside, too, and I'm going to take care of her like the other children. I've let the angel do it and the higher self. Now I am back with Doug again. His vibrations are so strong. I can't believe it. I'm telling her to go with the angel.*

Having resolved many of her earlier childhood issues, it seems time for Connie to face later difficulties surrounding her addictive behavior. While her personality has always been dependent, it was not until her late teenage years and the period following her automobile accident, that substance abuse and addiction became dominant.

During this session Connie makes contact with her inner-teenager. Moreover, during her relationship with Doug the teenager was feeling that her dependent needs were being met and the breakup was confusing for her. But Connie was responding to the dependence issue with Doug. She knew she could not enter into a long-term relationship under such conditions.

The inner teenager began to feel that she was to blame for what happened with Doug. This response, of course, was common during Connie's teenage years. It occurred especially when she was involved with abusive boyfriends and men.

To resolve the conflict, Connie's inner teenager is brought into contact with the light of the angel and the higher self. In the process, the teenager becomes aware of her capacity to love, represented by her own light within. Having had much experience with releasing damaged children of her childhood, Connie appears to follow the same process in dealing with this teenager.

It is suspected that other teenage and early adulthood parts of herself will emerge in Connie's imagery as representatives of the many facets of her addictive and dependent personality. It should be noted that she returned to Doug at the end of this session, as if to suggest a more permanent relationship with him, following her work with her dependence and addictions.

PART 30
Christ Consciousness and the Self-destructive Teenager

In the last session Connie became acutely aware of her teenage self and its connection to her addictions. During the intervening week Connie has been binging on cigarettes and food and has taken pills, apparently under the influence of her addictive inner teenager/teenagers.

Connie says, *the presence of the Master (Christ) is with me. It seems like he's with me more than my angel. My angel is always there, but I guess I'm more aware of the Master. It's like that is all that matters to me now is the Christ light. It's the light that's within me, too. It's the same thing. It feels like I'm coming home again. It feels good.*

Connie indicated that she has gotten back with her friend, Doug, and has been spending a lot of time with him. Further, she says, *I can also see the teenager within me. She's coming back now. She hasn't been. She came back the weekend I broke up with him. I think that's the one that smoked cigarettes, binged on cigarettes and food. I haven't had any encounters with her since things got settled down with him again, until just now. So, it's been my teenager that's reacting in an addictive way. I took some pills, too, that weekend. I've been writing this sentence over and over again; "I surrender all my addictions to Christ." It seems that they're being brought up more. I couldn't believe the pain I went through within a few days again. I was so tense and there it's gone again. It's amazing that it does go away because there's a part of me that believes that it's not ever going to go away.*

It was suggested that the teenager never took herself to be one who could be loved. Further, I encouraged Connie to ask the teenager, "who hates her?" *She seems confused. Maybe it's the emotions that keep running through her, thoughts that she can't quite put together, seeking to get a few moments of pleasure here and there."* Connie responds, *I think she's been listening to you. She's beginning to believe that she can grow with the Master. She's asking a question. It's, she wanted to release this addiction real bad and just has been confused and worried about my writing the mantra or the thing about addiction, her addiction. I don't know, this is getting confusing but you know what I mean. I think the fact that I made the decision about Doug and other stuff too, that gave me a lot of strength and she knows it.*

Next, Connie is encouraged to accept her inner teenager and not be judgmental or condemning toward her. Further, while she is not to judge her or be angry with her for her addictions, she should not let her take charge of her life. Instead it might be best to reach out to her like a mother would with a suffering child. Connie follows this suggestion and begins to cry, saying, *I can feel the heat leaving my body. It's so wonderful. Even though it's painful, she's ready to go now, with the Master. She wants some help. You're holding her and taking her there. She wanted you to be there with her. She trusts you. What's the link? I think she wanted a loving man, a loving father or just a loving male, I guess, to help her through with this because she never had it as a teenager. She's been watching you real closely and learned to trust you (laughs). My body feels much better.*

Connie's identification with the Master (Christ) has progressed to a deeper personal level. It appears that she is returning to her religious roots with a different perspective to resolve the self-destructive part of herself, personified in her inner teenagers. The primary emotion that appears to be associated with this teenager is the pain of self-hatred and the addictive response appears to be a way to gain some relief from such suffering.

The teenager seems to want to be released from her addictions. However, she appears confused about what will happen to her in the process. Her past week's attempts to take charge of Connie may have been due, in part, to her fear of change and growth. But Connie's decision to stay away from Doug until her dependent needs could be resolved seemed to bring her the strength needed to block the teenager from actually taking over. This act also brought her more strength and power to take control over her own life.

Before the teenager could be released, she needed Connie's love and acceptance. She could then feel more comfortable and trusting about being integrated within the larger system. Two additional factors also emerged in the process of integration. First, I the therapist, seem to have become a trusted loving father figure for the teenager. Second was the presence of Christ, another male figure representing divine love. It seems significant that the human father symbol would be a part of the process of giving the teenager over to the light. Perhaps even more significant is the fact that after having felt condemned and rejected by the religious community because of her anti-social behavior, she now returns to a deeper, more forgiving, loving and healing religious experience. However, it should be noted that this experience is not part of organized religion.

PART 31
The Clinging Teenager

Several weeks have passed since Connie has had an imagery session. During this time, it seems that another less self-condemning but more dependent teenager has surfaced in her consciousness and her clinging feels oppressive to Connie.

Connie begins, *I feel real heavy right now and it's real hard to respond to anything. I can see her now. She is clinging to me and draining all the energy out of me. She's like almost in a panic. She's afraid of being hurt. How can I keep her to stop being so afraid, afraid of just facing life?* It is suggested that Connie needs to be willing to face life on her own. This is to say that when she makes her own decisions and becomes more independent and self-sufficient, the inner teenager will feel free to go.

Connie responds, *I feel like she's tired of me too. There are cords, the Karmic cords or whatever.* The angel appears and the teenager is encouraged to go with the angel. *She's resisting*, Connie says. *I have never had this much resistance, I'll tell you.* It seems that there is quite an attachment between her and the clinging teenager. Similar to the other teenager, she takes aspirin and pills to relieve the pain. However, she is told to consider that while this form of escape relieves the pain for while it is only temporary. Again, Connie is encouraged to release the teenager so she can start her life anew and start growing up. Connie expresses an insight, *I guess the reason why is because I'm real afraid to let her go. Because, there's a grieving that goes with it. And it's like an emptiness.* She is reminded of other children who have been released and who have come back healthy, happy and whole and that is what she needs to want for this teenager. She agrees, *yes, and I'll be really loving her if I release her. Ok, I see her with Christ rather than the angel, with the Master. I can feel myself getting a little more energy. I feel like I'm letting go. I feel a little light right here. I can see her going now.*

It appears that this part of Connie represents two characteristics. First is her feeling of being dependent on others. Second is her tendency to escape into substance abuse when faced with the loss of significant others.

Surprisingly, Connie is reluctant to let this teenager go, apparently because this inner self is still an integral part of her personality. To give up this teenager is to give up a very important part of her own personal mode of survival. Presumably the task of this teenager was to absorb the fear and panic associated with a loss of dependent relationships. By assuming a self-sufficient role Connie shows her capacity to face life as an adult. She has already demonstrated this potential by her decision concerning her friend, Doug.

After it appears that Connie's potential for self-sufficiency had been established, she sees the teenager with Christ, the archetypal symbol of love and healing. This is a sign that the teenager is ready to be released for integration within the greater system. It is clear that we have processed and healed much of her early childhood and now we are processing her difficult teenage years.

PART 32
The Depressed Teenager

Doug took Connie to his parent's home where she experienced some phobic reactions, especially the inability to urinate and the fear of eating in front of his parents. It is not certain whether a different aspect of Connie's inner-teenager has surfaced or whether this is a different identity altogether. For therapeutic purposes a specific differentiation is unnecessary beyond a recognition that we are dealing with her adolescent fears, sadness and depression.

Connie begins the session, *it seems like lately I've been spending more time with the Master than I have with the angel, but it's back again. It was always there. I'm just not aware of it or something. Today it has wings and some form to it rather than just being light. It wants me to fly with it somewhere so I'm going to go. It's taking me back to the teenager again. She looks so passive and so sad. It's just that she's been sad. She doesn't know how it is not to be sad. I'm feeling compassion for her today. Sometimes I get real angry with her because she hangs around and it seems like she's always tugging at me and haunting, almost like a little kid who I want to be free of. She won't let go but I'm not feeling that today. I'm feeling more compassion for her.*

It appears that this teenager looks for anything to bring her out of her sadness, such as chemical substances and alcohol. Connie continues, *yes, anything that would bring her out of the sadness, fatigue too. She's really tired, lethargic and depressed.* Further, it seems clear that this is one of the primary basis for her addictions. She agrees, *yes, it seems like it. It seems like a long process of dealing with her, with the addiction. The progress is real slow and I think that's part of my anger with the teenager.* Connie seems to realize that she has been trying to push this teenager away. However, she has not been successful in doing this. She says, *there were times last week when she came on so strong and I got real tired of struggling with her. It was almost as though I was ready to let her come back and take over again. I guess it's just easier to do that sometimes.*

Connie appears to be feeling tired over the struggles she has been having with this teenager and her addictions. It was especially difficult when she was visiting with Doug's parents. She indicates that *a lot of fears came up when I was at Doug's parents' house. A lot of teenage stuff came up again for me, and I've been in awe of her coming back, the images of her, this whole process.* It was suggested that she convey to her teenager that not all families are the same. Some families are healthy and not dysfunctional. This is to say that her own experience in family situations cannot be used to define all families. Her experiences are of the past and not of the present.

I really have images of us separating more and more, says Connie. *You know, there still are connections, but it's a lot less than what it was*. It has become clear that the teenager is no longer needed to help Connie deal with unhealthy, abusive family situations. Since she is no longer in those kinds of situations in which there was a lot of pain and suffering, she does not need to take aspirin, drugs or alcohol. Hence, it is time for the teenager to be released to the light where she can be happy and without pain.

When asked if the teenager is ready to go, Connie responds, *yes she does. She can hardly believe that that could ever happen to her, though. She wants that. Yes, I have been wondering. It just hit me, too, that if every time I take an aspirin, I keep her hanging on, feeling her.* It was noted that the teenager helped her survive a very difficult time in her life. Further, it was suggested that she love her and feel compassion for her because she absorbed a lot of the pain and suffering during her teenage years. Then Connie says, *and, I need to accept her.*

Connie makes the observation that, *she's (teenager) just frozen with fear. It's incredible. I can see you with her now and what you're saying to her in the physical world is what you're saying to her in the other world too, in her world. When you are with her it comforts her, too. It helps her. I can feel the release of energy in me as she lets go of me a little bit. I think she's beginning to trust you more and more. Yes, to her it is almost like dying. I think to me it is too, to let her go because sometimes I blame it on her, what I'm going through. It's really amazing to watch you with her in the imagery world. It helps me to separate from her. I think you're going to take her on a walk now. You're walking towards the light.*

The teenager of Connie's Collective Consciousness appears to represent the passive, tired, lethargic and depressed state of her adolescent years. It seems clear that the task of this part of her personality was to absorb the sadness and depression of this painful time of her life.

By this time in Connie's therapy she is able to see the light at the end of the tunnel. She is becoming anxious to move on to the caring relationships of her future. Having already dealt with her early childhood experiences, she seems to be feeling some anger and resentment toward these emergent teenagers who represent the suffering of her adolescence.

Clinical experience tells us that this is a common feeling, especially after about a year of very painful and difficult work. Fortunately, once Connie gained some positive growth experiences from her work in therapy and sees the potential for a healthy creative life, she has little difficulty getting back on track with little need for encouragement. Unfortunately, many clients become discouraged with all the difficult and painful work. Often they abandon imagery therapy right when they are about to reach the summit, where the work becomes easier with more dynamic growth experiences. To be sure, this kind of therapy requires a good deal of courage and determined persistence.

It seems clear that Connie's phobic symptoms were tied to feelings of worthlessness and especially the fear of rejection that she often felt during adolescence. Her recent experience with a loving and caring family helped her understand that her own dysfunctional family was not the norm.

Another interesting theme in the process of releasing these adolescent parts of herself is my presence in her imagery. I seem to be a part of the process both externally and internally. I appear to be projected into her imagery to help develop a sense of trust needed to complete the integration phase, "walking into the light."

PART 33
The Teenager of Loneliness, Isolation and Rejection

This imagery session appears to be a continuation of Connie's work with her painful adolescence. Each inner teenager with whom we have worked has been related to the dependence and addiction issues of her life. Each one seems specific in its capacity to absorb a particular emotional response to given painful situations.

With regards to the next teenager who emerges in Connie's imagery she says, *she's standing right in front of me looking at me. She wants to go back to the school and re-experience that stuff just real fast like. I can feel a blackness come over me as I walk up to the school. There's so much negative energy there. She is looking at everyone who was there, who were significant. There was this one girl that gave her a real hard time, just made it miserable for her for three-four years. She let her do it until, until one day the teenager got so angry that she couldn't contain the anger anymore. She got the other girl in the bathroom and took her by the shirt and told her to shut up. She was calling her a whore and after that the girl left her alone.*

Connie continues, *God, she is just in so much pain. It is unbelievable. I remember that. I used to, I used to crack my bones because it felt good. I used to crack my arms and my knuckles and I think it must have relieved some of the pain. And my mom got real mad at me. Yes, she told me I looked like I was retarded. She took a belt and she (crying) tied it around my arms so I couldn't move. I forgot about that. And the pain is still there, the pain of loneliness, of isolation, of rejection. I think I know the aspirin I took started taking the edge off of it because I abused it right from the beginning. It was an expression, well not an expression but like you said it numbed me because I couldn't express the pain.*

Realizing that Connie is in a painful state reliving certain experiences of her adolescence, I asked her if the teenager needs to show her anything else or if she is in need of a rest. (Crying) She continues the imagery with the teenager. She says, *I just told her that I would be a channel for the pain and she could let it come through me. She could release it through me. There were the other ways to release the pain. I started writing on myself with razor blades. I think I told you that. And there was grandfather's booze when he moved in with us and we got other people to buy it for us. Doing something real rebellious and exciting would help to take away the pain. But it made more pain. I'm asking her if there's more of it. Oh, I just can feel some of what she went through. It was really a nightmare. I'm just sort of talking to her now.*

We follow a similar process as was followed with previous teenagers. The purpose of the process is to release the teenager to the light where she can become healed of her painful experiences. She is told that she is loved for helping Connie deal with the pain and suffering of her difficult adolescent years. She is told that we do not want her to suffer any longer and that Connie is strong enough now to manage her life on her own. In response Connie says, *I think she feels for the first time that somebody cares about her, you and me. Doug is here, too. She's looking at him though he doesn't fully understand. She trusts him, too, and that is unusual, and she trusts you*. She is told the reason that we relive the past is so that we can let it go, put the past in the past. What is unresolved in the past remains in the present until it becomes resolved. Hence, one remains trapped in the past until it can become resolved. With regard to the past, Connie continues, *she put herself into situations where she could be abused sexually, many times and there's a great deal of hurt with men. It made her sick, it just. The angel is here now. I think it's time for her to go back with the angel. The angel is showing her again the innocent baby that is the child. She's holding the child in her arms. I can feel a lot of light inside as she does that*. In doing this the teenager becomes aware of her own capacity to love and care.

It appears that another aspect of Connie's adolescence has emerged. As part of the process of resolution she takes the teenager back to her old school. One significant experience was her fight with the other girl. This seems to be the first time she had stood up for herself.

The pain of isolation and rejection was so great that she sought artificial means by which her suffering might be alleviated, such as alcohol, aspirin, "cracking her bones", and cutting herself with a razor blade. Further, sexual promiscuity would probably be among those exciting behaviors. However, what felt good to her was only temporary and led to further feelings of worthlessness, loneliness and isolation. These insights may help us to comprehend why many teenagers seem drawn toward similar behaviors. It might also help explain why sex education may not help in reducing certain instances of sexual promiscuity since it does not reach such girls at the level of their deeper suffering.

In the resolution of Connie's teenage selves, we experience some consistent themes. The major elements of healing, growth and change seem to be; (1) reliving painful experiences, including the emotions connected with them, (2) understanding the experiences objectively and without judgment, (3) gaining acceptance of oneself and significant others, (4) loving oneself and being loved unconditionally. Hence these elements, when present, seem to provide the conditions for the release and integration of these transpersonal parts of the self. It might be noted that elements one and two are especially important because of the need to place the experience in the past. In many cases painful past experiences are repressed and not part of one's Ego consciousness. One cannot face what one does not know. Moreover, when such repressed material is brought into Ego consciousness it is done at a time when the person has developed a greater cognitive ability and the ability to develop deeper insight into the painful experiences. This combined with accepting oneself without judgment or expectation is very important to releasing these inner parts of oneself to the divine, healing light.

At the end of this session a little baby is brought forward for the teenager to hold. This innocent baby seems to be the one who has just surfaced in Connie's imagery over the past few weeks. Holding the baby appears to bring out the teenager's own capacity to love and care for another, which is also Connie's own capacity for love and care. I hypothesize that this child represents a rebirth and transformation of her adolescent years. Presumably, as it grows in healthy ways it will provide Connie with a sense of a more natural adolescent development, despite her painful teenage experiences.

PART 34
The Integration of the Teenager and Connie's relationship with Doug

It appears that Connie may be coming toward the end of facing her very painful teenage years. This seems to open the door to a more enduring relationship with Doug. This session starts with Connie seeing Doug's face. *He's here. He's taking one hand and the angel is taking the other hand. I can see the teenager. We're walking up to her and I can see the light in her, too, the light within. I think she is going to be OK. She feels more distant now. I don't feel like she's holding on to me. I can feel that she's really separated or I've separated both, whatever. She's thanking you for being patient with her, for loving her and accepting her. She's actually excited now to go. She's not afraid or distrustful anymore. She's real excited to go. She's telling me to stay with Doug, that she won't interfere anymore. I feel such a relief. She went with the Master and Doug isstanding in front of me now. I can see a light within him. It's like his higher Self. You know, I'm having that light experience with my arm again, and I haven't had that for a while. It's been gone. I feel like touching Doug's face and blessing him. I can see you there, too. I can see us in Doug's home now. I've sort of resisted being there. It's like I'm sort of afraid to settle into it. I think maybe I'm going to get comfortable now. The home has light in it, too. It's like the core of the house and I'm, I guess I'm just feeling the light, the vibrations of the light in the home. It feels comfortable, too.*

Connie continues, *we're going to go for a ride on horses or something. It's like a ride through the woods. It seems like the angel is there and the Master is there. They're blessing us, our relationship. I can see Mary, too, all of a sudden. I don't know why she's there.* (Mary is a friend who is having to deal with her own painful, difficult past). *It's just good to be with her again. I haven't seen her, been with her, even in imagery. We're by a pond in the woods and it's really beautiful. Mary is there and she does look sort of sad, and we're hugging. I think we're going to ride back out of the woods now on the horses again. We're going to Doug's house.*

The teenager of the previous session appears ready to be released. As the teenager goes with the "Master," Connie seems to begin an internal process of committing herself to a relationship with Doug. Previously she was reluctant to become too deeply involved with him until her dependency issues had been resolved. Even though she had just moved in with him, a difficult decision for her to make, there remained a hesitancy on her part.

This imagery session appears to suggest that Connie may be moving away from her past toward issues of the present and future. For example, the adjustment to living with Doug and becoming comfortable in his home, is a present consideration for now.

Connie seems to be freer now to be with Doug as symbolized in her imagery, by taking a horseback ride through the woods together. This activity may be a "redoing" of an earlier imagery experience when she was riding a horse behind an abusive man. Riding together on separate horses might suggest a more mutual and individually self-sufficient relationship in her life. Since the woods are frequently found to be a symbol of the Collective Consciousness it would appear, she is now comfortable to share the deeper levels of her life with Doug. Moreover, since they received the blessing of both the "Master" and the angel, it might be concluded that she is to perceive their relationship as one "made in heaven."

   An interesting ending to Connie's imagery session is the sudden emergence of Mary, one of her friends. She seems very sad as they meet in the woods near a pond. A pond of water as a symbol of the unconscious and spirituality would also be a fitting symbol of Mary's personality. Whereas Connie's ordeal and suffering may be slowly coming to an end, it is suggested that Mary's future may hold some painful experiences for her. The only reason we can speak in such terms is that a few years have passed since this imagery session occurred and we have knowledge of what has since transpired in both their lives. It is pleasing to note that Mary's painful therapeutic journey, like Connie's, came to a positive conclusion.

PART 35
A Rebirth Experience

Typically, this imagery session seems to be an extension of the previous session. Connie's imagery appears to support her decision to move in with Doug. It is suggested that she continue with their marriage plans. Of great significance also is her apparent birth experience. This time, instead of giving birth to an innocent baby, she is the baby being born.

There's like an opening into another world, says Connie. *There's a lot of brightness there. It's funny, there's a lot of blackness on this side of the eye but looking through the eye there is a lot of brightness in a new world. Now, I'm seeing this Indian saint. He's a saint that passed on. I'm seeing his face, and we're going to walk into a light together. The light is brilliant. It's just, almost, it's more brilliant than what my eyes can stand. He's saying to look through this other eye. Doug is there. I am seeing our wedding again. It's like a marriage, a union, and I'm feeling once again trust for him. It's almost like I'm being shown that I can trust him and he's going to treat me good and it's OK. Everything that I'm doing, moving out of my apartment, moving in with him, is all OK. He's smiling at me. He's just such a glorious person to be around. Now I'm seeing that child again, in that kneeling position with her head tucked between my legs.* It is observed that the child is growing and it is assumed that the child is what Connie is becoming.

Connie observes herself in the kneeling position. She indicates that, *it's like a part of me is in complete surrender in that position and I'm real helpless and yet there's nothing that can hurt me either. The cocoon around me is part of that protection and the Christ light that I'm seeing. Whenever this happens, I feel, again, that it's a letting go of my body, of worry and letting go of all the old stuff. I feel that instead of watching the child I am that child now and that I am in the cocoon and I'm being healed as I'm in there.* It is further suggested that the cocoon may be symbolic of the womb and that it is like a rebirth of her.

Connie responds, *and something is placing flowers around me. What keeps coming to me is that I'm in for a real positive lifetime ahead of me. Not that I won't have my trials but maybe the rebirthing is letting go of all the suffering, the constant suffering.* It appears that with the rebirth of herself she is able to see the potentiality of her future as a positive, creative person, one who is capable of helping others heal their own lives. She continues, *part of my future is that light experience in my right arm, that's coming back again. It goes and comes. When it goes away, people don't ask for help but when it comes back, people just come and ask for help. It's really weird. I don't have to look for anyone but they come around. It looks like I'm going to come back through the eye. I'm going to come back. Where I am is in this room. It's just me, and I'm hearing a voice say, you're going to be OK, Connie. I'm feeling my strength again and that radiance, that light within.*

There are several apparent archetypal images that surfaced in this session. First, is the image of the "eye" through which Connie sees a brilliant image. She is evidently seeing a symbolic image of her future in a bright new world, full of new births and transformations.

The eye is noted for its symbolic meaning and is generally associated with spiritual and mental perception. It also represents the "mirror" of the soul and is considered the organ of spiritual and mental expression. At times, one sees a huge eye in imagery which has a number of archetypal meanings. It is sometimes associated with the discerning eye of God that sees through the dualities of life. (19)

Next Connie passes through the "eye" with an Indian Saint. After being instructed to look through the eye, she sees her wedding with Doug. Everything appears to be as it should be and she feels she can trust the development of their relationship. The images of the past few sessions appear to strongly support their union. Significant, it appears, is the absence of her ex-husband. Apparently, there has been a complete break with him, combined with the resolution of adolescent dependency problems. This seems to have paved the way for a deeper and more permanent relationship with Doug.

Another significant image is that of the growing and undamaged child. It is assumed that this baby represents a rebirth, a birth of a new life for Connie.

One interesting element that appears consistently when Connie is immersed in transcendent images is the sensation of light in her right arm. As we have concluded before, this likely has to do with creativity and helping others. Images pertaining to her future seem to support this hypothesis. Indeed, it appears that when she feels the light in her arm people tend to come to her for help. When the light is not present people do not seem to be drawn to her. However, there appears to be one more life experience that has to be faced before Connie can fully realize freedom from her past.

PART 36
The Bikini Woman Goes to the Light

About three weeks prior to this session Connie was making plans to spend a week with her parents when suddenly a young adult part of herself surfaced. She became very depressed and experienced an uncontrollable craving for drugs and alcohol. At first she could not understand what was happening since the disturbance came upon her without warning.

When Connie was finally able to go into an imagery state on her own she visualized a young woman with blonde hair wearing a bikini. This helped her identify the era of her life that she was facing. She became panicky since she was only a few days away from her visit with her parents. There was little time to process this part of herself. It was so strong and overwhelming.

Rather than take a chance of being overwhelmed, Connie decided to check into a drug and alcohol rehabilitation hospital. She called me to tell me of her plan to stay only the weekend and leave the following Monday for her parent's home. Her strong intuition indicated that all she needed was a few days in a controlled situation to make sure she did not relapse into an uncontrolled addictive state from which it might take weeks or even months to recover.

I soon received a phone call from the hospital asking for information about Connie. She had listed me as her therapist. The hospital counselor indicated that liver tests had been conducted and that her system was full of drugs and toxins. He indicated that the situation was so critical that if she were to check out of the hospital on the following Monday she would go into a severe shock of withdrawal and die. He seemed most insistent on gaining my help to force her to stay in the hospital.

I explained to the counselor that Connie had not released me to offer information about her case and until such release could be obtained, I was bound by the law of confidentiality. To this he responded that I was being uncooperative and unprofessional. I suggested that Connie knew what she was doing and if she felt that all she needed was a few days to get her addictive behavior under control, I trusted her judgment. The counselor accused me of enabling her and questioned my competency as a psychologist.

Under ordinary circumstances the counselor's objections might have been justified. Of course, I could not discuss Connie's work with her inner selves of the Collective Consciousness. Experience with her case strongly suggested that once she was able to differentiate this latest inner self her addictive behavior would come under control.

It is noted that an unusual and fascinating physiological phenomenon emerged in connection to Connie's hospital experience. To my knowledge (and to this day I have no reason to doubt her word), the only drugs she had consumed were aspirin and nicotine from cigarettes. Yet, according to the hospital counselor, tests showed medical evidence of lethal quantities of drugs and toxins. It would be most interesting, if the same medical tests could have been conducted at the time of her self-release from the hospital, to determine if significant levels of toxic substances remained.

What we do know for sure is that Connie did leave the hospital on Monday following her Friday admission. Further, we also know that she did not suffer any of the predicted withdrawal symptoms. Nor did she experience any further cravings for drugs or alcohol. Instead, she had a delightful time with her parents and was able to share some touching moments with her father.

Evidently, since Connie had dealt with the inner-young woman privately during her hospital stay of only a few days, I would hypothesize that no drugs would have been found had she been retested upon release. It is noted that this hypothesis is based on my work with Multiple Personality Disorder (MPD) clients. In my clinical work with MPDs, now referred to as "Dissociative Disorder," I have encountered an interesting phenomenon. For example, I have found that the primary personality may be ill without other personalities being affected or the primary personality may wear glasses while others personalities do not. If Connie's inner identity had absorbed all of her drug and alcohol abuse, then it seems reasonable to me that when she came forward into consciousness the body would manifest high toxicity. I am all but sure that she had not been drinking or taking drugs except for aspirin and nicotine. Indeed, she checked into the clinic because she did not want to start using and wanted to get control over this addicted aspect of herself. At any rate, it is a fact that Connie showed no symptoms of withdrawal after leaving the hospital as predicted. Nor did she have any further compulsions to take drugs. Indeed, had she left with such high levels of toxins in her system, she would most certainly have experienced life-threatening symptoms of withdrawal.

The session offered below includes Connie's latest experience with the woman who represents her young adulthood when she was actively using drugs and alcohol. It appears to be that part of herself who first surfaced during the aftermath of Connie's automobile accident. Connie begins the session with a description of the addicted self. *She has blonde hair and a tan and laying outside in a bikini. I don't feel any higher self or any angel. I just feel a lot of anger and I think that has me wanting to protect her, too. She really absorbed the hurt. It was tremendous. I mean a lot of it was covered over by the drugs and alcohol, but she absorbed a lot of it. She was like a zombie just going through the world existing, growing marijuana out in the backyard, having parties for the kids that ended up in beer bashes for the adults and there were fights. I can see myself in that accident, too, lying in that hospital bed. That's when it all started. That was when it emerged. That was when I passed over into chronic addiction, and I'm feeling so angry at Ted over the fact that he was dating other women while I was lying in that bed.* It seemed to be such an injustice being visited upon her as she was in a complete state of helplessness. There was nothing she could do while her husband was dating other women.

Connie says that she could see *herself pregnant with her daughter a couple of years after the accident. Ted was dating other women and treating me really emotionally abusive, doing things in front of other people to belittle me. And I would always allow him to do it. Afterwards, I would get really mad and holler at him, but I never got anywhere with him. He was unapproachable. I even ran up behind him and attacked him with my hands and I got beat up.*

Connie is encouraged to tell the bikini woman that while she has done a great job of absorbing a lot of pain and suffering, she is no longer needed to do this. After all, Connie has started a new life where there is no need for drugs or alcohol to numb the pain. Hence, while her help during some very difficult times of pain and suffering is greatly appreciated it is time for her to go where she will be able to heal her life. Connie indicates that, *you know, I'm feeling like, and she's looking like, right now, more ready than any of the other ones to go. Yes, it's like part of that permission for her to go is that I'm going to stick up for myself. I'm going to do what I need to do to make myself better, to see a lawyer, tell Ted off or whatever I need to do. I can see her smiling now. Another thing I need to do is not let him take anything, to at least fight and get what's mine.*

Connie's need to fight for herself and what is hers is reinforced. She is encouraged to stand up for her own integrity and not make everything a win or lose situation. Rather, fight for her own rights and a release from all the conflict and suffering that she had to endure during her marriage. She continues, *I think I've been wanting to tell him how I feel. Tell him off is telling him how I feel. From the last year of my life, I have not told him the depth of pain that I've gone through. When I think about him doing what he did, I want to tell him how I feel about it. I want to do that.*

After some thought Connie says, *I'm having an image. You're going to get a kick out of this. Last week I pulled up in the parking deck waiting for a parking space. This girl came to her car and she got in it. I was waiting for her to pull out and this guy came up behind me in a car and kept blowing his horn, laying on the horn. All at once I couldn't believe what I did. I gave him the finger and told him to go to hell. I couldn't contain all the anger and it wasn't for him. He was just acting like Ted acts. He thought the parking place was his or something, like he owned the deck. And then I thought, "Oh my God, he's going to come up to the class or he's going to follow me or slash my tires or whatever." I felt awful afterwards, but you know now it's funny. I couldn't even believe that I did that, that that was in me. Doug said, he said that the finger is a wonderful thing and it's a wonderful way to communicate. It's a universal symbol.*

Connie is told that all these things that she does, by way of standing up for herself, says to the bikini woman that she can handle things on your own and she no longer needs her to help with such situations. She responds, *yes, she was, just as you said that, looked up into the sunlight. She spent so much time out in the sun. That was her only comfort.* Then a beam of light appears and *she's standing in it and she's waving goodbye. She's going to hug me first. She's telling me, "thank you." And now the sunlight is drawing her up through the beam.*

It was surprising when Connie's imagery revealed a young bikini-clad woman of her post-accident days. Since she had felt no further addictive symptoms for over a month, we had assumed that this part of herself might have been set aside. The "bikini woman" seemed to have been the primary figure in absorbing Connie's addictive response to her painful existence during and following the accident. A significant part of her emotional pain came from the awareness that her husband had been involved with other women while she was suffering in the hospital. Also, during this period, Connie's husband was emotionally abusive and would belittle her in front of other people. Although she became very angry and once physically attacked him over these matters, she seemed to have little impact on his belittling behavior.

As we have observed with other inner selves, Connie's "bikini woman" appears ready to be released into the light, since Connie is strong enough to take a stand on her own behalf. This becomes apparent in the way she is conducting herself in the divorce process. Connie's recollection of her aggressive action toward the rude driver in the parking deck further demonstrated her capacity for taking charge of her life and breaking with previous patterns of dependence.

Having demonstrated her capacity to take care of herself and keeping abusive men out of her life, Connie has no further need for the "bikini woman." Moreover, her relationship with Doug indicates her commitment to a more positive, healthy and creative life. The "bikini woman" has little difficulty with being drawn up through a beam of light since her only comfort in life had been the warmth of sunlight. Apparently, she had already been a woman of the light.

As we shall see, this woman of sunlight would be the final part of Connie's inner self to surface during the therapeutic process. She was perhaps the most difficult of the many inner selves for Connie to face because of the intense addictive component. The final phase of the therapeutic process seems at hand after many months of painful struggling. As past Clinical experience suggests, the inner selves from the Collective Consciousness who suffer the most on our behalf, are often those who are the most highly developed.

PART 37
Walking with Love

Connie has just emerged from some difficult times related to having moved in with Doug and defining what she wants in a relationship. She wanted to resolve all her dependency needs before entering into a long-term relationship. At least her fears are now in the present rather than remnants of her distorted past.

Connie's relationship with Doug continues to grow and weather all of her struggles over the past few months. He has proven to be loving and patient. It is clear that he represents a healthier life for her. This imagery session further reinforces her progress and all seems right for her to proceed with future plans.

Connie begins the session, *the "Master" is saying to me "see I told you it would be OK." Now I see Doug's face. I guess Doug is going to hang around and go through this imagery with me. We're at the ocean and there's a real softness in the air. I feel like it is really OK. What I went through this week was necessary and that I shouldn't judge myself for acting crazy. It helped me to draw more clear lines. This is what I see in my imagery now, more clear lines about what I want in a relationship, to be more firm. We're still at the ocean and it's really beautiful. We're going to go for a walk. You're there with us, too, but you're almost in an, it's not a solid physical body. And I see a seagull just sort of swooping around us almost in a teasing sort of way*. Clinical experience suggests that Seagulls often represent one's guardian angel and this observation is shared with Connie.

Connie responds, *it might be. I haven't had any connection at all with my angel for quite a while that's for sure. Maybe it's been there but I just haven't consciously been aware of it. I feel like I have a lot of support with you being there, almost like in spirit and with the "Master" being there. The seagull just swooped down and got a shell and brought it to me. There's a piece of paper in there in the shell. I'm opening it and it says, "I love you Connie." Now I'm seeing the, I don't know, what did you call her, the woman of the light or something?* (I had earlier suggested that the bikini woman was actually a woman of the light because of the tremendous suffering that she had to absorb). *She tells me that I'm doing a good job with all that's happening around me.*

It is further suggested that Connie thank the "bikini woman" for all that she brought to her life and for what she did and absorbed on her behalf. After all it is likely that Connie would have been overwhelmed by all of the abuse and suffering during that time of her life, had it not been for the "woman of light." Connie indicates that, *I am telling her that.*

At this point I ask if the bikini woman was aware of being sent to help or did she just emerge? Connie responded that, *she knew, she knew what she was there to do.* I also asked if the bikini woman's coming to help her had something to do with fulfilling her own life. *Yes, she just told me that before you asked it,* said Connie. *Her reward, you know, when I thanked her for, for all that she's done, her reward is the fulfillment of her, what she was supposed to do here with me. It helped her transcend immensely. And just watching what's happened with me has helped her a lot.* Clinical experience suggests that such entities as the bikini woman and those we see with Multiple Personalities or multiplicity in Connie's case are those who emerge from the core of the self. They are brought forward to help in particular circumstances fitting to their own knowledge, experience and potentiality. They are allowed to do this in order to fulfill their own lives, that part of their lives that was otherwise unfulfilled. It is as if they are given a second chance. Moreover, they are actual entities that were past lives with their own personal history and life experience. They are often brought forward to help absorb pain and suffering and to help guide the primary personality through difficult times. In Connie's case, the bikini woman came to absorb the addictive phase of her life and to respond to her husband's abusive behavior toward her. Now that she is no longer needed, as with the others before her, she is free to go to the light and return to her place of being. She also seems to have a great deal of awareness and development that was necessary given the horrendous task that she had assumed on Connie's behalf.

Connie indicates, *yes, she needed that to transcend, to move on. She's been the easiest one to let go of, for me to let go of, and for her to let go of me. It's like we're ready and she trusts me. She trusts that I am doing a good job. She's been right here with me, but she's let me do the whole thing by myself. She's saying that there were times when I tried to kill myself in the seventies, but that I couldn't have because it was her that took over at those times. It was part of her job to help me get through this so that I could transcend rather than having to go back into another lifetime, and having to go through it again. She took some years out of her time. Actually, it's more of a timelessness for her. She's not linked to the physical time that we are, but she came here for a while in this world to, to help me.*

Next, Connie indicates that, *I'm back at the ocean again and I'm myself. There is this light there that I'm going to walk into. It feels good to be in the light again. I think I'm just going to experience it for a little bit, a couple of minutes. What it is telling me is that I can begin to prepare for a fast, but a different kind of fast. This fast is going to be away from aspirin for a while, just to prepare myself for that. The fast is that I'll eliminate aspirin. I think it is time to come back now. The light is swooping me up in the air now, and we're over this room and it's going to come down with me and it's going to stay with me.*

Connie's imagery session was very positive after a "crazy" week in which she was able to develop some very clear direction regarding her relationship with Doug. It seems that their relationship can move peacefully forward into the future. Interestingly her perception of me in her imagery was without a "solid physical body." This may indicate that my influence on her life is beginning to fade and that the end of our therapeutic relationship is near. This was confirmed when Connie completed her therapy within the next two sessions.

Of particular interest is the return of the "bikini woman" or "woman of the light," for a discussion of her role in Connie's life. Her case, combined with others, seems to confirm the hypothesis that many of the "identities" that surface in relation to abusive or overwhelming life circumstances, are actually identities of the Collective Consciousness or past life entities. Moreover, this does not rule out the possibility that a natural dissociation may occur when developmental issues require it. This is to say that an entity may surface, especially with children, when given difficult developmental issues require.

During my work with Connie I was trying to formulate some ideas about the structure of the unconscious. In those days I had not differentiated between what I identified as the Supra-Consciousness (Light), and what I later referred to as the Transpersonal Psyche or Collective Consciousness. The "light" is considered to be that part of the Self that has its origins in the divine world. One might consider it as one's Soul. The Collective Consciousness is assumed to be that part of the self, that while its spiritual origins are derived from the Supra-Consciousness, its life experience is of the earth. Further, I have concluded that most of the inner selves emerge from the Collective Consciousness, but under the direction of the Supra Consciousness, to which it returns when its life becomes fulfilled. Hence, each life is created by the Supra Consciousness, but which accomplishes its development through life experiences while living on the earth. Further, it seems that it does not return to the Supra Consciousness until its life becomes fully developed and fulfilled. Experience also suggests that an entity whose life has become fully developed or fulfilled may return to assist the primary personality to achieve given developmental and creative tasks.

It might also be important to note that the reader may have assumed that I had diagnosed Connie's case as one of Multiple Personality Disorder or Dissociative Disorder. I did not venture a specific diagnosis of Connie's case because as a therapist I am much more interested in the process, content and dynamics of each case. If I were pressed to give a diagnosis, it would likely be Post Traumatic Stress Disorder. However, to avoid any misconception regarding Connie's case, for those who are interested in diagnostic categorizations, her case is not one of Dissociative Disorder for the basic reason that she did not lose Ego consciousness when her inner selves emerge. She was able to differentiate herself from her inner selves. In cases of Dissociative Disorder, the primary personality may lose conscious awareness for hours or perhaps a few days, while an inner self or selves take over conscious awareness. I have worked with a number of MPD's, but most of my research subjects were like Connie, those who experienced a multitude of inner selves, especially during very difficult times. However, she was consciously aware of her behavior even though such behavior at times might have come close to overwhelming her. While she may have been unaware of these inner selves surfacing into her conscious reality, she rarely lost a sense of Ego consciousness. The exception to this would be during childhood when the ego is not fully developed and inner selves may naturally emerge to help accomplish given developmental tasks. Another exception was when the Bikini woman took over when Connie was trying to commit suicide.

Interestingly, Connie did report on having "out of body" experiences following the auto accident when she was in severe physical pain. I have had many persons tell me of such "out of body" experiences that they experienced during times of intense pain and during surgery. Others have told me similar stories when they were giving birth. This conscious orientation is more common than might be imagined. It is something that most people would not normally share with others. Since my research was related to different forms of consciousness, I was one who listened to such stories with acceptance, validation and without judgment.

Another hypothesis confirmed by Connie's imagery sessions is that the purpose of a given "inner self" is often to absorb the pain and abusive situations and respond in specialized ways, such as with fear, dependence, anger, and rejection which are sometimes referred to as defense mechanisms. The reader will notice that each inner child or teenager seemed to involve a specific issue and set of emotions. This is similar to what Grof describes as a "COEX System." (20) Moreover, when an inner self comes forward it does so to gain experiences important to its own growth and transcendence which may be related to some issue that has been left unfulfilled in its own life and growth.

Finally, one function of the inner self is to take over for the primary personality when external circumstances become too overwhelming. As indicated above in Connie's case, the "woman of the light" took charge during times when she tried to kill herself. This might also explain why many suicide attempts with others are not successfully completed.

PART 38
Centering

It would seem that in this session Connie's attempt to take charge of her life is being reinforced. She begins the session with, *I was thinking this morning that I haven't seen my angel at all or communicated with it. I think one reason is, is what I'm seeing the angel holding up. It is a sign that says, "take charge of your life." It's like it is there to remind me of that all the time.*

Connie continues, *Christ is there. There is a boat there. He wants me to get into the boat with him. We're going to go for a ride. We're out on a body of water, and I'm trying to discern what the water is whether it's a lake or the ocean. It's a lake. It's a real quiet, peaceful lake. It feels good to enjoy the quietness for a change, the solitude. Christ is telling me to relax, that he is going to row the boat. He's going to take the oars and do the work. It's hard for me to let go of that, that wanting to help. What he's telling me is that I've asked for the light within and that it's there. It's coming, coming into my awareness. I see this fire. It's like real bright, almost like a divine fire. Now I see Christ placing it within me. It's like an archetype or symbol. I see on either side of the fire the opposites; the addiction is on one side and the purity is on the other. In the center of the fire is where the opposites come together. The fire within is also the light within that I've been seeing within me. I'm being told now that the expression of the addiction was, was to confront the archetype. It's like a denial of what was within me. It was, in order to get rid of it, I needed to face it.*

It seems that the addiction itself or being dependent on something like a chemical substance is part of an archetypal pattern. Connie responds, *yes, the dependency because it's addiction to all things, not just to one substance. It is the passive-dependency sort of thing that I'm finding within myself. The answer to all of that is I don't have to look on the outside anymore, to people or to substances.* It is suggested that when one is centered in the light in the center of the opposites or such archetypal patterns one is then in control, such that each opposite becomes the potential for action rather than what controls our behavior.

Connie continues, *in the center, the light, it's beautiful. There is this light that's like pulsating. In the center of the cross is like the symbol for the coming together of the opposites and it's also the light, Christ's light. I won't have to have this underlying worry about the addiction. I'm keeping it under control because I'm transcending it, if that makes any sense. I'm still experiencing the light and the cross, the pulsating cross. I feel this pull to go toward the center of the cross. I'm just sort of letting my whole being be drawn into that area. I'm there. It's like there isn't any other. It's just a center. There are no boundaries, no limits. It's almost like a nothingness, but it's all a, it feels good, it's not scary. It's a, maybe it's like being in a womb. There's a lot of light there and there's, um, a feeling of union with the universe. This pulsing light is the same light that comes down my arm. Its source is from me. It's my light. It's growing stronger. It's funny because I feel that when I'm here in the center and when I have the experience of the light in my arm, I can't tell where my arm leaves off and other people start. It's a good feeling. It's a real feeling of oneness. I've been starting to write my mantra with my left hand also and that's good. I'm going to bring the cross back into the center. I'm coming back into the room now. It sure does take all the craving away if I'd use it, if I'd draw on it.*

A theme that has emerged in Connie's imagery recently has been to take charge of her life. It is interesting that she finds herself in a rowboat with "Christ" who presumably represents her own divine inner resources such as unconditional love, forgiveness, growth, healing and creativity that will take her across the waters of life. It would appear that these are the values that she is adopting to guide her own life. The divine fire being placed within her would seem to be symbolic of acceptance and the integration of the essence of such archetypal values within her personality. From this centered perspective she is able to see the duality of the archetype of dependence (addiction) versus independence, which has greatly influenced her life.

During Connie's childhood and young adulthood, she was obviously polarized by the dependent side of the pair of opposites. In recent years she has struggled to achieve independence by leaving her husband, going back to school, learning to live alone and working to become self-sufficient. As we come to the end of her lengthy therapeutic journey, it appears that she is moving to the center of these opposites. As she says, *I'm to confront the archetype. It's like a denial of what was within me. In order to get rid of it I needed to face it.*

It is important to note that from Connie's centered place the pair of opposites become potentials for action rather than controlling factors in her life. Hence, she is taking charge of her own life in order to enter into a satisfying inter-dependent marital relationship with Doug. Also, important to note is the discovery that Connie realizes that dependence in its extreme form is addiction to everything. Her answer to the additive side of her passive-dependent personality is what she is finding within herself, a center from which she can take charge of her life without having to look outside of herself to "people and substances." It would seem that some treatments of alcoholism and drug addiction fail to recognize that it is a dependence/independence polarization problem which needs to be addressed more than an addiction to a specific substance.

It is interesting that Connie sees the image of a cross with a pulsating light at its center. The cross image that she had before differed somewhat because it seemed to represent her suffering, and a death and rebirth of the self. (21) Rather, she takes the light at the center of the cross to be where the dependence vs. independence opposites come together. According to her imagery, it seems that one must transcend the opposites such that they become potential responses to given situations in life. It is noted that resolving the dependent vs. independent opposites is a developmental issue to be resolved in early childhood. To be sure, Connie's disruptive and difficult childhood made it impossible for her to accomplish this developmental task.

Connie continues to describe the transcendent experiences she is having by being in the beautiful light at the center of the cross. When she is centered in this experience, she appears to have no addictive cravings. This imagery session seems significant because it reinforces the idea of Connie taking charge of her life and deciding for herself what she wants her life to be. To gain control of her dependent needs she needs to find her orientation at the center of herself. The center of herself seems to be a transcendent experience perceived as a pulsating light, a divine light. This light appears to represent a psychological state of unconditional love where the archetypal opposites come together.

It might be noted that following her imagery therapy Connie no longer experienced addictive cravings. She is one of two people who I have had in therapy who have accomplished this task, considered by some to be an impossibility. She came to realize the resolution of her addictive cravings while at a social gathering. During the party someone came up to her and handed her a glass of wine. She took it and drank several sips from the glass. Then with little thought she put it down. After socializing with others, she suddenly realized that she had taken a drink of alcohol but had put the glass down without thinking about it. In the past she would never have been able to do that. She would have continued to drink until she had reached a state of intoxication. Her feeling at this time was that she was "just not interested." The other person I referred to had almost the same experience and reaction, "I was just not interested."

PART 39
The Communion

This was Connie's last imagery session, the completion of her imagery therapy and the journey to healing her life. It is one of communion and celebration and the beginning of a new life. She returns to the "light." *The light of the Master. I'm asking him, "what's next?" I'm seeing Linda's face. I don't know if it's because we were just talking about her or what? It's just staying with me. Her face is really vivid and real clear. She's smiling. She looks fine. There are no troubles or anything and she's taking me into a garden. I'm integrating into my center in the light within. I feel a lot of light within again. It's a light in my head especially, and I feel a lot of sensations in my third eye center, a lot of movement. And, the Master is here in form. He doesn't have a face but he has like a body to him and he offering me communion again. There's a golden chalice. I'm kneeling before him. I'm going to take it, and I feel as I take this communion a lot of warmth throughout my being, my physical being.*

The communion experience in imagery, while not common, has occurred with a number of other cases. (The reader is reminded of Theresa's case study given above). It is likely related to one's Christian background in which communion is a significant part of one's religious tradition. As suggested in many of Connie's imagery sessions, she also has an orientation to Eastern thought that she has acquired through the practice of yoga and meditation. It appears that she does not find any inner conflict with either orientation as would be the case with more fundamentalist Christian traditions. However, Connie is not involved in Christian church activities as she had been subjected to the self-righteous and judgmental attitude of many fundamentalist Christians. This may well have been a basic reason for turning toward Eastern thought, yoga and meditation. In any case, she is accepting of the "Christ" or "Master" images of her imagery and the communion experience seems significant for her. Generally, the symbolism of communion represents coming to a "union," between Ego consciousness and Divine consciousness. It is also a commitment to life, one's willingness to participate in this union, an integration of divine consciousness as represented by the "light" within oneself.

Connie continues, *he says that he's in the process of healing me, that I need to be patient. I am feeling a pulling in my third eye. There is like an energy that's pulling it. It feels like a magnet. I guess it's drawing in Christ's energy or it's awaking or whatever. I see a woman in a nun's habit. She looks real joyous. She's a little bit, she has a round face. I'll find out who she is. It's one of the saints. I don't know which one. It's St. Therese of Avila. She's smiling at you. She's giving me some of her healing energy also. It's so warm. I feel a real sense of nurturance with this. We're just looking into each other's eyes. It's really a good experience and she's holding my hands. The love is so intense, so deep. She says that the love is healing, that what I've been looking for in my life is manifesting. It's being integrated at this point. She is reaching over to touch you now, on the shoulder. I can see a real bright light within. I'm tasting that sweetness in my mouth again. It's been coming more and more lately. What's coming now is that sharing this light with other people will help it grow brighter.*

Taking communion from the hand of Christ is assumed to mean a union with the divine center of the self. Presumably it represents a commitment to life and life-giving values. The Golden Chalice is also of great symbolic value. (22) It has a number of possible meanings. However, in Connie's case we assume that it represents divine nourishment and immortality. Further, it might be noted that there was also a reference regarding communion in Theresa's case study. Moreover, communion in her case also came toward the end of her imagery work.

It seems fitting that Connie would finish her final imagery session with an image of St. Therese of Avila, who is reported to have said as she neared death, that after death she would shower the earth with flowers. She was hoping to bring faith and hope to a world of suffering.

The reader might recall that Connie's first imagery session contained a similar image of a saint. It is difficult to understand the specific reason for this to occur except that St. Therese, like Christ and a mutual friend, Robert, represents unconditional love and nurturing to her. She is getting the strong impression that love is what heals and stimulates new growth. Another significant message of her imagery is that it is important to share this light/love with others and that this is what helps it grow brighter.

DISCUSSION

It seemed that what Connie had to face as an adult was an unsuccessful attempt to resolve the growth stage of dependence vs. independence during her childhood. We can see from her relationships with given family members, especially her mother and brother, that the conditions were not compatible with a healthy progression through this phase of her development. To be sure, her life during childhood and into early adulthood was one of being polarized upon the dependent side of the duality.

Later after Connie came to face her dependency needs, as manifested in her alcohol and drug addiction, she began the courageous journey toward independence and self-sufficiency. Entering a rehabilitation hospital, going back to school to earn her high school, college and graduate degrees are clear examples of her quest for greater independence. Her divorce proceedings were also indicative of her intense struggle to break with her addictions and dependence related to relationships with abusive men.

The reader may recall that many of Connie's imagery sessions began with transcendent experiences. Such experiences are not unusual in imagery work. However, their constant presence at the beginning of each session would seem unusual. In her case, the idea of transcendence appeared to be a major theme in her work. The process involved seemed to be an attempt on the part of her unconscious to lead her toward the center of herself, the divine self, with its sense of healing and unconditional love and spirituality. The intent would appear to be one of providing the means by which she might transcend the many dualities that she would be facing in her life, including dependence vs. independence.

At the center of Connie's work was dealing with a void in her life created by a lack of "unconditional love." Her idea of love seemed defined in terms of sentimentality. Further, loving and being loved had more to do with the ability to please someone and make them happy. Moreover, sexual feelings and sexual intimacy were often confused with love and being loved. Love then had become defined as the fulfillment of one's dependent needs.

Connie's imagery work seemed to place a great deal of emphasis on her dependence and the void that was created by a lack of unconditional love in her life. This seemed to be a major aspect of the process of centering within herself and moving to a position of transcendence. Another significant part of the process was to alter her external orientation regarding the fulfillment of the deprived needs that she felt. This is to say that she sought fulfillment in others and in drugs and alcohol. She had become polarized externally. While an external perspective is important with regard to conducting one's life in a given culture and society, an internal orientation is equally important when the quality of transcendence is needed to resolve the many dualities one faces in life.

By centering within herself, Connie was able to feel in progressive degrees the unconditional love that had been lacking in her life. As she began to integrate her inner experiences of being loved by internal forces, she was able to establish relationships with more loving and caring people. Further, she was able to break away from the negativity of abusive, non-loving people of her past.

Another part of the imagery process was to help her view situations and people from the transcendent position of unconditional love. It is from this perspective that one is able to transcend and resolve such dualities as dependence vs. independence. Moreover, from a position of transcendence and non-judgment she was able to review and relive her very difficult childhood experiences and relationships with a more loving and objective attitude. The importance of this attitude change cannot be overemphasized because it sets aside the personal and judgmental aspect of one's point of view and enables one to see the truth of a given painful experience. For example, Connie was able to see that her mother's rejection and abandonment of her was really a result of her mother's own personal problems. Perhaps her mother was unable to resolve her confusion over being a young mother, wife and homemaker. In any case, her mother's response to her was not personal and had nothing to do with her inadequacies as a child or her inability to please her.

Moreover, Connie was able to see that her brother's rejection and abandonment had more to do with his own growth necessities than her unworthiness. It was a time for him to pursue his own freedom and independence from parents and family as part of his own natural growth needs of adolescence. His being mean to her was most likely a result of his trying to break with her dependent clinging. Of course, the more he tried to gain his freedom the more Connie tried to please him and cling to him. Indeed, her actions were in conflict with his own developmental needs. Presumably this created feelings of anger that he may have projected upon her which caused her to feel rejected and unworthy.

Finally, from a loving, transcendent and non-judgmental perspective Connie could acknowledge her own contributions to the unconscious development of the rejecting and abandonment circumstances of her youth. It seems clear that her own innocent dependent needs were very draining to others and that they would have to use anger or some other rejecting type of behavior to defend themselves against her. It was never a question of intending to do harm or displease others. Rather, it was a matter of not being developed mentally and emotionally enough to understand such difficult life circumstances to which she might have otherwise responded with wisdom and maturity.

Like many persons it became important for Connie to relive many of her damaging life experiences in order to heal her neurotic responses. Connie's case was consistent with this theme as many of her imagery sessions took her back to such past experiences. Often this process is preceded by an initial transcendent experience, followed by a guide from the unconscious, generally the "guardian angel," who takes her back to unresolved experiences in her life. Some examples of such experiences were when she was a newborn baby being left alone, hurtful times with her mother, the sexual episode with the neighbor boy, difficult school days, moving to another school, and the automobile accident, to name a few.

The key therapeutic concept appears to be that we often experience traumatic events in our lives, when we have not the maturity or fully developed mind to comprehend what has happened to us. As with Connie, with proper development through adult life experiences and therapeutic intervention, such as with imagery therapy, she was able to develop an adult mind with the capacity to center and transcend the dualities of life. When the time is right one returns to given traumatic experiences, not as a child, but as a mature adult. Given this growth process for developing maturity, wisdom and new insights into life experiences, one can view such painful events of life as being part of life and for them necessary learning experiences, without the need for feeling shame, guilt, inadequacy, worthlessness or anger and resentments.

Often in imagery sessions, one can observe the unconscious actually leading the client through inner experiences, such as Connie's transcendent images, like one playing a role in a drama of life as preparation for meeting given external events in the present. This is why it is important for the therapist to try to cooperate with the wisdom of the client's unconscious during the preparation process to help reinforce the ideas and knowledge being developed. It is also important to be patient with the unfolding process because it is the client's Supra Consciousness alone that knows when preparations are complete and when the time is right for facing and reliving painful past events or relationships. Finally, during the reliving process the therapist needs to be very loving and supportive while reinforcing the client's awareness of the ideas and knowledge that need to be applied to reliving a given situation or external event. A close review of Connie's imagery sessions will reveal such therapeutic themes consistently emerging.

DISCUSSION OF RESEARCH QUESTIONS

The Unconscious: Its Structure and Content

In the introduction I posed a number of research questions that I kept in mind while working with research subjects. One question had to do with the nature of the Unconscious. The term "Unconscious" has been a central focus of Analytical Psychology since the days of Freud. While I also use the term, I view it as something that is actually full of consciousness. Further, a primary goal of psychotherapy is to bring into conscious awareness, what has otherwise been unconscious. To be sure it is difficult to solve a problem of which one is unaware.

Generally, the unconscious is comprised of material and content which is unknown to Ego consciousness. Some of the content are memories of experiences that have merely been forgotten over time. These memories may relate to early childhood and since they serve little purpose in one's adult life, they have merely been forgotten. There are other areas that we might refer to as the shadow side of the self. These areas contain parts of the self that are unacceptable to oneself and to Ego consciousness. These are parts of the self that may relate to childhood behavior that was unacceptable to parents and the adult world. Hence, what threatened to cause a loss of love from parents and significant adults was rejected and repressed. Often such behaviors were related to one's natural development and which became rejected by parents, teachers and of necessity one's own self. The shadow side of the self is full of repressed materials that have become unacceptable to the self.

In the past I have also identified the spiritual side of our individual lives as the Personal Psyche. The Personal Psyche is our own spiritual identity that contains all of our personal life experiences. It is related to Ego consciousness as means to establish a relationship between our inside and outside worlds. It also establishes a relationship with the Collective Consciousness and at times with the Supra Consciousness. Like Ego consciousness it has its own conscious identity and awareness including, but not totally limited to Ego consciousness.

The Unconscious contains what I refer to as the Collective Consciousness. It is a collection of entities who have had their own life experiences. They have their own identities and are independent of one's present life. We may never become aware of their existence or influence in our lives. They are fully conscious of themselves and generally of their role in relation to our own lives. Usually they are brought forward because of something unfulfilled or unresolved in their lives. They help to guide the present life through given experiences that lead to resolution in their own lives. Often these experiences are related to relationships with others. It might be noted that I have also used the term Transpersonal Psyche to describe the Collective Consciousness. Transpersonal means something that is independent of one's own personal life and does not owe its existence or content to our personal life experiences. The Psyche is used to identify these entities as spiritual in nature without physical form except that they sometimes project a physical form so that we can become visually aware of them.

Just as the Personal Psyche has a shadow side, the Collective Consciousness also contains a shadow side. This dark side of the Collective Consciousness contains thoughts and behavior that would otherwise be unacceptable to the self and our Ego consciousness. A significant part of healing one's life is to access such negative elements of the self, process them and release them to the light. During this process it is important for the therapist to reinforce the idea of approaching each inner self with acceptance and without judgment. Each of us contains the whole history of humanity including all of its inhumanity.

The Supra Consciousness is what might be referred to as Divine Consciousness or Light Consciousness because it often appears as a "being of light." At times it appears as the fire at the center of the self, such as was demonstrated in Theresa's imagery. It contains the archetypal patterns that inform us and bring direction to our lives. Often, they are represented as dualities. Common examples of such patterns are mother/father, brother/sister, Christ/Father, Knight/Warrior, feminine/masculine, etc. A common example in the clinical setting is the archetypal mother who appears to bring unconditional love and healing to an adult who had been abused as a child, especially by the mother. Further, the archetypal father may appear as the loving, caring father to help heal the wounds from having been abused by a father.

There are countless examples of when the archetypal mother informs the young mother who has just given birth. Suddenly the child becomes the most important thing in her life. The husband who had been at the center of her life finds himself feeling neglected and much less of a priority in his wife's life.

How might the "Unconscious" influence our everyday lives?

Another research question was whether the content of the unconscious affects or influences our everyday lives. After reviewing the structure of the unconscious and its content, some of the ways in which such content influences our lives is apparent. Primary are the archetypal patterns of the Supra Consciousness. This is where the blueprint of one's life is contained and certain patterns are brought forward in our lives to bring direction and energy to support that direction. Each developmental stage of human development is supported by archetypal patterns which help to lead us through the tasks of each phase. Indeed, each stage of development is an archetypal pattern. These developmental tasks are often described in terms of the resolution of given opposites such as Trust/Mistrust, Independence/independence, Industry/stagnation, etc.

Archetypal patterns provide direction and energy to certain roles that one assumes in life and in relationship with others. As indicated above, there are certain roles such as being a soldier in the military that one might assume in life. The warrior/knight archetype is brought forward to inform this role and provide energy to fulfill these activities. There are other career roles such as teacher, coach or any role in support of young people to help them grow and change in a positive way. To be sure, there are roles that are negative in nature.

The mob gangster is such a role. People whose lives are consumed by mental illness, even those who become murderers, are energized by certain negative archetypal patterns. Carl Jung discussed this with regard to the dark side of God. (1) This is to say that evil, the opposite of growth and change, is also an archetypal pattern and informs those who choose to be involved in such activities.

The Collective Consciousness also has an influence on our thoughts, feelings and behavior. Like the Supra Consciousness, the Collective Consciousness represents potentialities in our lives. Once we chose a certain life direction not only is the Supra Consciousness activated, but related aspects of the Collective Consciousness are brought forward. A very good example of this was when Julia was brought forward in Ellen's imagery. Ellen's desire to heal certain aspects of her life that were related to feelings of guilt and depression triggered the help that she needed from the Collective. Apparently, at the core of her feelings of guilt and depression were related to Julia's life experience. Ellen's experience with Julia, as is common, had mutual benefit. Julia was able to tell her story and bring into consciousness the core problem. Ellen's job as an older and more experienced person in a position of authority, and whose life was in the present was to bring all the factors together and help bring resolution to the problem. This released Julia to continue with her growth from where it had stopped following the accident. When the core problem that was within her Collective Consciousness was resolved, Ellen's symptoms of guilt and depression were eliminated. This is not to say that Ellen did not continue to have problems. However, her problems and emotional responses were directly related to situations and relationships in her present life.

In addition, we have numerous examples of how certain parts of the Collective Consciousness affected Connie's life and which became significant factors at certain stages of therapy. There were many who were brought forward including children, adolescents and young adults. Paychotherapy seemed to progress from early childhood to early adulthood. Such aspects of the Collective were present during traumatic childhood experiences and helped to absorb a lot of the pain and suffering that would have otherwise overwhelmed her. The Collective often assumes this role so that the present life and Ego consciousness can survive given trauma until such time that one is strong enough to face the traumatic situation. The same was true of similar experiences during her adolescence. Later during her years of addiction and alcoholism younger adults were brought forward to assist during this part of her difficult life. All of these parts of the Collective had to be processed during imagery therapy and released to the light from whence they came.

Natural Processes of Healing and Growth.

As suggested above, there are natural growth patterns that have been well documented by Developmental Psychologists. Each person passes through given phases of growth from childhood through adulthood and even into old age. The only exception to these natural growth patterns is when a given person is raised in an abusive or highly restrictive environment. We saw clear examples of this in the case studies of Sara, Connie and Theresa. These archetypal growth patterns are informed and supported by unseen life forces of the Supra Consciousness. To be sure such patterns have existed and have been evolving since the beginning of humanity. They are the result of millions of years of interacting with one's environment and significant relationships. The nature of growth is characteristically in constant evolutionary change. The primary archetypal pattern is a process of learning in which there is a constant reciprocal exchange between the inside of oneself and the outside of oneself. The Ego system is part of establishing this reciprocal relationship. As we have seen in the case studies presented above, such natural growth patterns can become interrupted or blocked by traumatic life experiences. It should be noted that the very nature of the Supra Consciousness is that of unconditional love, growth, healing and creativity. The processes of healing are as archetypal as those processes that support and inform human growth and development. The primary process is that of bringing what is unconscious into one's Ego consciousness, into the light of consciousness.

There is one natural unconscious process that helps to enable one to grow toward adulthood despite certain wounds or traumatic experiences. We tend to call these processes defense mechanisms. By means of repression or suppression certain negative experiences become walled off from Ego consciousness, permitting the rest of the system to continue to grow and mature. As suggested above, such wounding and negativity may also be absorbed by significant elements of the Collective Consciousness as we observed in the case studies. Were these natural processes and mechanisms not in place one might become overwhelmed, resulting in Ego disintegration.

Growth continues despite debilitating traumatic experiences in life. Once one has grown sufficiently, cognitively, emotionally and especially with significant Ego strength, these negative experiences are brought into consciousness. Further, those related parts of the Collective Consciousness are brought forward, as well. This is to say that those parts of the Collective Consciousness that helped to absorb the pain, suffering or addictive patterns related to given life experiences are brought forward as part of the healing process. Elements of the Collective Consciousness may take over and help us function or get through difficult situations or life circumstances. We see a number of examples of processing such related elements of the Collective in Connie's case study. Often the healing process includes that part of the Collective being released to the light where it can become healed. We observe a number of instances in which archetypal beings, such as the guardian angel, Christ or other divine entities become involved in helping to process negative experiences and bring them to resolution.

It might be noted that a given individual may have cognitive memories of debilitating traumatic experiences and can describe such experiences in detail during the use of Cognitive Therapy techniques. What has not been healed are the related emotional feelings such as anxiety, depression, hurt, wounding, etc. that have not been faced, processed and released. To a certain degree such emotional responses may have been absorbed by the Collective Consciousness. Hence, that part of the Collective is brought forward for processing and healing. When this occurs, the individual will be faced with some very difficult times until the total experience can be processed and released. In a certain sense the traumatic experiences are re-experienced in detail, processed and then released. During such re-experiencing, it is not uncommon for the client to feel disbelief and to consult with friends and family members to verify the experience. In many cases family members will verify such experiences, experiences that may have been family secrets for many years.

Another example of an archetypal healing process was demonstrated in Sara's Case Study. Her story is a classic archetypal rebirth experience. Her life experiences were so rigid and restrictive that she was unable to successfully pass through the natural stages of growth. Hence, we observed her processing the effects a restrictive environment such as putting herself in a "Red Church" to escape the realities of life which she believed to be dirty and imperfect. Further, she struggled with her moralistic and judgmental beliefs regarding her relationships with others. Such judgmental attitudes were often polarizing, and we observed dream segments in which a wedding was taking place, often symbolic of a union of the opposites. Following the resolution of such moralistic and judgmental attitudes she was ready to reenter the womb and experience a rebirth. The reader might recall her journey through the symbolic birth canal and merging with given figures representing each developmental stage of human development. A rebirth is one of the natural archetypal processes of the unconscious that moves one toward growth and healing.

Other symbolic and natural processes may be represented in dreams or imagery such as a death or a funeral in which part of oneself dies and is reborn into a more healthy and positive part of the self. We have already mentioned the wedding as a process that heals polarizations and forms a union of the opposites. A death in the unconscious is often a transformation process such that a negative trait or life dies to be transformed through a re-birth to something more positive and growth oriented.

In other instances, there is a re-enactment of a given negative experience. We observed this in Ellen's case study. Once elements of Julia's specific traumatic experience were resolved, "forgiven" and released, she repeated her experience of traveling with friends to the west. However, she could re-experience the trip with a free spirit and an ability to grow and learn from the experience. This is similar to recording something new over an old tape recording such that the old is erased as the new growth and healing experience is recorded.

There is another phenomenon that I have observed over the years that seems to have a significant impact on growth and healing. At certain stages in therapy a newborn baby appears, as was observed with Connie's case study. There are two types of births that seem to occur. First, it appears that certain parts of two or more entities of the Collective Consciousness are brought together to form a newborn child. It might be said that DNA is taken from a number of entities of the Collective Consciousness to form a single child. This child becomes integrated within the primary personality to provide needed traits and insights for further growth and healing. Second, at times there is what seems to be a birth of a "divine child" (2) that emerges from the Supra Consciousness. These inner children, like those originating from the Collective Consciousness, follow normal growth patterns. However, they grow much faster and within a few months the child grows to adulthood and becomes integrated within the primary personality. They often represent deeper insights into life and may lead to creative thinking and activity.

Finally, as was demonstrated in Ellen's Case Study there is the "guide" phenomenon. At times these guides can be very helpful. We have discussed Julia and her role in guiding Ellen through a sequence of events from within her Collective Consciousness. Joseph seemed to be a spiritual entity who was not part of her or related to her. He seemed to be one who helped both Ellen and Julia experience and process a traumatic situation. He suggested that he helped Ellen and Julia in order to test some of his theories and solutions to human problems in the physical world. Apparently, there can be a number of these entities who are assigned to us for the purpose of helping and manifesting their thoughts and ideas in the physical world. I have run across these entities a number of times and the test regarding their validity is whether what they do is helpful, healing and growth oriented. It is my clinical experience that there are those who will pose as guides but who are really just trying to express themselves through one who is in the physical world. They tend to be otherwise benign, but are little or no help in the process of healing and growth. Once this is determined it is easy to dismiss them and continue with the healing and growth-oriented process.

Another manifestation of the guide phenomenon may vary in appearance. Some guides are animals, the most common being a dog. The reader may recall that a dog appeared in Theresa's imagery during the early stages of her work. The dog took her to see the old woman who was determined to be of her Collective Consciousness. Other common animal guides are deer, especially the maternal doe who guides one through the woods, the woods being symbolic of the Collective Consciousness. Guides can come in other forms such as mythological creatures like a unicorn or fairy like creatures. Despite the many different forms of guides, as long as they are growth and healing oriented in their behavior, they serve a productive and even creative function. Otherwise, they are to be dismissed as non-essential components of the imagery process.

Of course, the most significant form of guidance appears in the form of the Guardian Angel as shown in Figure 1. It knows the blueprint of each life and is in direct contact with the Supra Consciousness. His role is that of protector and support regarding life direction and is growth and healing oriented. While the Guardian Angel is part of the teaching of the Catholic Church, it appears that it is a more universal archetypal being without regard to specific religious or cultural differences. Depending on the client's perceptual preference, the Guardian Angel may appear as either male or female. Sometimes they may appear as an animal or bird such as a seagull. In other cases, they may appear as a beautiful, brilliant being of light. Interestingly, they rarely appear with wings as depicted by religious organizations.

It is likely that there are many more growth and healing processes that are natural and archetypal in nature. Those listed above are some of the most commonly observed during my experience with Spontaneous Imagery Therapy. It should be noted that there is no healing of one's life except that it be supported or initiated by the divine world or the Supra Consciousness.

Accessing and Facilitating the Natural Growth and Healing Processes.

The most appropriate strategies for accessing the unconscious and its infinite array of consciousness appears to be what might otherwise be referred to as hypnotic techniques. There are also a number of approaches to meditation that enhance one's relationship with his/her inner world. Moreover, there are certain drugs like LSD which make possible accessing the unconscious. Some of these drugs have been used in therapeutic circumstances by Grof (3) and others. However, they are not recommended without professionals who are specially trained to use them. I have known LSD to be used on an individual basis without professional help. In such cases it seems that the information obtained appears unreliable and tends to support an attitude of arrogance, spiritual superiority and narcissism. I also observed the same kind of attitudes being formed by those who practice Transcendental Meditation, a form of meditation that was more popular during the 1960s and 70s.

I much prefer more natural techniques in the presence of a skilled therapist or researcher. This is not to say that highly mature and developed individuals cannot access the unconscious, in natural ways, using meditative techniques. Indeed, I would recommend a meditative practice to anyone who would be inclined. I have noticed recently that there seems to be a movement toward what is referred to as "mindfulness" and approaches to wellness which include meditation and guided imagery. During my research with highly creative individuals, I was often impressed by their ability to move into a relaxed meditative state and access their inner worlds. It seemed to be part of their creative potentiality. Individuals in the performing arts such as music and especially the visual arts seem well adapted to inner work.

The approach to the inner world of consciousness that I have come to adopt over the years, is what I refer to as "Spontaneous Imagery Therapy." Hypnotic techniques used for the induction of moderate to deep relaxation, to the extent that the individual begins to access images from his/her inner world, appears all that is necessary. Once the individual begins to experience spontaneous images, not imagery suggested to him/her, a Rogerian approach of listening, reflecting, interpreting, support, etc. (4) can be utilized to encourage and enhance the images being experienced. Moreover, unlike clinical hypnotic strategies, I never block from memory anything that has been experienced during the imagery session. The idea is to bring into consciousness what is otherwise unconscious to Ego consciousness. This makes possible an interpretative discussion of what was experienced during spontaneous imagery. The therapist does not suggest or "tell" the client what to see, think or feel. Rather, the important thing is that the client experiences what emerges on a spontaneous basis. I have discovered that such imagery tends to be the most valid and reliable with regard to the therapeutic process.

An exception to this approach is when the client is initially unable to experience spontaneous images. This being the case, I generally suggest that the client choose where he/she might wish to go to start the imagery work. Often, I suggest that it be a safe and calming place. There tends to be three places where clients tend to go to start their imagery. The most common is a beautiful beach, like Theresa experienced in her imagery. The next most common initial imagery is a natural setting, like a meadow in the midst of a wooded area. Finally, a mountain top with a spacious view is the third most common imagery. The idea is to create imagery space within which the consciousness of the unconscious can appear and with which the client can begin to interact.

There are times when the therapist might take charge and become more directive such as when an entity might try to interfere with the process in a way that is not healing or growth producing. There may be times when the client may be feeling overwhelmed by his/imagery. However, this is somewhat rare and jumping in and interrupting even when things appear out of control may actually be harmful or at least not helpful.

The Attitude and Conditions conducive to Spontaneous Imagery Therapy

Perhaps, more important than a particular hypnotic or meditation approach to Spontaneous Imagery Therapy is the attitude of both the therapist and Client. It is important to approach each session with an attitude of non-judgment and without expectation. Each person needs to be open to what emerges without resistance. As indicated above, the shadow side of the self often contains that which is unacceptable to the self and hence rejected. Accordingly, there is the need to approach the unconscious without judgment, accepting all that is brought forward. Indeed, approaching the unconscious or one's inner world with a sense of openness and without judgment or expectation, invites those positive unconscious forces to come forward and reveal themselves and the processes of healing and growth. I taught a regular class in imagery therapy, which was quite popular with the students. Much to my surprise, one fundamentalist Christian faculty member tried to undermine and eliminate my course from the departmental course offerings based on religious beliefs about the evil of the unconscious. This person had had no experience or training in hypnotic techniques or knowledge based on scientific evidence. These were things I had to continually fight against within my department and in other segments of the University. Further, I had to be very careful and secretive with regards to my work for fear that my work might have been shut down by such bias and prejudice.

Contrary to these beliefs it is necessary to develop a trust in the unconscious to know what it is doing when it is in the process of creating, healing and growth. Behind all that is going on is the wisdom and knowing of the Supra Consciousness or Divine Consciousness that is always behind whatever is going on, no matter how it might appear on the surface. Many of my medical colleagues would become frightened when a patient experienced an abreaction while in a hypnotic state. Their reaction was to immediately intervene and stop what was going on. This is when a client is experiencing something that is creating a strong emotional reaction and other reactions that appear out of the control of the clinician. Control is very important to many therapists, especially those in the medical profession. However, it is the very thing that blocks the process of healing and growth. For example, there are times when a client will go into a childhood traumatic experience. They re-experience the trauma of their childhood and it can manifest quite a display of emotional and physical responses. Sitting with a client in a calm, empathic and supportive way, without interruption, while they are going through these experiences is very important for healing such experiences. During such times one must trust those forces involved to know and direct what is going on for the purpose of healing the given traumatic experience. I have sat with clients hundreds of times during such episodes and have only seen positive outcomes. Occasionally, when there becomes a threat that the client is becoming overwhelmed by the experience, those underlying forces will gently lead the client out of the experience, only to revisit it at a later time when the Ego system has become stronger and better prepared. It is during such experiences, along with the experiences of other phenomena from the unconscious, that have led me to develop an inherent trust in the wisdom and processes of the unconscious. If one examines closely the case studies provided above, one may get a sense of a greater wisdom and direction operating below the surface and sometimes within the explicit content of the imagery work. Only once did I try to take charge of the process with significant negative results; a lesson learned and remembered.

Once one becomes familiar with the unconscious, especially the Supra Consciousness with its array of archetypal patterns, one can develop a sense of trust in its divine wisdom. Indeed, this part of the self is pure love and its only goal or motivation is to bring healing, growth and creativity to the whole self. In my case, my work evolved over time in which I was taken through each part of the unconscious in a gradual matter. Finally, the Supra Consciousness revealed itself in some very dramatic ways. I might note that I took myself to be a scientist, and I had to be shown through objective data and experiences before my belief system could incorporate the dynamics of the unconscious. Further assuming the role of a scientist, I am not bound by given religious dogma, beliefs or assumptions. This helped me to view the data in an objective way without a need to prove anything. My only limitation was in the questions I formulated. Sometimes the questions I asked were formulated as I progressed in my work with the unconscious. Knowing the right questions to ask is not always easy but very important because without them there can be no answers.

When the Divine Consciousness began to reveal itself, we started to experience the appearance of what is referred to itself as the "guardian angel." At first, I thought it was another aspect of the Collective Consciousness. However, we soon learned that this was a different and more highly developed entity manifesting in the imagery. We also learned that everyone has a guardian angel no matter their religious background, cultural background, race or gender, etc. During this time there were often flashes of light that would appear in the therapy room when these creatures were present.

At a later time, what I refer to as the "Christ" archetype or Consciousness appeared. During one session with a young woman, this phenomenon appeared as a being of bright light, with a sense of tremendous power. It was quite frightening at first because the light permeated the whole room and there was a feeling of thousands of volts of electricity or ions being present. The client seemed to have no fear of this being of light and my fear was calmed when it became evident that this being manifested tremendous unconditional love and what I have come to call "divine wit." As indicated, there was tremendous power associated with this being of light, enough power that I imagined could level our whole city. However, I knew that it was the power of love and healing and not of destruction. It was nothing to fear, rather something to embrace. This session had a life changing, healing impact on the client, that to my knowledge was sustained for the rest of her life. It might be noted that this being of light seemed delighted that we would welcome its presence, as we were told most everyone runs away when "He" comes to them. Over time I came to develop an implicit trust in the underlying forces of the unconscious that were always present in the imagery work.

Further, both the therapist and client need to have a certain degree of courage, especially during the initial stages of work with the unconscious. Later as the therapist develops sufficient experience with the unconscious and a sense of trust is developed, this sense of trust can become a supportive factor for the client. After all, things can appear a bit wild and out of control at times. It does take courage as one never really knows what is going to manifest from the unconscious at any given time. Many times, I sat on the edge of my seat while a client was experiencing what appeared to be an out of control abreaction. It did take some courage to sit there without jumping in and assuming control. Finally, I learned to trust that while something may seem out of control to me it does not mean that it is really out of control. Indeed, there are underlying forces that can be trusted to be fully in control of whatever situation might arise.

The Question of Evil

I have often been asked about the presence of evil in the unconscious by students, colleagues, and others, especially those with a fundamentalist Christian background. My answer is that just as there is evil in the outer world, there can also be the presence of evil in the inner world. The important thing is to develop the ability to discern evil from non-evil whether in the outer world or inner world. This takes wisdom developed from life experience. Generally, that which represents unconditional love, healing, growth and creativity is of a divine nature and not evil. That which is destructive and devoid of these qualities is evil. Creativity and a sense of humility is the absence of evil. Arrogance, narcissism and parasitic tendencies toward relationships with others tends to be characteristics associated with evil. M Scott Peck's (5) writing with regards to evil provides deeper insight into this question which we rarely see coming from a well-respected mental health professional.

Those of us who have worked with people diagnosed with Multiple Personality Disorder (MPD), more recently referred to as Dissociative Disorder, know well of the existence of evil in the therapeutic process. Interestingly, the more progress one makes in such cases, and in cases in general, the more dynamic evil forces become to oppose this progress. Such persons almost always have been severely abused as children and young adults, a condition which invites the involvement of demonic entities. While it is rare for clinicians who work with MPDs to publicly write or talk about this phenomenon for fear of ostracism, they may be eager to enter into private discussions with those who have had similar experiences.

When these demonic entities surface in imagery therapy they can be quite frightening and intimidating. However, that is generally the extent of their ability to do anything of substance. My initial reaction was feelings of anger and rage which only tended to make things worse. Now I just dismiss them and continue on with the work. In other words, there is little that one needs to do about such creatures when they surface.

It is a matter of choice on the part of the client. Choice is held sacred by the divine world. The threat to such demonic creatures is that when they reveal themselves the client becomes consciously aware of them. When he/she decides that he/she does not want them, they are expelled by the divine forces of the Supra Consciousness. So, when demonic creatures come to the surface, they have become desperate because they feel themselves losing ground with the client. It is worth mentioning again that when such creatures surface it means that significant progress with healing and growth is being made. The therapist does not need to do anything regarding such phenomena. When it is brought into the conscious awareness of the client and he/she decides that it is not wanted, forces from the Supra Consciousness will expel it, sometimes in a rather dramatic fashion.

I am only mentioning this aspect of the imagery work because of the number of times over the years I have been asked questions regarding evil in the unconscious. This is just a brief introduction to my experiences with such entities. I really see this aspect of the work as minor, despite their scary presence to those who lack experience with such matters. Otherwise, I have no interest or curiosity in these matters. My intent and role are to facilitate growth and healing. I am a therapist after all, and that is my major focus. It is from this prospective that my research questions have been formulated.

Summary Statements

The unconscious contains three major aspects: one is the Personal Unconscious or Psyche. It has its own consciousness and contains all of one's personal life experiences; the second is the Collective Consciousness which is a collection of past life entities who have had their own life experiences and are autonomous individuals; the third aspect of the unconscious is the Supra Consciousness or fire or light consciousness. It contains all the archetypal patterns that inform our lives and seek to fulfill the blueprint and inherent direction of our lives. These archetypes often surface as autonomous entities and are what I refer to as divine. While the guardian angel is not part of ourselves it is none the less a divine creature and works closely with our own Supra Consciousness and on behalf of our growth and healing.

The Collective Consciousness and Supra Consciousness has a great deal of influence on our thoughts and behavior. They can lead us into given experiences and guide us through these experiences for the purpose of healing and growth. What is unresolved in the system, whether it be a few days ago or thousands of years ago remains in the present. Such wounds of the past that block certain aspects of our growth and change are brought forward into the present to be healed and all those related elements of the Collective Consciousness are released. On a greater scale the Supra Consciousness and its archetypal patterns support our life direction and the fulfillment of our broader life purpose.

There are natural growth processes that each person passes through during his or her life. These growth processes are easily observed during growth from childhood into adulthood. Further, there are natural healing processes that help to resolve wounding experiences such that our natural growth processes can be released and implemented. What is behind these processes are often the unseen forces of the divine Supra Consciousness.

Spontaneous Imagery Therapy is one way to invite those inner forces and content of the unconscious to become experienced and integrated within ego consciousness. The intent of the inner world is that it becomes brought into the sphere of consciousness. Growth through increased consciousness is a primary goal of the unconscious. However, Spontaneous Imagery Therapy is not for everyone. It is fitting to those who have the desire, openness and courage to access and experience their own unconscious.

The most productive way to approach one's inner world is with an attitude of non-judgment and without expectation. Those who have the courage and a non-judgmental attitude will often open to the richness and wisdom of their inner world of humanity and divine nature. While it can be very painful at times to face one's own shadow, the light of divine consciousness is well worth the effort. The work often leads to a more creative and productive life for those who take the journey into their inner worlds.

In the final analysis, it seems that what we are is pure consciousness. As Connie experienced, when she was without a body, was that she was fully conscious of who and what she was. Moreover, she appeared conscious of others and of her surroundings and circumstances. Those who have had out-of- body experiences often express themselves as formless but with a sense of consciousness and conscious identity.

Notes and References for the Introduction

1. Cottone, R. Rocco, *Theories and Paradigms of Counseling and Psychotherapy*, Allyn and Bacon, 1992, pp. 97-11.

2. Hannah, Barbara, *Jung, His Life and Work*, Perigee Books, 1976 (paperback edition) p. 108. Hannah reports on Jung's discovery of a technique in which feelings and fantasies become objectified, such that one can interact with them at an ego consciousness level. She indicated that he "learned to take an active role in it himself, and he found that he could have an influence on its development and that he was no longer a passive spectator in an unending flood of fantasies."

3. Jung, C. G., *The Structure and Dynamics of the Psyche*, Bollingen Series XX, Princeton University Press, 1975 (paperback edition), pp. 151-152. Jung uses the term "personal unconscious" which I refer to as the Personal Psyche. He indicates that this part of the psyche contains contents that have been forgotten because they have lost their significance to Ego Consciousness or contents that have been repressed because they are unacceptable or rejected by Ego Consciousness.

4. Cornelia B. Wilbur, MD, was a pioneer in the field of Multiple Personality Disorder (MPD) later referred to as Dissociative Identity Disorder listed in the *Diagnostic and Statistical Manual of Mental Disorders (DSM)*. She is best known for her work that was featured in the book, *Sybil*, by Flora Rheta Schreiber. While her work with Sybil came under criticism she was considered a primary authority in treating this disorder. I was fortunate to meet her during a workshop on MPD where a number of patients were in attendance and told their own stories.

5. Jung, C.G., *The Archetypes and the Collective Unconscious*, Bollingen Series XX, Princeton University Press, 1990 (paperback edition), p.42.

6. Ibid., p. 183, p. 285.

7. Newton, Michael, *Destiny of Souls*, Llewellyn Publications, 2003 (paperback edition), pp. 201 – 257.

8. Jung, C.G. *Four Archetypes (Mother/Rebirth/Spirit/Trickster)*, Bollingen Series XX, Princeton University Press, 1992 (paperback edition), pp. 35-44.

9. Newton, Michael, *Journey of Souls*, Llewellyn Publications, 2004 (paperback edition), pp. 201-220

10. Jung, C.G., *The Archetypes of the Collective Unconscious*, Op. Cit., pp 46, 113-115.

Notes and References for Case Study I

1. Cliness, David W., *The Journey of life*, Banausic Publishing, 1996, p. 6.

2. Campbell, Joseph, *Creative Mythology*, Penguin Books, 1976 (paperback edition), p. 332.

3. Erickson, Erik, H., *Childhood and Society*, W. W. Norton & Company, New York, 35th Edition, 1985, pp. 247-269.

4. Rogers, Carl, R., *A Way of Being*, Houghton Mifflin Company, Boston, 1980, (paperback edition) p. 116. Rogers used the term "unconditional positive regard" to describe the climate for change in the therapeutic relationship, including acceptance, caring and non-judgment. I have observed that when the client is able to return this kind of regard for the therapist and toward others, healing, and growth occurs.

5. Cliness, David W., *The Journey of Life*, Op. Cit., p. 73.

Notes and References for Case Study II

1. Woolger, Roger J., *Other Lives, Other Selves*, Boston Books, New York, 1988, (paperback edition), pp. 122, 167.

2. Campbell, Joseph, *Creative Mythology*, Op. Cit., pp. 223-224.

3. Jung, C. G., *The Archetypes of the Collective Unconscious*, Op. Cit., pp. 3-4.

Notes and References for Case Study III

1. Matthews, Boris (Translator), *The Herder Symbol Dictionary*, Chiron Publishers, Wilmette, Illinois, (paperback edition), pp. 155, 219.

2. Ibid., p 75.

3. Jung, C. G., *The Archetypes and the Collective Unconscious*, Op. Cit., pp. 42-43.

4. Jung, C.G., *Four Archetypes*, Op. Cit., pp. 15-18.

5. *The Herder Symbol Dictionary*, Op. Cit., p. 187. While Christ is associated with the Sun, it is generally associated with the "highest cosmic intelligence" and of warmth, fire and a life giving and nurturing principle. In this regard, it is considered feminine in nature.

6. Cirlot, J. E., *A Dictionary of Symbols*, Philosophical Library, New York, 1971, pp. 38-39.

7. *The Herder Symbol Dictionary*, Op. Cit., p. 155. The rainbow is a common symbol in Spontaneous Imagery Therapy and usually means that the Supra Consciousness is surfacing in the client's imagery.

8. *The Herder Symbol Dictionary*, Op. Cit., p. 216.

9. Robinson, James M. (Editor), *The Nag Hammadi Library*, Harper San Francisco, (paperback edition) 1990.

10. *The Herder Symbol Dictionary*, Op. Cit., pp. 211-212.

11. *The Herder Symbol Dictionary*, Op. Cit., p. 72. See also in *A Dictionary of Symbols*, Op. Cit., pp. 99-100.

12. Jung, C. G., *The Archetypes and the Collective Unconscious*, Op. Cit., p. 285. Jung refers to the Wise Man or Wise Old Man as an archetype but does not seem to go beyond this definition. He does not seem to draw a relationship between the Wise Man and the "Christ," which I also refer to as an archetype. At times He appears in imagery, in the clinical setting and also in my own dreams and imagery as a "Wise Man." Further, the "Christ" is often referred to by others in the imagery process such as the "Guardian Angel" as the "Master." Hence, I have come to equate the two as one and the same archetype. While Jung may disagree with my use of the two terms or concepts, I think it important to the reader that he/she knows the context in which I view the use of the term "Christ" or "Master" and the "Wise Man."

13. Cooper, J. C., *An Illustrated Encyclopedia of Traditional Symbols*, Thames & Hudson, London, (paperback) 1978, pp. 68-69.

14. *The Herder Symbol Dictionary*, Op. Cit., p. 63.

15. Campbell, J., *The Hero with a Thousand Faces*, Bollingen Series XVII, Princeton University Press, 1973 (Paperback). See also Campbell, J., *The Hero's Journey*, Shaftesbury, Dorset, Boston, 1999.

16. *The Herder Symbol Dictionary*, Op. Cit., pp. 219-220.

17. *The Herder Symbol Dictionary*, Op. Cit., p. 187.

18. *The Herder Symbol Dictionary*, Op. Cit., p. 113. See also in *An Illustrated Encyclopedia of Traditional symbols*, Op. Cit., pp. 92-93.

19. *The Herder Symbol Dictionary*, Op. Cit., p. 77.

20. *An Illustrated Encyclopedia of Traditional Symbols*, Op. Cit., pp. 41-42.

21. *The Herder Symbol Dictionary*, Op. Cit., pp. 83-84.

22. *The Herder Symbol Dictionary*, Op. Cit., pp. 110-111.

23. *The Herder Symbol Dictionary*, Op. Cit., p. 87.

24. *The Herder Symbol Dictionary*, Op. Cit., p.72.

25. *The Herder Symbol Dictionary*, Op. Cit., p. 5.

26. Cirlot, J. E.,*Dictionary of Symbols,* Op. Cit., p. 43.

27. *The Herder Symbol Dictionary*, Op. Cit., p. 140.

Notes and References for Case Study IV

1. Whitfield, Charles L., *Healing the Child Within*, Health Communications, Inc., Dearfield Beach, Florida, 1987 (paperback) pp. 39-41.

2. Ibid., pp. 9-15.

3. Jung, C.G., *Man and His Symbols*, Doubleday, Garden City, NY, 1964, pp. 194-195.

4. *The Herder Symbol Dictionary*, Op. Cit., pp. 61-62.

5. Jung, C.G., *Psyche & Symbol*, Ed. By deLaszlo, V. S., Doubleday Anchor Books, New York (paperback), 1958 pp. 113-131.

6. *The Herder Symbol Dictionary*, Op. Cit., pp. 10-11.

7. *An Illustrated Encyclopedia of Traditional Symbols*, Op. Cit., pp. 146-151.

8. Jung, C. G., *Four Archetypes*, Op. Cit., pp. 9-18.

9. Whitfield, C. L., *Healing the Child Within*, Op. Cit., pp. 25-41.

10. Jung, C. G., *Four Archetypes*, Op. Cit., pp. 9, 36, 39, 40.

11. Cirlot, *Dictionary of Symbols*, Op. Cit., pp.105-106.

12. Campbell, Joseph, *Occidental Mythology, The Masks of God*, Penguin Books, NY, 1964 (paperback), pp. 230-232. It is noted that the wisdom of Socrates is based on beauty and love. While he valued the beauty of the body he felt it was nothing compared to the "beauties of the soul." Further, Diotima said of Socrates, "there bursts upon him that wondrous vision which is the very soul of the beauty he has toiled so long for. It is an everlasting loveliness which neither comes nor goes, which neither flowers nor fades, for such beauty is the same on every hand, the same then as now, here as there, this way as that way, the same to every worshiper as it is to every other."

13. Mishlove, Jeffrey, *The Roots of Consciousness*, Random House, 1975, pp. 14-15.

14. Ring, Kenneth, *Heading Toward Omega*, Quill William Morrow, New York, 1985, (Paperback) pp. 41- 44. Ring discusses the out of body experiences (OBE) in relation to Near Death Experiences (NDE). It seems that Connie may have been near death from her accident and also experiencing unbearable pain. These two factors fit with Ring's description regarding the relationship between NDE and OBE.

15. Jung, C.G., *The Archetypes and the Collective Unconscious*, Op. Cit., p. 170, also see Figure 37, a Mandala of the Divine Child.

16. Campbell, Joseph, *Creative Mythology, The Masks of God*, Op. Cit., pp. 20, 168, 204, 415.

17. Campbell, Joseph, *Occidental Mythology, The Masks of God*, Op. Cit., pp. 334-335.

18. *An Illustrated Encyclopedia of Traditional Symbols*, Op. Cit., pp. 45-46.

19. *An Illustrated Encyclopedia of Traditional Symbols*, Op. Cit., p. 62.

20. Grof, Stanislav, *Realms of the Human Unconscious*, Observations from LSD Research, E.P. Dutton & Co, 1976, (paperback ed.), pp 44-94.

21. *An Illustrated Encyclopedia of Traditional Symbols*, Op. Cit., pp. 45-46.

22. *The Herder Symbol Dictionary*, Op. Cit., 53-54.

Notes and References for the Summary/Discussion

1. Jung, C.G., *Memories, Dreams, Reflections, Vintage Books*, New York, 1989 (paperback edition) p. 58. Jung seemed to struggle with developing some understanding of the nature or character of God. Part of the struggle included what he sometimes referred to the dark aspects of God, including traits like vindictiveness, wrathfulness, and His incomprehensible conduct toward the creatures His omnipotence had made.

2. Jung, *C.G., The Archetypes and the Collective Unconscious*, Op. Cit., p. 158.

3. Grof, Stanislav, *Realms of the Human Unconscious, Observations from LSD Research*, Op. Cit., pp. 44-46.

4. Rogers, Carl R., *Client-Centered Therapy*, Houghton Mifflin Co., New York, 1951

5. Peck, M. Scott, People *of the Lie, the Hope for Healing Human Evil*, A Touchstone Book, Simon & Schuster, New York, 1983 (Paperback edition).

About the Author

David W. Cliness earned his AB and MA degrees from the University of Kentucky in 1964 and 1965 and his Ph.D from the Ohio State University in 1973. He is Professor and Chair Emeritus of the Department of Counseling at Youngstown State University where his teaching focused on student development and his administrative role concentrated on program development. He is a licensed Psychologist in the State of Ohio and has held a Psychologist license since 1975. Moreover, he is certified in Clinical Hypnotherapy by the National Board for Certified Clinical Hypnotherapists. Following retirement from the University he served as the supervisor of the Department of Psychology at Woodside Receiving Hospital in Youngstown, Ohio until it closed in 1996. Since then he has served in various positions in the private sector as a psychotherapist.

His 20 years of clinical research focused on the Unconscious and its capacity for unconditional love, growth, healing and creativity. His research subjects have included emotionally and mentally disturbed persons, including those diagnosed with Multiple Personality Disorder, and also those diagnosed with terminal illnesses. Finally, his book of poetry, *The Journey of Life*, which was first published in 1996 is now revised and available on Amazon. His own journey of life has been a quest for the healing and integration of the psyche.

Printed in Great Britain
by Amazon